BRENDA COLVIN
A career in landscape

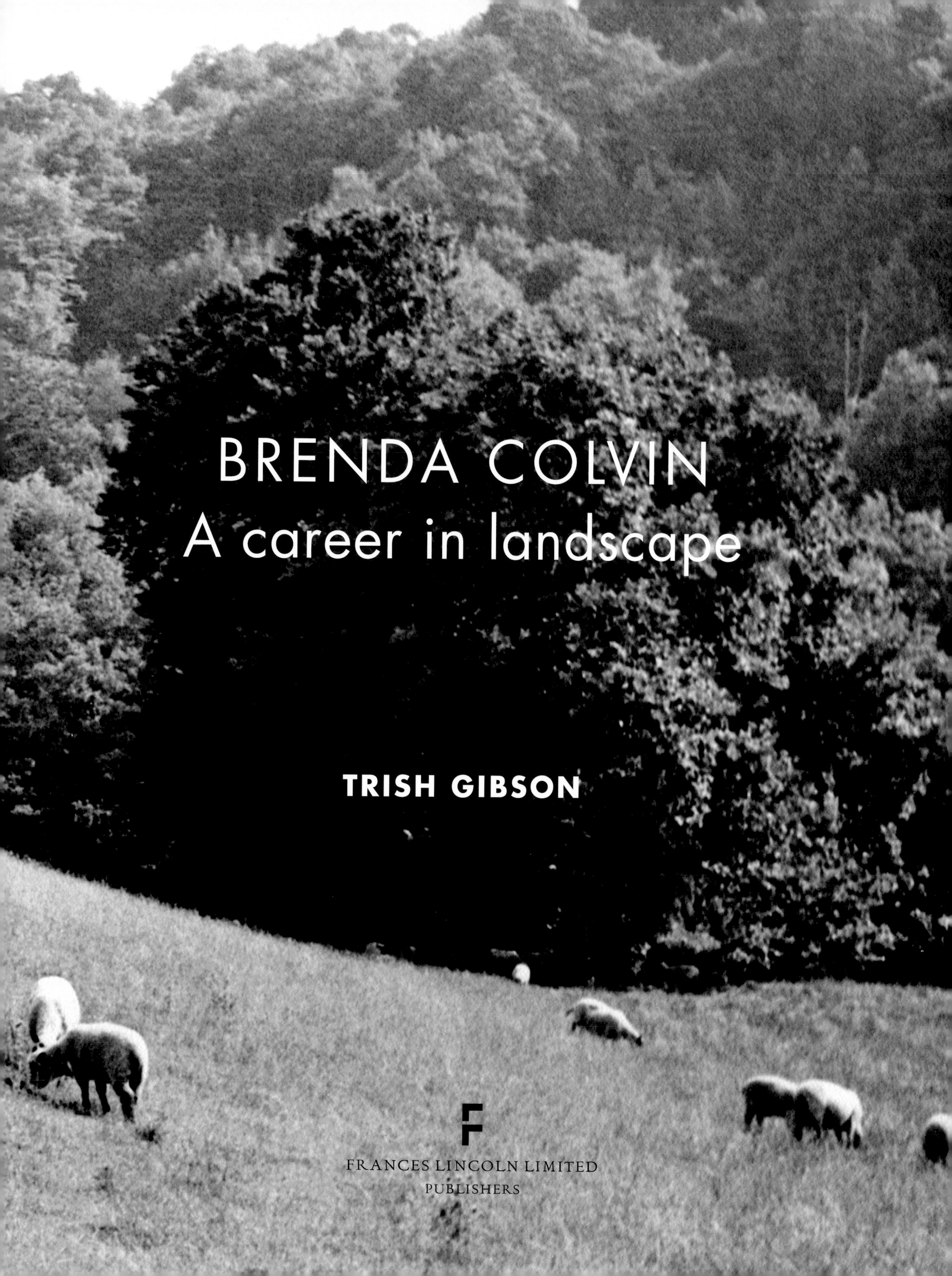

BRENDA COLVIN
A career in landscape

TRISH GIBSON

F

FRANCES LINCOLN LIMITED

PUBLISHERS

For Jeremy, Sam and Hannah

and for my mother, for her insistence that her daughters
should have the education she was denied

Frances Lincoln Limited
4 Torriano Mews
Torriano Avenue
London NW5 2RZ
www.franceslincoln.com

Brenda Colvin: A Career in Landscape
Copyright © Frances Lincoln Limited 2011
Text copyright © Trish Gibson 2011
Illustrations copyright see page 255
Foreword copyright © Hal Moggridge 2011

First Frances Lincoln edition 2011

A catalogue record for this book is available from the British Library.

978-0-7112-3171-9

Printed and bound in China

1 2 3 4 5 6 7 8 9

Commissioned and edited by Jane Crawley
Designed by Anne Wilson

HALF-TITLE PAGE Brenda Colvin photographed
on her election as president of the Institute of
Landscape Architects.

TITLE PAGE At Trimpley reservoir, the outer face
of the embankment was to be maintained by
grazing sheep. The base of the embankment is
shaped to a gentle curve where it joins the bank
of the river Severn.

Contents

Foreword

IN APRIL 1969, forty years ago, I became Brenda Colvin's partner and the practice of Colvin and Moggridge, Landscape Architects, evolved.

Brenda's practice had been established in 1922, forty-seven years earlier, while mine had hardly started. I was only thirty-three years old and thrilled by this opportunity; it was indeed the chance of a lifetime for me. Brenda was seventy-two, still highly active in landscape design, writing and work for the Landscape Institute. We found ourselves surprisingly compatible. Her wisdom and experience tempered my too extravagantly enthusiastic ideas, helping to mould them into practicality. I found her deep understanding of the natural world and its creative possibilities an inspiration. I believe that she valued my hopeful optimism and belief that landscape designs come out of familiarity with each individual site.

Brenda was always insistent on looking to the long term and the need for proper aftercare of newly modelled landscapes. By creating, for the first time in her long professional life, a partnership, she succeeded in perpetuating her practice, uniquely amongst her distinguished contemporaries. Colvin and Moggridge is still thriving, now under the guidance of another new generation of landscape architects.

Though a frequent guest of the Jellicoes, I had been surprised in late 1968 to find myself at a dinner party of older members of the Institute of Landscape Architects, gathered to discuss its foundation in 1929. Before, during and after dinner I was seated beside Brenda Colvin, a founder member of the institute, whom I had never previously met. We hit it off excellently. She telephoned a few days later to ask me to visit her in Filkins to discuss the possibility of my joining her. On the journey down in a car borrowed from a friend, I was involved in a minor car crash, and so arrived late and shaken. Nonetheless we again found that much was shared in our approach to the art and science of landscape architecture and a three-month trial period was agreed upon.

Within a few weeks we were both certain that we wanted to work as partners. Brenda's principal condition was that I and my family would move to West Oxfordshire, so that I could work in and help to manage the Filkins office, which was situated in the garden of Brenda's home following her retirement from practising in London. Filkins has proved to be an excellent location for a landscape practice, central in England and Wales and accessible to London and airports.

Brenda was extraordinarily generous in her management of the partnership's work. She invited me to join her in completing some of her splendid industrial landscape designs such as Trimpley Reservoir and the grounds of Drakelow and Eggborough Power Stations, each project several square kilometres in area. I had previously only had the opportunity to design small gardens. She also handed whole large new jobs on to me to design and run, always helping in the background with wise and penetrating assessment of how to analyse a site or solve tricky problems.

She liked powerful cars and would lend me her 3-litre Rover for more distant site visits; this car provided a status and comfort not attainable in my own modest old family banger. She meanwhile continued to run her favourite jobs herself, such as Aldershot where the tarmac military town was being converted into a green place, using ecological perception to extract tree growth from derelict parade grounds at minimal cost and finding methods to convert the processes of rubbish disposal into the creation of habitats for nature, wooded hill and bird-filled lake.

We would have lunch together in her kitchen or garden whenever we were both in the office; her kitchen garden provided delicious fresh vegetables including asparagus in early summer, the whole considerable crop of which we consumed together while discussing jobs, the office, the profession and the nature of our planet. Hers was a wide-ranging intellect. She also encouraged Chris Carter to return to the office from Cornwall County Council. After her death in 1981 he became my partner. He shares her great gift as a plantsman, an essential skill in a creative landscape design practice. Thus she arranged for a rounded future extending beyond her own lifetime.

This book is a worthy, and overdue, tribute to this pioneer (whose outlook to landscape design I have sought to continue). It moves seamlessly through her life's work, expanding from her garden designs in the 1920s and 1930s into a two-part look at her large scale work of the 1950s and 1960s, the first of which is so nicely entitled 'A landscape worth living in'. The chapter 'Working for splendour' outlines her energetic promotion of the landscape for public benefit. Her strength of purpose and personality led to her being elected president of the Institute of Landscape Architects (now the Landscape Institute) in 1951, certainly the first time that a woman headed an environmental or design profession in the United Kingdom, perhaps even in Europe and America as well. I hope that the appeal of this book will spread much wider than the landscape and building architectural professions to touch the imaginations of all who can agree with the prescient opening line from 1948 of Brenda Colvin's *Land and Landscape*: 'The control which modern man is able to exert over his environment is so great that we easily overlook the power of the environment over man.'

Hal Moggridge
Colvin & Moggridge
Filkins
near Lechlade
April 2010

Prologue

ARLY IN 1973, a secret party was being planned for Brenda Colvin. The invitations from her 'junior staff' went out with an instruction that there was 'an embargo on notice of this occasion to Miss Colvin before the end of February'. They knew her well enough to suspect that her innate modesty was unlikely to allow her to agree to any such public celebration. A thank-you letter after the event from her doctor John Groundes-Pearce reveals that they 'were entirely successful in keeping from her [their] secret of the plan for the Party until the moment intended'.[1]

At the age of 75, Brenda Colvin, 'landscape consultant and senior partner of Colvin & Moggridge', had been awarded a CBE in the New Year Honours. She had been working as a garden designer and landscape architect for more than 50 years and the honour was given in recognition of her outstanding contribution to the cause of the landscape.

The award was noted in a brief three lines in the February issue of the Institute of Landscape Design's journal *Landscape Design* and certainly it would have been recognised by her fellows on the council of the institute in London at their next meeting, but to many of her peers this recognition was long overdue. It was, however, entirely in keeping that Colvin herself would never have expected it. She had a mistakenly low estimation of the value of her own work.

The presentation of the award was made by the Queen at a formal investiture in the Ballroom at Buckingham Palace on 20 February to which Colvin was accompanied by her professional partner Hal Moggridge and his wife Cass. When she heard she was to be awarded the CBE, this able yet, as will become apparent, sometimes difficult woman who bowed to no one was anxious about how to observe correct procedures at the palace and asked Cass Moggridge to help her prepare. As the daughter of a high-ranking member of the Indian Civil Service, Colvin would certainly have had to curtsy on many occasions in the distant past but now she was nervous about her ability to do so correctly and without wobbling. Together they practised in Colvin's sitting room and at the palace all went well. Ordeal over, Colvin would have appreciated the much more relaxed feel of the party organised for her by her staff.

THE JUNIOR STAFF OF COLVIN AND MOGGRIDGE

INVITE

TO A CELEBRATION IN HONOUR OF BRENDA COLVIN CBE
ON SATURDAY 3RD MARCH 1973 AT EIGHT OCLOCK IN THE
NEWLY CONVERTED OFFICES AT LITTLE PEACOCKS FILKINS

*There is an embargo on notice of this occasion
to Miss Colvin before the end of February*

RSVP TO WOODRUFF COTTAGE . SHILTON . OXFORDSHIRE

It was held on the evening of Saturday 3 March in the village of Filkins in a newly converted barn at Little Peacocks, her Cotswold home and, since 1965, her office. Fittingly, this building was about to provide some very welcome extra space for Colvin & Moggridge's expanding business. The firm was engaged in two particularly long-term, large-scale projects – the rebuilding of Aldershot Military Town and an ash disposal scheme at Gale Common, Eggborough. Both projects provided a clear indication of just how successful Colvin had been in her career – and of the confidence and ability she had acquired in the course of it, a rare woman in what was still largely a man's world.

The private party was intended to have a light-hearted friendly feel but, without her knowledge, Colvin's staff also wanted to celebrate her philosophy and remind everyone exactly how much she deserved the award. It was a clear sign of their great affection and deep respect for her, and they made sure that the guests were those people with whom Colvin would wish to share the occasion. Among them, they invited the fellow landscape architects that Colvin regarded as personal friends – Bodfan Gruffydd, Geoffrey Jellicoe with his wife Susan, and Sheila Haywood, a regular visitor to Little Peacocks. Otherwise, the guest list consisted almost completely of her staff – in many ways her surrogate family – together with local friends and neighbours, and local builder Mervyn Swinford and his father, master mason George Swinford, who had carried out the conversion work on the barn. On the walls a copy of the guest list was pinned up and, in keeping with the family feel of this evening, alongside the names were written some not entirely serious reasons as to why the guests themselves should receive awards. For example, Geoffrey Jellicoe, whose garden design work had included the Royal Lodge, Windsor, for the Duke and Duchess of York, was rewarded

LEFT The invitation sent out by Colvin's 'junior staff' for the secret party they organised to celebrate her CBE.

ABOVE Colvin's garden at Little Peacocks, Filkins, her Cotswold home and office.

'for introducing Royalty to Landscape Design', Keith Heming, husband of one of Colvin's assistants and a contractor, was 'awarded the J.C.B.', Sir Gordon Russell was honoured 'for not being connected with the lupins or sprouts of the same name' and, appropriately, his wife was commended 'for explaining the procedure at the Palace'.

In contrast to this informality, Colvin's staff also displayed photographs of some of her work and the text of an extraordinarily visionary statement on the subject of 'ecological health', written by Colvin the previous month.[2] This confirmed her carefully considered belief that the basis of landscape was biological and that human endeavour was – and had to be – dominated by the laws of nature:

> To appreciate the meaning of 'ecological health' we must realise that human existence is bound in the bundle of life on this planet. It is a part of and utterly dependent on the rest of the biosphere…the living envelope, made up of soil, air, water and the life they nourish, encircling the earth….We can apprehend the biosphere as a single dynamic organism [whose] life…is maintained by a delicately balanced cycle of movement and change.

Given this, she considered that humanity should be seen simply as 'one of the components of that life, a member but not the master of the organism'. Powerfully, she went on to observe:

> Humanity has acquired power to damage and even wreck [the organism], but not to direct it. To assume that humanity can usurp absolute power over the cycle is to risk extinction. The words in the biblical account of the Creation, indicating man dominant over every living thing, have led to suicidal arrogance. The word 'steward' or 'trustee' might have been a better application and the words of the New Testament, 'members one of another' come closer to the modern interpretation of man as a member of the whole body of life on earth.

In her mind, 'biological health' meant 'the relationship of land, water and air to the whole cycle of life'. These were the 'matrix of life on earth and landscape is the form in which we see them'. Crucially, she concluded, 'Any area, large or small, for which any one of us may be responsible, with its complement of living individuals… contributes to the health of the whole.'

Although Colvin wrote these words late in her career, her profound belief in our ecological relationship with the landscape and the possibility of our having a positive impact on our surroundings was a long-standing and remarkably prescient one, a philosophy she had developed and refined throughout the course of her long and influential career as one of the pioneer landscape architects of the twentieth century. In the course of that career her dedication to the cause of the landscape was absolute. Her role was crucial to the foundation of a professional body for landscape architects in the 1920s and to ensuring its continuation during the 1930s and 1940s; by her writing and lecturing she educated and influenced the following generations. During and after the Second World War she committed herself to 'working for splendour', following an exhortation to those of her generation not to be bowed by the threat of chaos. The influence of her beliefs can be found in the way our gardens have developed, in the way our post-war landscape has been managed, and the way ecological considerations have increasingly come to be taken into account by anyone concerned with the landscape. All this she personally instilled in her staff. It is all the more surprising therefore that the vital contribution of her career in landscape has on the whole remained unrecognised for so long.

RIGHT Brenda Colvin photographed in her garden when she was in her seventies.

Beginnings

'My earliest schooling was in a houseboat on the river Jhelum [in Kashmir]...
I remember the wealth of wild flowers and the almond blossom orchards on the
lower terraces of the surrounding mountains. I remember picnics on the banks
and islands of the lakes and in the gardens of the Shalimar.'[1]

O N A CHILLY September morning in 1918, a tall, reserved but remarkably self-assured young woman walked through the iron gates of Hextable House in Swanley. At the age of twenty-one, Brenda Colvin was leaving behind the comfort and independence of her life at home for the constraints and rigours of life as a student at Swanley Horticultural College. She intended to specialise in fruit growing. The First World War was coming to a close, and her father, at the age of 57, had recently moved back to England after 36 years with the Indian Civil Service. Colvin had led a cosmopolitan life up to that point and to date her schooling had been far from usual. It had included from a young age a variety of private schools in England and France as well as the exotic-sounding houseboat she recalled on a Kashmiri river. In fact her education was so unconventional that she used to say on the census forms that her upbringing would class her as 'an illiterate immigrant'.[2]

From her memories of wild flowers and almond blossom in Kashmir, Brenda Colvin was profoundly affected by the plants and the landscape around her even as a child. From a surprisingly early age, too, she knew instinctively that she aspired to a professional life, to do something that mattered. Unconventional from the start – and yet born into a very conventional family – she disliked having to wear pretty dresses and did not behave as young girls were expected to do.[3] Her early interest in flowers and plants was eventually to prompt her to follow a career spanning almost 60 years in which she rose to play a leading, pioneering role in twentieth-century garden design and landscape architecture in Britain. But her career might not have taken that direction. For a brief while in her teens, before the First World War, she was torn between the prospect of studying art in Paris and training in horticulture, but by September 1918 she had, with typical pragmatism, decided that 'horticulture was more likely to produce some returns'.[4] Nevertheless that earlier interest and training in art – and in looking carefully at shape and form – guided her keen appreciation and developing understanding of plants and plant design.

LEFT Colvin (in the foreground) working with fellow students in the Conservatory at Swanley Horticultural College in 1919.

Colvin was born on 8 June 1897 in Simla (now Shimla), a popular hill station in northern India that was also the country's summer capital during the British Raj. Her father Elliot Colvin's family had ties with India that went back four generations and her mother Ethel's family also came from a long line of Indian Civil Service officers. In fact family traditions were so strong that Colvin was even given her maternal grandfather's name as part of her own: Brenda Gwyneth Steuart.[5] She spent the early part of her childhood in India, as did her elder sister Helen, born in 1890, and her younger brother Hugh, born in 1901 and, much to his irritation in later life, always known by her as 'Bay', short for 'baby'.

At the time of her birth, Colvin's father was Political Agent for the Eastern Rajputana States. He then became Revenue and Judicial Commissioner in Baluchistan and in 1903[6] he was selected for appointment as Resident in Kashmir. It was from this time, at around the age of six, that Colvin remembered her early schooling in a houseboat on the river Jhelum. Two years later, Elliot Colvin was appointed Agent to the Governor-General in Rajputana and Chief Commissioner, Ajmer-Merwara.[7] At times the young Colvin would accompany her father on his tours round his district, riding on camels and living under canvas.[8] Later in life, she would describe these 'progresses', confessing how, at the age of about ten, she was always intrigued by how the elaborate camps came to be set up. After breakfast, she and her father would

leave their lavish camp, set up with carpets and furniture, and when they arrived at their destination at the end of the afternoon, without any servants having passed them, there would be the next camp ready and waiting for them. As a child it had taken her a while to realise that in fact there were two identical camps and that one was already set up while the other leapfrogged to the next location.

Life in the Colvin household was a privileged, relatively formal one, with plenty of exalted guests visiting – even the Prince and Princess of Wales in 1905 – but there was also a lighter side to life in the British Raj. Elliot Colvin's childhood enthusiasm for cricket never left him and he passed it on to his children. A cricket tournament begun in 1911–12 was even named after him and remains Rajasthan's foremost cricket competition. In June 1912 Elliot Colvin's long service in India was rewarded when

OPPOSITE ABOVE Brenda Colvin with her younger brother Hugh at home in India with an exotic backdrop of lilies.

OPPOSITE BELOW A family photograph of Hugh and Brenda in fancy dress.

LEFT One of the Colvin family's homes in India.

BELOW The Colvin children playing cricket with friends.

he received the warrant granting him the 'Dignity of a Knight Commander of the Most Exalted Order of the Star of India'.

Although Colvin spent her early years in India with her family, like many generations of Raj children including her father before her, she was sent 'home' to England when she was a little older to continue her education. She lived with a widowed friend of her parents in one of the grace-and-favour apartments at Hampton Court. There she spent much time playing in the grounds, especially after hours when they were closed to the public.[9] Here, as in India, she was much affected by the plants and landscape around her and it is most likely that her early memory of a yew grove 'carpeted with silvery moss' is from this time: 'The yew stems were like fluted pillars, and the dark canopy of leaves was the roof. Through this shadowy hall, one saw the open lawns and the bright garden flowers beyond.'[10]

There were trips back to India, too, of course. One occasion was for Helen's marriage in May 1917 in Rajasthan to Harold Hill 'of Burford Manor and Kenya'.[11] Colvin, now aged twenty, was there as a slightly reluctant-looking bridesmaid. Towards the end of 1917, though, as her father's period of service in India came to an end, her parents undertook the hazardous trip home on a P & O liner travelling for safety in a war-time convoy. Her sister, unable to get a passage home to England with them, went to stay with relatives in Kenya. Later Colvin was to visit her and Harold at their home in Kitale. Once in England her father found war work in the form of an appointment as Secretary to the Surrey County Agricultural Committee – of which he said drily that he 'knew little about agriculture in England and, if possible, less about county administrators' methods'. At first the family lived in Chelsea but in 1918 they bought a long lease on a house in Kensington.[12]

It was at this point, at the age of twenty-one, that Colvin decided to leave behind her comfortable lifestyle to embark on something she was to find altogether more regimented and, as events turned out, something that would necessitate some hard decisions. At Swanley the college's rules and regulations were strict, uniform was worn at all times, each student had a tiny cubicle

ABOVE A portrait of Brenda Colvin, taken about the time she was sent 'home' to England to continue her education.
LEFT Helen Colvin's marriage in Rajasthan in May 1917 to Harold Hill. Brenda Colvin is the bridesmaid on the left; her mother Ethel is seated beside the unsmiling bride with her husband Elliot standing behind her.
OPPOSITE, CLOCKWISE FROM TOP LEFT Hextable House, home to Swanley Horticultural College, which Colvin entered in 1918; a typical student's cubicle bedroom at Swanley; Swanley students follow the digging example; Swanley students pose with hoes around a newly planted tree.

bedroom in which to sleep, and there was plenty of hard, physical work. As the syllabus explained: 'No gardening operation is considered as too menial, the method being that actual work accompanies, under skilled supervision, the theoretical instruction.' She was to study botany and beekeeping, chemistry and entomology as well as learning how to dig and hoe, prune and weed. The days were long too: the gardens opened for work at 6 a.m. in the summer, 9 a.m. in winter. To complete the course to the college's satisfaction, students had to 'satisfy the authorities by their general conduct, industry, punctuality of attendance....They must each produce a diary of horticultural work performed during that time and make a collection of injurious insects and weeds.'[13]

Colvin would certainly have been prepared to work hard at her chosen course but, as the Swanley instructors were to discover, she was not one to submit to anything with which she disagreed. Throughout her life, she would always make her opinion known. At Swanley,

within a year, she had changed from the compulsory general horticulture course to the landscape design course; within two, she was head student at the college and was writing to the principal to point out the shortcomings in her course and to question a rise in the fees. Her nonconformity, though, was about to provoke profound change. Before the second year ended, she had left, taking a group of students with her, in protest at the inadequacy of the teaching.

The roots of this rebellion lay in a change of management at the college. The horticultural college at Swanley had been established in 1889 as a private venture with just 13 male students enrolled in the first year.[14] A women's branch started in June 1891 with five students, but just seven years later the 35 women had overtaken the 20 men, and in the next year it was decided not to take any more male students. It was the first horticultural college in England to take women[15] – and became the first to be exclusively for women – but, even when Colvin arrived to study there, it was unusual for the daughters of professional families to contemplate a career. There was still much prejudice against – and derision about – the mere idea of 'lady gardeners'. It was not all that long since the Revd William Wilkes, Secretary to the Royal Horticultural Society, in a reply to the Hon. Mrs Evelyn Cecil's request for a recommendation of a lady gardener, had written that '(a) the work is not suited to women (b) women are not suited to the work. [Then, underlined in red:]…to put women to it is to go back a big step in the emancipation of your sex'.[16] Swanley students had to be determined young women and, although she was not to be there for long, Colvin's career was shaped by her time at the college and the contacts she made.

The college principal in 1918 was Miss Georgiana Sanders who, unusually, had come to Swanley from a school of landscape design in the United States. Under her, a new course in landscape gardening was introduced; it was taught by a former Swanley student, Madeline Agar, a woman whose experience and professional approach were to have a significant influence on Colvin. Agar had also studied in the States with a firm of civil engineers and was at that time practising professionally in England as well as teaching. When she had first left Swanley as a student, Agar had taken the post of Horticultural Instructress at Wycombe Abbey School for Girls, opened in 1896 by Miss Frances Dove, one of the earliest students at Girton College and a woman keen to improve the education available to young women. Encouraged by Miss Dove, Agar produced *A Primer of School Gardening*, which appeared in 1909, and two years later she published her *Garden Design in Theory and Practice*, a book that was to go on to a second edition in 1913. In 1907 she had also started Hollybush Nursery at Amersham with a Miss Holmes.

Agar's garden design clients were mostly private garden owners but from 1906 she was also employed as landscape gardener to the Metropolitan Public Gardens Association (MPGA). The association relied much on women for its work rescuing derelict sites and turning them into public gardens.[17] Later Agar was employed by the Conservators of Wimbledon Common on restoration work, so she was one of the first women in Britain to practise landscape design in the wider field of public works.

Later in life, when listing her training, in addition to the more traditional elements of college and working as an assistant in an architect's office, Agar credited her time working for the MPGA as having enlarged her 'experience in laying out and planting' and also noted a 'wise old Scotch foreman' who had taught her 'much

RIGHT A rare picture of Madeline Agar (back right), here aged 15 in her uniform as a member of the Wimbledon Ladies' Hockey Club, 1889–90.

about structural problems and the handling of labour'.[18] Such a down-to-earth approach and Agar's wide range of practical experience made her the ideal teacher for the new course which, according to the college magazine, was established with seven students. 'We are fortunate in getting Miss Agar to come to Swanley…to organize the start of the course,' it acknowledged. 'The students… have a maximum of two hours gardening daily, working chiefly in the flower gardens and walled-in garden.'[19]

By now Colvin had realised that 'in garden design my tastes for design and an outdoor life were brought together.'[20] Having changed to Miss Agar's course, she 'found the subject absorbing'. Consequently it was to be a blow for Colvin and the others on the landscape design course when, in 1919, Miss Sanders resigned. The vacant post of principal was taken by one Frances M.G.Mickelthwait. Mickelthwait's successor Dr Kate Barrett was later to say of her that she 'had rather revolutionary ideas. She would have no compunction in shutting a girl up in her room for a day with just bread and water if she considered she deserved the punishment.'[21] Following Miss Mickelthwait's appointment, the college went through a troubled period and in a very short space of time 19 instructors, lecturers and demonstrators – including Miss Agar – left. As the college magazine version of events put it in May 1920: 'Miss Agar has, we regret to say, found it necessary to relinquish her direction of the Landscape Gardening Course.'[22] Clearly Miss Agar – and the other 18 members of staff who resigned – did not see eye to eye with the new principal and her methods.

Miss Agar was replaced by a Miss Donaldson, a pupil of Thomas Mawson, probably the best established professional garden designer of the day. Once again the college magazine reported the change: 'Some of [Miss Agar's] work is being carried on by Miss A.Donaldson who has been working for the past 2½ years under Mr Mawson. The latter has promised to supervise the work and to give lectures himself or send one of his staff for that purpose.'[23] For Colvin, though, the replacement's 'lack of experience was scarcely compensated for by occasional lectures from Mr Mawson himself, and our small group of six or seven students became aware of

some serious gaps in the syllabus, though still totally unaware of the range of subjects required. In particular we asked to be taught surveying and levelling, which was due to start in the term Miss Agar left.' The last straw was when their 'youthful tutor' set them to do 'kindergarten exercises in model making' with plasticine rather than teaching them the basics of surveying. Colvin rebelled and left the college with her fellow students, having arranged private tuition with Miss Agar in the home of one of the group who lived locally – a move symptomatic of her determination to progress in her chosen field of garden and landscape design.[24]

In spite of her relatively brief time at the college and the trouble over her course, Colvin clearly formed a strong attachment to Swanley and did not bear a grudge. While there she had established some good friendships with both staff and students even though all her life she remained reserved, masking her shyness with an abruptness that could appear arrogant. In spite of this, everyone who knew her found her a kind, considerate and generous person and she inspired great loyalty. To stay in touch with the college and the friends she had made, she joined the Guild of Old Students and reported her news to the college magazine in successive years. In November 1931 she attended the annual conference and read a paper about a visit she had made to America earlier in the year, including her observations on American gardening and landscape architecture. By 1934, with the title of 'Adviser in Garden Design', she was a visiting lecturer at the college on 'the decorative side of horticulture' and she continued lecturing there until 1937. In the magazine for 1934 she wrote a piece on the problems of finding good training in landscape architecture and on the benefits of a period of apprenticeship with a working practice. At the following year's winter conference the subject was landscape work and Colvin spoke briefly on the subject, again advising that students should take a paid post to gain experience and self-confidence before starting to work on their own – a route she herself had followed when she started her career, working for Madeline Agar.

While still at Swanley, Colvin had won an award and the prize was a visit to Gertrude Jekyll's garden at Munstead Wood. That Colvin met Jekyll is confirmed by

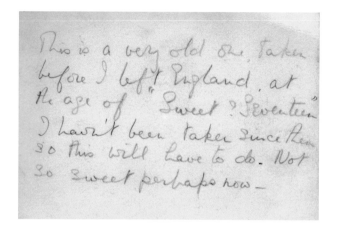

This is a very old one, taken before I left England, at the age of "Sweet ? Seventeen" I haven't been taken since then so this will have to do. Not so sweet perhaps now –

LEFT AND OPPOSITE A portrait of Brenda Colvin aged 17 that she gave to her father some years later – perhaps when he was in Bulgaria – with a handwritten message on the back.

the biographical note on the jacket of the second edition of her *Land and Landscape* which refers to 'memorable meetings' with both Jekyll and with William Robinson at Gravetye Manor. She also mentioned the prize and the meetings to her employees in the 1950s.[25] As a keen student of garden design, however, these visits must have been a profound experience and certainly she found Munstead Wood a revelation in the way that plants, foliage and colour could be used to create very specific effects. Robinson's Gravetye must surely have been the beginning of her interest in 'wild' gardening which was otherwise largely unknown at the time. Much later she was to write of Jekyll's partnership with Lutyens that he was lucky to find in her 'an artist sensitive enough to give his gardens an interior decoration harmonizing intimately with his own intention and a remarkable unity was achieved'.[26]

From today's perspective, however, where we can see the pervasive influence on garden design throughout the twentieth century of the Jekyll–Lutyens style – Lutyens's architectural stonework softened by Jekyll's colour-themed herbaceous borders – it is striking that in Colvin's view, Agar's skill and professionalism were more impressive. While she acknowledged that Agar never became as well known as Jekyll, 'who was widely known through her work with Lutyens and books on garden matters', she added the telling phrase, 'though [Jekyll's] design work was largely confined to planting Lutyens' architectural gardens'.[27] She considered Agar 'much more professional than Jekyll – she did working

drawings for construction and taught her students to do the same'.[28] At this time the practice of landscape design was far more advanced in America than it was in Britain and encompassed work that was done here by engineers. Agar had experienced this and obviously was determined that her students should acquire the additional skills they needed.

Having left Swanley, Colvin maintained her link with Agar, working for her in 1921 as clerk of works and site assistant on a five-acre war memorial garden at Wimbledon. Although Colvin was not involved with Agar's later work replanting the part of Wimbledon Common that had been occupied by Guards Regiments during the First World War,[29] she knew that Agar worked there with direct labour and that she visited the sites weekly, instructing a skilled foreman – that wise old Scotsman, perhaps – who was employed by the Conservators. When asked to list her training for the Institute of Landscape Architects' records in the 1940s, significantly Colvin listed 'Pupil to Miss Agar' first, with Swanley and the Regent Street Polytechnic School of Architecture in second and third place. Agar's influence at this early stage, setting an example as a skilled professional and opening Colvin's eyes to the importance of the wider landscape, was to be crucial to the development of her own career.

Before she set up her own practice, however, in the spring of 1921 she travelled to Sofia in Bulgaria to be with her parents. Her father had been seconded there as British Delegate on the Inter-Allied Commission, settling the treaty under which Bulgaria had to recognise the existence of Yugoslavia and pay reparations.[30] Her experience with the family in this remote spot was undoubtedly to stand her in good stead in her future travels in Europe.

In time Colvin travelled back to England. Her extensive connections through family and friends meant that very soon she had enough garden design business to set up her own private practice.

A good connection

'I have worked up a good connection, mostly in the class
that calls itself now the "new poor". '[1]

I N 1922 Brenda Colvin was invited by her cousin, William Gladstone, to design a garden for his house in Dorset.[2] What a challenge this was for a first commission – to create a garden for this stark new house stranded on the wild, exposed hillside above Lulworth Cove. Colvin was just twenty-five and only two years out of college, and it was her very first solo job. Whatever her feelings about it, the result was phenomenally successful and remains so today.[3] The ideas she brought into play here in this garden are absolutely perfect for the site.

Stair House is something of a rarity – few of Colvin's earlier gardens have survived. Many of them have been lost as a result of changing fashions or just the passing of time; many others disappeared as new owners came in and made their own changes. Here, though, although the original plans have been lost, it is possible to see that there has been virtually no structural change since the photographs of the garden taken in its heyday.

From the house to the clifftop is a steep climb up towards the south, and the site is completely exposed to all that the English Channel can throw at it. Colvin began by building a wall along the east side of the plot, then she planted shelter belts of wind and salt resistant trees and shrubs such as holm oak, sea buckthorn, euonymus, macrocarpa, eleagnus, fuchsia and laurestinus all round. At the same time she made sure to take the greatest possible advantage of the wonderful views to Lulworth Cove and out across the Channel – through squints and peepholes – without exposing the garden to the full blast of the predominant southwesterlies. Today some of the shelter has outgrown its space but it still works perfectly, lifting the wind up and over the garden which remains completely calm even on gale-rocked days.

Within the garden there are a number of fairly traditional elements from the 1920s – steps and terracing close to the house,

RIGHT AND OPPOSITE The well worn cover and first page of the notebook in which Colvin recorded her commissions.

1922?

List of Gardens in Order	Addresses
1 Lulworth	W. B. Gladstone
2 Acton Round	Wotbryche Whitmore?
3 Rodwell	through Penrose-Thackwell
4 Frognal (Planting Hans)	
5 Wishaw, Scotland	Lord Belhaven & Stenton
6 Wesprings	
7 Mr Roxburgh's garden	a Stowe School (through Joy Conyby)
8 St Margaret's Bay	through Penrose Thackwell
9 Lady Blennerhasset	
10 Mr Harrison	
11 Mrs Penrose P— Thackwell	
12 Mrs Fowler	Trull, Somerset (through Newtons)
13 Mrs Buckland	
14 Mrs Verney (Planting Hans only)	
15 Catchbells	Colvin, Stanway Sussex.
16 Mrs Tucker	
17 Pamflett	The Yanells
18 Hartcup	9 Elm Tree Road
19 Goodenough	Lilhurs Lechlade Glos
20 Mrs Cleghorn	
21 Mrs Blackett-Surrey	Taunton through Newtons?
22 Mrs Radcliffe	
23 Sesame Club.	through Penrose Thackwell

a sunken rose garden with pergola, herbaceous borders, Irish yews marking gateways, a rose parterre and the essential grass tennis court. Other elements, however, are far from conventional. There is a great sense of fun and excitement here – a positive labyrinth of paths, each bend leading you on round the next corner on an exciting voyage of discovery. There are seats hidden in every nook and cranny and one found on the cliff-top path is in a little stone semicircle known as 'the saucepan'. It is possible even on the windiest of days to sit in the calm sunshine here gazing out to sea and Portland Bill in the distance. There is an intriguing narrow, twisting, tunnel-like path to the Cliff House, an earlier fortification on

ABOVE Newly built, Stair House stands alone on the cliff top above Lulworth Cove.

CENTRE A 1905 postcard of West Lulworth Cove Hotel showing Stair House above, exposed on the cliff beside the new road.

BELOW In this 1921 postcard, Stair House is on the far right.

the top of the cliffs, and to one side near the top there is a mossy rockery. In this steep garden, Colvin did not forget to make provision for the gardeners either – there were four full-time posts in the garden's heyday – and she arranged for pipework to supply water on three different levels.

Sales details from 1972 describe:

This delightful garden is entirely enclosed and was originally laid out by the well known garden architect Miss Brenda Colvin….There is a stone terrace with views into Lulworth Cove, and below this a sunk rose garden. There are good herbaceous borders and a second rose garden leading to the major portion of the grounds which have been planted as a wild garden with an extensive and varied display of matured shrubs. This in turn leads up to the cliff top with its own cliff walk and a uniquely placed summer house

ABOVE A postcard view of Lulworth Village showing the garden taking shape around Stair House and the wall built along its east side.

BELOW Many years later Colvin's planting of trees has matured and protects the house from the prevailing winds.

looking out on a magnificent coastal panorama across to Weymouth Bay and in the distance to Portland Bill.

It is a garden that, even though her first, shows many of the characteristic elements of her designs: a profound respect for the 'genius of the place'; skilled plantsmanship with an emphasis on choosing the right plant for the right place; the use of curves and bends – whether paths or borders – that lead the eye on through the garden and excite curiosity in the visitor; careful use of axial lines and vistas; consideration of the practicalities of maintenance; and, not least, meeting the clients' expectations with some more traditional, conventional elements.

As Colvin herself admitted,[4] her early commissions were for friends and relatives but, even though this first commission came through a family connection, the Gladstones must have been pleased with the result because over the years they recommended Colvin to other garden owners, and Mrs Gladstone commissioned Colvin to design her London gardens as well.

Such connections are typical of Colvin's early years. From 1922 until the outbreak of the Second World War, the basis of Colvin's practice, working from her home at different addresses in Chelsea,[5] and later from her office at 28 Baker Street, was the creation and improvement of private gardens. In that year, under the neat heading 'List of Gardens in Order', she made her first entry in the small red notebook in which she continued to keep a complete numbered list of her commissions. This slim book, just 8 cm (3 in.) wide and 20 cm (8 in.) tall, contains 41 pages of entries and, eerily, by the time of her death in January 1981, it was exactly full.

ABOVE Glimpses of the sea and the countryside beyond are seen over the top of the formal pergola and 'sunk' rose garden at Stair House.
LEFT Traditional steps and terracing cope with changing levels in a formal area near to the house.
RIGHT Towards the cliff top, a path curves away beyond the rockery.

(A transcription of the notebook is included on pp.234-248.) The entries are brief – usually just the client's name and short address – and sometimes – more so in later years – a note of how Colvin came to be commissioned. And, a sign of her practical nature, several entries in the notebook also make a note of the gardener's name. Stair House, No. 1 in 1922 was simply entered as 'Lulworth – W.B.Gladstone'. The last is No. 675 in 1980: 'Thenford House (Heseltine) – through Basil Street'. This was a survey for the designer Lanning Roper who was drawing up planting plans for the Heseltines' garden.[6]

Study of the notebook shows how Colvin's garden practice grew, but it lacks detail and frequently it is not possible to identify precisely the place or the person for whom the work was done. Even where a certain identification of a garden can be made, there is often no further information available. An additional obstacle to identification is that many of Colvin's records and plans were destroyed by a bomb blast at her office during the Second World War. Of those that survived, many have simply been lost in the intervening years, were disposed of in occasional office clear-outs or were burnt by Colvin herself or her assistant Mac later in life.[7] Clearly she did not consider that people might one day want to discover more about her career and her influence on garden and landscape design – a typically unassuming attitude.

Nevertheless it is possible to draw some safe conclusions from the entries. Some recommendations are from people for whom she had recently completed work, often living fairly close to the new commission – so the garden at Stair House brought in work nearby in Dorset on the Gladstones' recommendation for a Mrs Bond in 1923 (No. 36) and in 1924 for the Swanns at Steeple Manor (No. 50) – who, incidentally, then recommended her in 1934 to Colonel Woodall at Netherbury Court, Beaminster, also in Dorset (No. 208). And the Gladstones' recommendation brought in other work around the country over the years, even as late as 1958: 'No. 424 Commander J Oram, Whitwick Manor, Herefordshire – through Gladstone Lulworth job'. Some names such as Penrose-Thackwell and Newton, presumably closer family friends, recommend her quite often.

Colvin's own photographs from this time include pictures of gardens she worked on, sometimes taken three or four years after the initial entry in the notebook, so at least a number of these commissions were ongoing projects.[8] A good example of her continuing input on the gardens she designed – and also her ability to mix socially with her 'clients' – is provided by the visitors' books of two sisters who lived near Tewkesbury. Colvin was first employed by Miss Nora Kennedy at Sarn Hill Grange (No. 177) in 1931. The Sarn Hill visitors' book shows that she stayed there in November 1931, February 1932 and again in February 1934. In the meantime, Miss Kennedy had recommended Colvin to her sister Mrs Alice Maxwell who was renting Conderton Manor (No. 199) from the Holland-Martins, and she stayed there in October and December 1933 and in November and December the following year. By December 1933, on the recommendation of Mrs Maxwell, Colvin had also started work at Overbury Court for Mrs Holland-Martin. And so, in these earlier years of her garden design practice, it is evident that frequently it was Colvin's network of contacts and the subsequent positive word-of-mouth references that led to further commissions.

Certainly, for her to be given all these personal recommendations, Colvin's work and her approach to it must have been popular. Many of her clients were women and no doubt preferred to deal with a woman who might be more sympathetic to their ideas. In the period leading up to the Second World War, it is a fact that the majority of garden design practitioners were male, whether garden designers or nurserymen. Another factor in her favour was that her designs were practical and revealed a sensitivity to the surrounding landscape and to existing trees and plants and therefore were not too disruptive. And she was not expensive. Writing to the Institute of Landscape Architects in July 1930 about a proposed scale of professional charges, she agreed with all the proposals except the *per diem* charge: 'A large proportion of my work is charged for entirely on a time basis; if the proposed 7 gns[9] a day is to be considered as a strict minimum, I shall be in a somewhat difficult position. I have worked up a good connection, mostly in the class that calls itself now

the "new poor", and were I to adopt the suggested basis, I should lose practically the whole of that connection.'[10]

The 'new poor' had been created after the First World War. The most significant result of that had been a more than tenfold increase in the national debt. Accordingly, to finance this borrowing, taxation stayed at a high level for several years into the peace. During the slump of 1921–22, unemployment had risen to its highest level for 100 years and it remained the biggest social problem of the 1920s and 1930s. The extra revenue the government needed could only come from yet higher taxation and this fell hardest on the rich with income tax rising to 4 shillings in the pound. For the owners of large gardens this created a vicious circle – high unemployment meant that there was plenty of labour available but high taxation meant that people could not afford to employ gardeners on anything like the pre-war scale. It was in these post-war years of austerity, after all, that the 9th Duke of Devonshire was driven to have the Great Conservatory at Chatsworth blown up. It demanded too much unwarranted expenditure.

Colvin's notebook also reveals exactly how well connected she was socially – it is like reading a *Who's Who* with many titled and high-ranking military names among her clients. Most of the recommendations were personal but some came through Swanley College, some from pictures of her designs featured in *The Studio Gardens and Gardening* annuals and some from photographs seen at the Chelsea Flower Show. Later commissions came as a result of her lectures and books and through the Institute of Landscape Architects.

Although she was not there every year, Colvin regularly exhibited plans and photographs of her gardens at Chelsea in the years before the Second World War.[11] She also reported to the Swanley College magazine that in 1925 she designed and was in charge of a garden exhibited by Clayton & Hammond of Baker Street at the Ideal Home Exhibition. In the years after the war at Chelsea, she showed a mixture of private gardens and more public projects – for example a garden in a small London square in 1952, a factory garden and sports ground in 1954 and some school gardens in 1956.

Most of the 296 commissions up to 1939 are private gardens at addresses in Yorkshire, Shropshire, Worcestershire, Wiltshire, Gloucestershire, Dorset, Somerset, East Anglia, Scotland, Wales and Ireland, and even France, Italy and Poland, as well as those in London and the Home Counties. The long distances involved in some of these journeys by road – as well as snowstorms on her trips to Poland in the later 1930s[12] – are a good indication of Colvin's intrepid nature. She spent a considerable amount of time travelling, and was a good, albeit by some accounts erratic driver with a preference for sports cars and soft tops at a time when most people, and certainly most women, drove saloons.

Later in life she was to say of this garden design work,

> When I chose the profession of landscape architect I believed that it would bring the great satisfaction of 'seeing results'. Let me warn every beginner that the hope is in vain. The pleasure is always in the imagination – the picture as we see it in the mind's eye – as we have tried to show it on plan, and as we hope it will some day appear.[13]

She was realistic but regretful about the chances of survival of her work on private gardens which she considered likely to be lost either through neglect or change of owner. Or, perhaps worse, by the introduction of some unsuitable ornament:

> Surely other designers beside myself on revisiting work carried out in the past must have found their whole intention shattered by the intrusion of a bird bath made of rustic concrete or an inscription about 'the kiss of the sun' making nonsense of the ideas underlying the design.[14]

As well as the private gardens, there were commissions too for a number of more public spaces in these earlier years. In her first year in practice, 1922, Colvin worked for J.F.Roxburgh, the inspirational headmaster of Stowe School, shortly before the school was founded in May 1923. The entry in the notebook (No. 7) reads simply 'Mr Roxburgh's garden, Stowe School' and is most probably the 'parterre' or enclosed area to the east of the South Front steps, just next to Mr Roxburgh's living quarters.[15] In a note to the Swanley College magazine at that time, she also included 'restoring landscape at Stowe' among her work this year, so she may have carried out some additional work there. She was invited back by Mr Roxburgh two years later to design a garden or planting for what she refers to as 'New House' (No. 55).

There were commissions for other schools, too: University College School (No. 38, 1923), Wycombe Abbey (No. 173, 1930), Queen Margaret's School in Scarborough (No. 179, 1931-2), Sebright School, Wolverley (No. 204, 1934), St Felix School, Southwold (No. 209, 1934 and No. 296, 1939), and Roedean School, Brighton (No. 278, 1938). Photographs among Colvin's papers show a small formal iris garden at Wycombe Abbey.[16] This particular garden was also featured among 'Members' work' in the autumn 1937 issue of the ILA's journal *Landscape and Garden*, where it was specified that the pattern was carried out in box and thyme, and a photograph of it formed part of Colvin's display at the Chelsea Flower Show in 1953. At St Felix School, Colvin's own photographs taken in the summers of 1935 and 1936 show planting around the new chapel and wooden steps leading up to a seating area referred to as 'Sheila's Garden'. Her work here led to a commission on the

ABOVE Colvin's formal iris garden at Wycombe Abbey School with a pattern carried out in box and thyme.

recommendation of the school's bursar, Mr Tweddle, for work at the memorial garden in Southwold for Colonel Mallinson (No. 215).

There were several other ventures outside the world of private gardens too. In 1922 Colvin was employed in London by the Sesame Club (No. 23), a liberal, predominantly women's club which had been formed by a 'group of friends' who had children and who wished to study and discuss how best to educate them. She also designed gardens or provided planting plans for the Governesses' Benevolent Association at a house in Beckenham (No. 61, 1924), the Mariners' Charity in Lewes (No. 89, 1926), Stoke Poges Putting Green (No. 152, 1929), the Chelsea Housing Scheme at World's End Passage (No. 172, 1930), the City of

TOP 'Sheila's Garden' at St Felix School, Southwold, is seen in Colvin's own photograph from June 1936.
ABOVE Another of her photographs shows some of the planting around the school's chapel.

London Maternity Hospital (No. 218, 1935), and the Lambeth Housing Movement in Clapham (No. 260, 1937). In 1927–28, anticipating her later work on roads, she did some work on the Barnet bypass (No. 118), and in 1939, with the Second World War in the offing, on Madeline Agar's recommendation, she was employed by the Metropolitan Public Gardens Association to work on trenches being prepared as air-raid shelters in Eaton Square and Shepherd's Bush (Nos. 292 and 293).

The war was to bring great change to the nature of the work Colvin was commissioned to carry out. Although her work in these pre-war years was almost exclusively involved with the design of private gardens and school gardens, she had been increasingly concerned with the question of landscape design and was closely involved from the start with the establishment of a professional body for its practitioners.

A self-sown seedling

'The idea of landscape design evolved by cross fertilisation between horticulture and architectural design and grew like a self-sown seedling in a carelessly maintained garden, which when it reaches its flowering stage, almost unobserved, proves to be a new and valuable life form.'[1]

N 1929 the Chelsea Flower Show was witness to the birth of a new organisation. On Thursday 23 May of that year between 30 and 40 people interested in landscape design gathered in what the catalogue referred to as the 'art tent' at the show. This was where 'Paintings, Garden Plans etc.' were being exhibited. By this stage Colvin had been in contact with the organisers for some time and was one of the key figures behind the move. It was to be a momentous meeting. Colvin made certain she was there, accompanied by her assistant Kate Hawkins.

In early February she had seen a notice in the *Gardeners' Chronicle*, inviting 'All who are interested' to a meeting at 7pm on 20 February at 9 Gower Street, Bedford Square, 'to discuss the formation of a proposed Society of Garden Architects'.[2] As one of those 'desirous of receiving an invitation', she had sent a postcard to Richard Sudell, one of the organisers, asking if she could attend that meeting. Two weeks later, in early March, she wrote to him again about a further meeting on the 6th.[3] Clearly she was anxious to be closely involved right from the start.

Of the Chelsea meeting, Colvin was to recall, 'We met standing in the centre of the design tent – and had an informal talk which led to the launching of the project with R. Sudell as president.'[4] Not everyone, however, was prepared to get involved: Percy Cane, an established garden consultant, was to be seen 'prowling around the small standing circle listening to our proceedings but taking no part'.[5]

One question led to much debate among the founders over the next few months: what was the new organisation to be called? The 'British Association of Garden Architects', perhaps, or should it be of 'Landscape Gardeners'? Colvin felt sure 'that at the earliest stage of the discussion the term Landscape Gardeners was the title considered, in continuation of the Capability Brown and Repton tradition'.[6] Soon, though, Thomas Adams, founder president of the Town Planning Institute in 1914, managed to persuade the founding members to use the American title and decide on 'Landscape Architects'.[7] This was significant. As Colvin recalled at the time of the organisation's

RIGHT The four covers designed by Sylvia Bergin for the Institute of Landscape Architects' journal *Landscape and Garden*, published from spring 1934 to summer 1939.

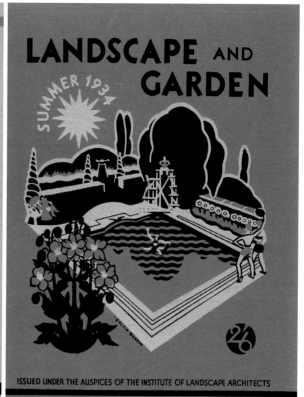

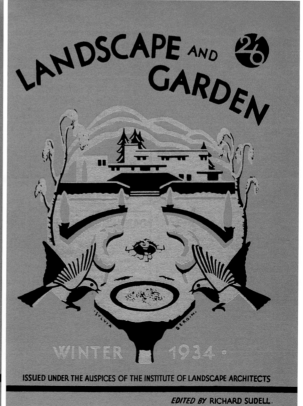

Golden Jubilee in 1979, 'Most of the people who started the institute were only doing private gardens....If we had called it Landscape Gardeners, it would have taken us much longer to arrive at the full scope the profession has today – if we had arrived at it at all.'[8]

Through the 1920s there had been a growing swell of feeling that some sort of professional organisation was needed. First Colvin and the other students on Madeline Agar's landscape design course at Swanley had considered it necessary but Colvin remembered that when they suggested it to Thomas Mawson, who had taken over their course from Agar, 'he responded that there was not enough work to justify founding an institute – that his firm and that of Milner White[9] would absorb all there was in this country. This theory was manifestly inaccurate.' At the Chelsea Flower Shows through the 1920s, Percy Cane and several other designers were exhibiting photographs of their work in the garden design section and the nursery contractors' small gardens were, in Colvin's words, 'evidently a profitable venture'.[10] As the 1920s progressed there was a clear expansion of the profession: several Swanley students had started practices in garden design, as had students from the Royal Horticultural Society gardens at Wisley and former pupils of Mawson, Edward White, Percy Cane and other consultants.

An International Exhibition of Garden Design held at the Royal Horticultural Society for a week in October 1928 proved to be something of a catalyst. The lack of unity seen at that time in the British section prompted two designers, Stanley V. Hart and Richard Sudell, to call a meeting in early 1929. Dismayed by the current state of affairs, they resolved to form some kind of professional association and placed the notice for the preliminary discussion meeting which, in its turn, led to the gathering at Chelsea.

The Chelsea meeting – from which Mawson was noticeably absent – was followed by one arranged by Sudell in his office in Gower Street. The architect and landscape architect Geoffrey Jellicoe recalled that, in addition to those who had been at Chelsea, Sudell invited some other architects known to be interested in gardens.

As well as Jellicoe himself, there were Oliver Hill, Gilbert Jenkins and Barry Parker. Sudell chaired this meeting but, according to Jellicoe, Jenkins whispered in his ear, ' "We must get Sudell out of the Chair and we must get Thomas Mawson in" and so at the next meeting, we proposed that although Sudell had done splendidly in starting the thing off, an Institute must have a great name to get it launched.'[11] Graciously, Sudell resigned and Mawson was invited to join the institute and lend his 'prestige' as its first president. So, after a very brief spell as the British Association of Garden Architects, the Institute of Landscape Architects (ILA) began its life with a constitution drawn up by Jenkins. Without the influence and support of the architects, Colvin felt that it 'could well have foundered or become confined to purely horticultural design'.[12] The committee set up to select other members included Jenkins, Edward White, E. Prentice Mawson (son of the president), and Marjory Allen (Lady Allen of Hurtwood, also known as Joan Allen). Stanley Hart was made honorary secretary. Early members also included Madeline Agar (who was encouraged to join by Colvin,[13] garden designer Russell Page and planner Thomas Sharp. (See p.112 for a group photograph from 1934 that includes several of the early members of the institute.)

Even though they belonged to the ILA, at first most of the so-called landscape architects were occupied only with private garden design: 'the enormous field of wider landscape planning was not foreseen until our attention was drawn to it by Thomas Adams, who was working in the USA and had seen the role opening there for landscape design. He was engaged on the regional plan for New York and the Westchester County Park system.'[14] The exceptions who were already working on the wider landscape were Mawson, who designed town parks, and Madeline Agar with her work for the Metropolitan Public Gardens Association and for the Wimbledon Common Conservators restoring Wimbledon Common after wartime damage.

In 1931 Adams delivered a public lecture for the institute on the 'Meaning and Scope of Landscape Architecture and Its Relation to Town Planning'. 'My eyes were opened by Thomas Adams,' Brenda Colvin admitted. 'I went to America on the strength of that talk.'[15] The continuing slump of the early 1930s had affected her business which was virtually at a standstill so, anxious to widen her own horizons, Colvin sold her car and used the money to pay for a visit to America.[16] In the spring of 1931 she went 'armed with introductions and advice' from Adams, and observed,

America, unlike Britain, was not a nation of gardeners and…its people felt the need for professional advice. Professionals such as Olmsted turned from formal gardening to the 'English' garden style of the eighteenth century to deal with these large-scale projects and the changing style was in evidence when I visited.[17]

The landscape architect Frederick Law Olmsted (1822–1903) first came to appreciate the need for public recreation spaces in cities following a visit in 1850 to Joseph Paxton's new park at Birkenhead, near Liverpool. In partnership with the English architect Calvert Vaux (1824–95), he designed many well-known urban parks in America, including Central Park in New York City, and shaped the development of public park design in the later nineteenth century following the mid-nineteenth-century work in Britain by Paxton and his followers. His practice, taken over by his two sons, who were also founding members of the American Institute of Landscape Architects in 1899, later designed many high-profile projects including parkway systems, universities, exposition grounds, libraries, hospitals and state capitols.

While Colvin was in America, Mr Pond, a lecturer in landscape design at Harvard, was a great help to her and she attended lectures and visited many sites with his pupils – including some of the Olmsted Brothers' work and their offices, which employed some 60 people at their peak in the 1930s. She travelled from Boston to New York along the length of the Westchester Parkway, which she considered marked 'a stage in the progress from garden design to landscape planning'.[18] As she told the Swanley Old Students' Guild after her return, she found the treatment of the main roads or parkways an example of

the splendid results achieved by proper co-operation among the authorities concerned…they are, in a sense, extensions of the parks in the various towns…

RIGHT Colvin visited the Westchester Parkway in 1931 and felt it marked 'a stage in the progress from garden design to landscape planning'. This picture of it featured in a double-page spread in *Landscape and Garden*, Autumn 1936, under the heading 'Modern Highways'.

A wide strip of land is reserved all along both sides of the road and this is all treated as park land, and well planted with trees and shrubs.

In spite of appearing to be a costly way of making roads, it seemed that the parkways were self-financing – the bathing beaches and amusement parks incorporated in the plan more than paying for their upkeep.[19]

In New York she met more landscape architects and then finally moved on to Philadelphia and Washington but had to 'give up hopes of California and other centres as funds ran out'.[20] She returned home in June and promptly wrote to Stanley Hart at the institute to let him know she was back, expressing the hope that she was 'still a member of the Council'.[21] She found a few jobs and, 'by buying a second-hand car for £25 [the equivalent of about £1,000 today], was able to limp along until times improved'.[22]

The economic depression had affected the other members of the institute too. According to Geoffrey Jellicoe, it was 'a period of consolidation by a very small number of practitioners – enough only to form the council'.[23] Colvin felt they 'had only the faintest notion of how the Institute might develop or how the work and influence of the profession could expand through joint efforts'. Beyond the need for communication and the sharing of information, better education and more public recognition, their 'sights were still set low'.[24]

Nevertheless communication was important and Edward White, who followed Thomas Mawson as president in 1932, took a much more active role than his predecessor, and his son, L. Milner White, became honorary secretary and started the 'Quarterly Notes', the first newsletter for members of the new organisation. These continued with Geoffrey Jellicoe and H.R. Dixon as honorary editors and, written by Brenda Colvin, became a regular feature in the institute's new quarterly journal, *Landscape and Garden*, which was first produced in spring 1934. This was an ambitious and attractive publication, produced on heavy quality paper with illustrations. Sylvia Bergin designed four avant-garde seasonal covers for it and these were used until the last issue was published in

summer 1939. In the same way that its members were largely involved in garden design, the journal featured many articles on gardens and garden plants but it also included writing about the wider landscape both in Great Britain and abroad, and discussion about the role of the landscape architect at that time.

Public concern about the rapidly increasing damage being done to the countryside by indiscriminate development and land use had been rising since the start of the 1920s. After the First World War there had been an acceleration in the change from 'a world of horses, wagons, dusty lanes, oil lamps, thatched roofs, cob walls and labour-intensive farming…to the world of cars, lorries, motor buses, tractors, tarmacadam roads, council houses, electricity, telephones, wireless, piped water, mains drainage, standardized household articles and mass entertainment'.[25] The rapid growth in car ownership – there were 177 different car manufacturers exhibiting at the Olympia Motor Show in London in 1922 – meant that people were no longer tied to living in towns and cities. With their own transport to take them to shops and workplaces, they could live further out into the countryside. The unplanned spread of housing that grew to meet this demand was known as 'ribbon development' – the building of straggling lines of housing along the main roads, the random building of small houses along country lanes. In his best-selling *In Search of England*, first published in 1927, H.V. Morton sets off on his journey, trying to get beyond 'The Place Where London Ends':

> In a field some way off the high road were scared-looking pink and white villas….Wives as new as the gardens and the houses busied about their work…. The most significant item on the landscape was an empty omnibus…. The history of London is the moving on of that red omnibus another mile along the road; more pink and white houses; more shops.[26]

RIGHT The contents page of the first issue of *Landscape and Garden* to which Colvin contributed 'Quarterly Notes'.

LANDSCAPE & GARDEN

A Quarterly Journal devoted to Garden Design and Landscape Architecture

VOL. I   SPRING, 1934   NO. I

BEAUTY

"I have seen the Lady April bringing the daffodils,
Bringing the springing grass and the soft warm April rain."

JOHN MASEFIELD

Garden by Edward White

CONTENTS

Edited by RICHARD SUDELL

EDITORIAL, ADVERTISING & PUBLISHING OFFICES: 4, BEDFORD SQUARE, LONDON, W.C.I.

TELEPHONE - MUSEUM 2288

TRADE SALES : 34, BLOOMSBURY STREET, LONDON, W.C.I.   TELEPHONE MUSEUM 5728

13

The country's increasingly commercial culture also led to the proliferation of garages and petrol pumps, broadcasting masts, advertisement hoardings and litter, and further threats to the landscape came from the new roads, mineral workings, electricity pylons and other industrial developments. This process of urban growth and its sprawling spread was seen as an 'octopus' – the city's tentacles reaching out and strangling the countryside, an image that was originally used by pioneering planner Patrick Abercrombie in a 1915 essay but one that was popularised by the Portmeirion architect Clough Williams-Ellis in his *England and the Octopus*, an anti-sprawl polemic that was published in 1928. 'Everyone', he says, 'knows that England has changed violently and enormously within the last few decades. Since the War, indeed, it has been changing with an acceleration that is catastrophic….It is chiefly the spate of mean building all over the country that is shrivelling up the old England.'[27] Two years previously, Abercrombie had published his *Preservation of Rural England* which called for a national joint committee to preserve the countryside and to plan for change. This was indeed formed in December 1926 as the Council for the Preservation of Rural England (CPRE), with Abercrombie as its honorary secretary.[28] The CPRE immediately started campaigning, first in the war against ribbon development by urging that local authorities could use powers granted by the Public Health Act 1925 to charge street work costs to new roadside building – a major disincentive to developers. The campaign continued with the CPRE supporting Raymond Unwin's proposed 'Green Girdle' for London which was to become Britain's first Green Belt. Finally, in 1935 the Restriction of Ribbon Development Act was passed.

In support of such campaigning, by 1934 in the 'Quarterly Notes' in the first issue of *Landscape and Garden*, Colvin was writing that while one of the institute's chief aims was to maintain a standard of qualification, it was also to 'co-operate with any organization whose object is to preserve the beauty of England and to foster and encourage the appreciation of beautiful surroundings'.[29] Later that year she reported on a lecture by Thomas Adams that dealt with the need for the art of landscape design as a branch of town planning. It was not enough just to provide open space 'as is seen in some of the worst examples of ribbon development which are often very spacious'. What was needed were 'the proper grouping of the buildings on the site and the treatment of the open spaces'.[30]

The notion of landscape design approached through the planning process – something far removed from garden design – was developing, something Colvin's professional partner Hal Moggridge has more recently described as 'landscape without boundaries'.[31] An example was Patrick Abercrombie's plan for Sheffield in the late 1920s, which included a layout of open spaces to run from the city centre out into the Peak District. In 1935, in his presidential address to the institute, Gilbert Jenkins made an appeal to 'all who have a knowledge of landscape design, whether they call themselves planners, town planners, garden designers or architects to join us…in fighting the battle against the growing tide of utilitarianism'. He also appealed to all who were interested in 'the beauties of landscape and garden' to help in this great work. 'With a strong Institute', he went on, 'it will no longer be necessary to talk of preserving the beauties of our Island, as new forms of beauty will arise throughout the land.'[32]

In 1937 the man who had inspired Colvin to make her trip to America became president of the institute. With Thomas Adams at the helm, a man who had worked with the Olmsteds' office in America, a man who had been recently involved in planning in New York and the Westchester Parkway, the institute moved further down the road to becoming a body concerned with much wider questions than simply park and garden design. However, although this period was very much a time of expanding ideas, almost all the work available was still limited to garden design. It would not be until after the Second World War that a new political and economic climate would enable the landscape architects to put into practice those wider notions of landscape design linked with planning. Meanwhile, alongside her work for the institute, Colvin had been developing her own style of garden design and ideas about the wider landscape.

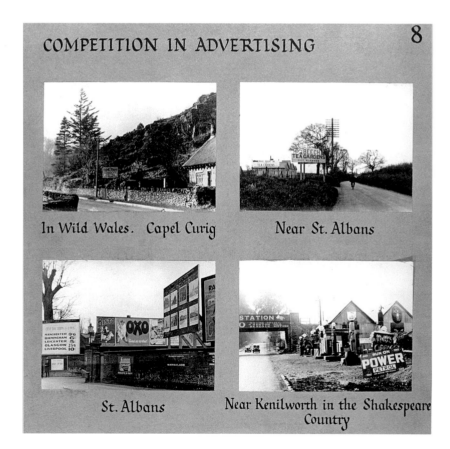

OPPOSITE LEFT Ribbon development seen in one of Colvin's contact prints, captioned by her, and below it is a version cropped as she suggested.

OPPOSITE RIGHT Colvin captioned this contact print herself, later calling it 'A garage typical of many that spoil our villages' when it appeared in her book *Land and Landscape*.

LEFT Part of an exhibition panel put together by the Council for the Preservation of Rural England in 1928 to warn of the horrors of advertisement hoardings. Later, Colvin was to forbid anyone staying at her Cotswold home from buying any products she felt used inappropriate advertisements.

A small but satisfying livelihood

'I then began doing a few private garden designs for friends and relatives…
and found that a small but satisfying livelihood was available at very low fees'.[1]

LOOKING BACK IN 1979, Brenda Colvin feared that only a few of the gardens that she had designed before the Second World War would have survived:

> The work of those following this profession is too easily lost by neglect or changed by new activity or ownership. This is especially true of private gardens and of the work I did before the war little evidence remains.[2]

In fact, though, there is plenty of evidence to be found of her earlier work. However much some have been neglected in the intervening years, a number of her gardens have survived, at least in part. Then there are Colvin's own photographs of the earlier gardens, a number of these mounted and captioned for display at Chelsea in the 1950s. And she herself commented in some detail on a few of them in her articles for the Institute of Landscape Architecture's journal and other publications. Finally, a few rare plans have also survived.

It is interesting, first, to look at three examples of Colvin's smaller, town garden work in London as seen in her own photographs. At Essex Villas, Kensington (No. 184 in her notebook), she designed a bright, private and easy-to-maintain garden for a Miss Pigot-Moodie in 1932. She used trellis and trees around the edge of the garden to screen it from its neighbours and whitewashed the walls to reflect the light and contrast with the cleared trunks of the trees and the dark trellis above. The curving walls of the pool-like sunken central section give the garden a feeling of greater width and a sense of movement and yet the planting softens the hard edges of the brick surrounds. Writing in *Good Gardening* magazine in 1936 and using a photograph of this garden, Colvin advocated the use of different levels – however slight – that give interest to a garden design: 'the banks or walls provide a surface at a different angle from the rest of the garden, which will accommodate different plants, and the steps can be an attractive feature in themselves.'[3] The repeated use of planted pots round the outside of the garden provides seasonal colour, breaks up the hard lines and brings rhythm to the row of trees along the side and end walls.

RIGHT Designed by Colvin in 1932, this bright, secluded garden in Essex Villas, Kensington, features many of her characteristic design elements.

Early the next year Colvin's cousin's wife, Mrs Gladstone of Stair House in Dorset, commissioned her to design their London garden in Stanford Road, Kensington (No. 188 in the notebook). In this slightly larger garden, again there is trellis and planting on the walls aimed at achieving greater privacy. A pair of clipped bay trees frame the view of the garden from the upper level; a path in a simple brickwork pattern leads the eye down the garden to a raised section which could be used for sitting or eating out at almost any time of year. Colvin uses changes in level throughout this garden to add interest, and yet the hard landscaping is skilfully softened everywhere by exuberant, cottage-style planting with an emphasis on striking foliage.

Several of Colvin's own photographs from the 1930s feature her own much smaller courtyard garden at 25

Cheyne Row in Chelsea. An overhead picture, taken from an upstairs window, shows a very private, leafy oasis. Although it is hard to be sure of the details of the planting, the emphasis here is on foliage rather than flower colour, the walls are covered with climbers – ivies and a Virginia creeper – and, to one side, use is made of a shapely small tree to give height and, no doubt, seasonal colour. A potted plant provides a focal point at the end – and the chance to make changes in the planting according to the seasons. Again, trellis to one side gives privacy and the basket-weave brick paving is simple and understated – and the ideal low-maintenance surface.

The close-ups of planting in this garden show broad-leaved hostas and bergenias – which became one of Colvin's 'signature' plants – contrasting with ferns and iris or some other strap-leafed plants, and again the use of pots. In a short article for *Landscape and Garden* in 1938,[4] she recommended using ordinary garden pots planted with a hosta and a royal fern to fill a dark corner in a small town garden or courtyard – and whitewashing the wall behind to reflect as much light as possible and to set off the soft grey-greens of the plants. The illustrations she used for this article included pots in her own garden and a photograph she had taken in Paris in June 1937 of a small Modernist courtyard by the Cubist-inspired French designer André Vera which showed the use of succulents in pots to add interest to an expanse of concrete wall.

These London gardens can seem rather unexceptional now but at the time they were totally original. In the 1930s people's back gardens in London were almost non-existent. These gardens are definitely extensions of their houses, 'rooms outside', a principle Colvin was to advocate many times. They are places that could be used in almost all seasons, and the emphasis in the planting

LEFT ABOVE Formal bay trees frame the view of the garden from indoors and the steps lead down to a simple brickwork path at Stanford Road, Kensington.

LEFT BELOW The cottage-style planting includes lilies and roses but the emphasis is on contrasting foliage; trellis and climbers screen the garden from neighbours.

LEFT Colvin's own garden in Cheyne Row, Chelsea, seen from upstairs in 1936, a leafy year-round haven.
BELOW The broad foliage of hostas and rheum contrasts with iris and other strap-leaved plants in Colvin's Chelsea garden.
BOTTOM Pots of succulents break up an expanse of concrete wall in this Paris garden by André Vera, photographed by Colvin in June 1937 when she was attending an International Conference on Garden Design.

is on form rather than colour, using mostly permanent foliage plants with large leaves that need little sun and that would have been able to thrive in London's sooty atmosphere at that time. Indeed, her own London garden's style was so timeless that Colvin used a picture of a corner of it to illustrate what could be achieved in 'Shady Corners' in her 'Our Gardens' report, published by the Central Housing Advisory Committee in 1948,[5] and it was considered sufficiently up to date to be included five years later by Marjory Allen and Susan Jellicoe in their *Gardens*, a small Penguin picture book that argued for good modern design, and again as late as 1977 in their *Town Gardens to Live In*.[6] And it is true to say that none of these town gardens would look out of date today.

Of the range of rather grand private gardens that she designed before the war, there is now little physical evidence on the ground, but again Colvin's photographs of a number of them, a few surviving plans, and descriptions and pictures in articles that she wrote for *Landscape and Garden* reveal the key elements of her design aesthetic.

Following on from her first, very successful design in 1922 for Stair House at Lulworth, Colvin's fifteenth commission came from a Colonel James Colvin, a distant

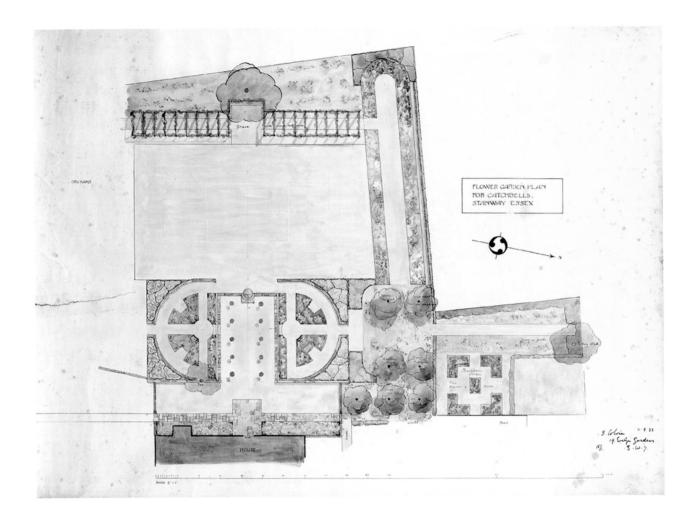

relation, who lived at Catchbells, a farmhouse dating from the fifteenth century in what was then a rural location on the London Road in Stanway, Essex. Here she designed a flower garden with a number of formal areas well suited to the house – a herb garden, a grass walk between double herbaceous borders, an oval rose garden edged with lavender and a gravel path through a nut walk. But within the formality she introduced a more relaxed feel with areas of long grass, and in the rose garden the detailed planting plan shows named varieties on the inside but a number of species roses on the outside – sweet briars, rugosa roses and *Rosa moyesii*.

In the next couple of years Colvin's commissions took her on the long journey to Scotland (No. 5) and to Varengeville in Normandy (No. 34), as well as to many other destinations in England.[7] She had returned

ABOVE Colvin's overall plan for the 'flower garden' at Catchbells shows a number of formal areas balanced by softer elements such as the unmown grass beyond the nut walk and beside the grass walk leading to the turkey oak (bottom right).

to Dorset in 1923, to Corfe Cottage (No. 33) and, on the recommendation of the Gladstones, to 'Mrs Bond, Dorset' (No. 36).[8] In 1924 once again she drove from London to the Isle of Purbeck for what was to be the 50th commission in her career as a garden designer, Steeple Manor near Wareham.

In the early 1920s Major Frederick Holland Swann bought Steeple Manor.[9] It was a derelict farmhouse and the Swanns employed the architect Morley Horder to carry out renovation work for them.[10] With no previous garden on the sloping site, the design for Steeple Manor must have been another real challenge for Colvin early in her career, but it was one she met magnificently. Starting work there in 1924, she created a garden of contrasting yet complementary compartments or 'rooms' on a number of different levels, with a range of styles and moods, matching perfectly the spirit of the seventeenth-century house and offering extensive views both within and without.

As she was to do elsewhere later in her career, almost her first move at Steeple was to re-route the access road to the house so that cars did not drive up to it and spoil the outlook from the main entrance.[11] As an interested driver, she was perhaps more aware of cars than many and conscious of the need – discreetly – to provide space for them. At Steeple this involved getting permission to move the road which ran close to the house and then turned at a right-angle towards Steeple Church. By

BELOW Steeple Manor had been a derelict farmhouse with no garden when Colvin took on the commission in 1924.
BOTTOM From neglected farmland, she created a garden that blended successfully into the countryside as can be seen in this photograph from the 1940s or 1950s.

making the road run on a direct line to the church and providing a turn-off towards the house for cars, with a small parking area away from the main façade, she gained an unencumbered vista across a lawn from the front door and, at the side of the house, space for a small orchard and access to the garden.

Today, to enter the garden down a couple of steps and through the oak door from the parking area is a journey into a secret garden, another world. The path has raised beds on either side and, a little higher, through shrubs to the right, there are glimpses of the orchard that Colvin planted with thorns and crab apples. Sadly, after more than 80 years, not many of these survive. The stone used here for walling and paving, as throughout the garden, is the local Purbeck stone from Lander's quarries. At the end of the raised beds, the path forks, to the right heading down into a small, separate damp spring garden that has

a small gulley running through it. This is planted with hellebores, violets, primulas, bulbs, ferns and hostas – a wild garden of mostly native flowers that looks out to the fields beyond. The fork to the left leads the visitor round to what comes as a complete contrast to the gentle, natural feel of the spring garden: the formality of the double hedge garden, a semicircular enclosure edged with yew and beech hedges.

This is a tranquil space with a peephole in the centre of the hedge that looks out to the landscape beyond. As Colvin designed it, four large blocks of yew, matched by four island beds, marched across the space to two large borders either side of a gateway that leads up steps back to the house. Carrying on past the gateway, one is led round, up steps and through an arch, to another room, formal in layout with its beds edged with stone flags, but relaxed in its planting – phlox and iris in Colvin's day –

ABOVE Colvin's sightlines at Steeple were carefully planned – this is the view back from the pleached lime walk, across the lily pond and up the steps to the formal garden close to the house.

OPPOSITE Closer to the house, Colvin used more formal planting, as in this hedge garden.

and back through a decorative cast-iron gateway to the walled garden in front of the house with its Irish yews. Here, against the side wall, there is a magnolia planted by Colvin with a mass of *Crocus tommasinianus* at its feet. From the walled garden she planned a sightline running through the formal garden, down steps to a lily pond edged with a row of upright conifers and with a small rill running into it and on to a small pleached lime walk – a hedge on stilts – and the woodland beyond.

Elsewhere Colvin planned a sunken tennis lawn and one of her own photographs, taken on the grass area above this, shows what she describes as a 'border on a formal terrace', divided into 'rectangular ranks of graduated colour enclosed by neat clipped Box hedges'.[12] In contrast, the background of the photograph of the formal box planting reveals a less conventional and more relaxed style in early examples of what were to become typical Colvin features: the sweeping curves of unmown grass running up to the stone summer house, and the unmown area, planted with many spring bulbs, under a single tree that has probably had its lower branches cleared.

Aside from the formality of the garden rooms close to the house with their clipped hedges and yew shapes, recently discovered photographs taken by the owners a few years later show some wonderful drift-planting of

bulbs, lupins and Dutch iris in grass, with softly curving grass walks mown through. Another of Colvin's own photographs shows the lawn garden that faces the front door of the house. A simple stepping-stone path winds its way across the grass towards a well-established tree. Other features that she included at Steeple were a clump of several different flowering cherries, a woodland walk beside a natural stream and two enormous herbaceous borders beyond the tennis lawn. And, throughout, where possible, she was sensitive to existing trees and retained many of them.

ABOVE Beyond a formal border above the grass tennis court at Steeple, a more natural area of the garden includes sweeping curves of unmown grass planted with many spring bulbs. This photograph was exhibited at Chelsea in the 1950s.

LEFT A gently curving mown grass path leads through drifts of planting to the pleached lime walk in the distance in this 1930 photograph of the garden.

RIGHT Stepping stones lead to the shade under an established tree in the lawn garden opposite the front door. This photograph was displayed at the Chelsea Flower Show in the 1950s.

between the paving stones. Neither Colvin's plans for the garden nor much of her planting had survived but the new owners' planting style was very much in tune with hers and the recently discovered photographs show how the garden developed in the years after her work there.[13]

Significantly, too, although she had designed this garden in the mid-1920s, Colvin had sufficient confidence in it to exhibit her photographs of it at Chelsea in the 1950s and also to use it to illustrate an article on 'Gardens to Enjoy' in the 1952 *Studio Gardens and Gardening* annual. In this she argues that a garden can be thought of as

> an extension of the house…[it] is a place to live in and should be designed primarily for that purpose, and be given all the shelter and seclusion and resting places needed. But it is also a place which provides endless variety and change as the year goes round, with rich contentment for the eye at every stage.[14]

The garden at Steeple Manor achieved all that.

At Boldre Hill (No. 138), a long-established garden in the New Forest, Colvin was commissioned in 1928 by Mrs Napier. Writing about her work there ten years later, she explained that it had consisted of planting and the 'drastic' removal of a formal garden, probably Victorian, at some distance from the house. 'Amongst informal surroundings and unrelated to any architectural features', she had felt it 'seemed curiously out of place.' She replaced it with a broad sweep of lawn

When new owners acquired Steeple Manor in 1979, they found a neglected garden full of brambles but, fortunately, the original layout and the bones of the structure were still intact. And they also found that many of the bulbs Colvin had planted in the grass re-emerged once the ground was cleared – swathes of *Crocus tommasinianus*, huge drifts of camassias, fritillaries and small narcissi. Colvin's layout has many elements that are typical of her garden designs: sightlines and axes are opened up, there is a sense of space and movement within the boundaries, paths curve round out of sight, tempting the visitor on, hedges and walls divide the garden into a series of rooms with different changes of mood, and there's a deliberate mix of formality and informality, light and shade, the hard edges of steps or balustrades contrasting with soft cascades of wall climbers and ground cover emerging

LEFT ABOVE The circular brick pool was a chance find during clearance work at Boldre Hill.

LEFT BELOW The shrub border seen from the silver and grey end, looking towards the red- and copper-leaved plants.

OPPOSITE ABOVE At Boldre Hill in Hampshire, Colvin replaced a formal garden with a broad sweep of lawn and gently curving herbaceous borders. She displayed this photograph at the Chelsea Flower Show in 1953.

OPPOSITE BELOW Reflections in the pond in the water garden were achieved by enlarging it and raising its level.

edged with herbaceous borders. This led down to a water garden where an existing pond was enlarged and the water level raised by means of a dam. Increasing the size of the pool in this way allowed for tree reflections, and planting the bank and trimming existing trees gave the area a feeling of width it had previously lacked (see p.84 bottom). While this work was being undertaken, the foundations of some former farm buildings were discovered, including a circular brick tank which was retained as a lily pool. Colvin felt it looked 'rather unexpected but having, nevertheless, the charm that such unforeseen features…often do seem to have'. Unexpected, perhaps, but as seen in Colvin's own photograph, the move from the formality of the brick pool to the more natural pond and out to the field beyond is perfectly harmonious. The contrasting sunlit foliage shapes of the plants around the pool show up well against the shadows of the trees in the background. She used a mixture of perennials: iris, libertia and crocosmia provide vertical lines to contrast with groups of comfrey, bergenias, 'decorative rhubarb' [*Gunnera manicata*] and hostas. This 'bold group planting' was another example chosen by Marjory Allen and Susan Jellicoe for their 1953 Penguin *Gardens* book. In addition to the water garden, Colvin also planned a shrub border with many red and coppery foliage plants at one end that contrasted strongly with silver and grey-leaved shrubs at the other. As 'intermediaries' between the two groups, she used shrubs such as *Rosa glauca*

and purple-leaved sage which she felt combined the qualities of both groups. 'The planting…was designed as far as possible to give interest of foliage, shape and texture' – key aims in Colvin's planting philosophy.[15]

At West Stowell House, near Marlborough, where she was commissioned in 1929 (No. 148) by Lady Phipps, Colvin's own photographs from 1937 show how her design developed after six or so years. By then the yew hedge backing the grey and silver garden is providing a good contrast to the luxuriant planting, and the herbaceous borders are impressively full and blowsy, softening the hard edges of the path and contrasting with the neatly clipped hedge beyond them. What Colvin captions the 'walled garden' by the house has a more restrained treatment, its architectural feeling with firm, formal lines suiting its position well. At West

OPPOSITE ABOVE Colvin's own photograph from 1937 shows the developing grey and silver garden begun in 1929 at West Stowell.

OPPOSITE BELOW Soft, billowing planting contrasts with the hard landscaping and the formal lines of the hedge and clipped arbour around a seat at the end of the path.

BELOW LEFT The 'walled garden' beside West Stowell House was given a simple, formal treatment.

BELOW RIGHT The formal lines of a maze planted with *Lonicera nitida* contrast with the informality of the surrounding trees.

Stowell, she also designed a sizeable, fairly complex maze (see p.84 top) which was planted with *Lonicera nitida*, 'a happy choice, as it is essential to have a neat growth and one which can be clipped'.[16] Perhaps her need for assistance on this meant she had closer dealings with the gardener here than on some other commissions – his name, Lynch, is noted in her notebook.

In the same year Colvin was invited to design two areas of the grounds at Attingham Park in Shropshire. The 8th Lord and Lady Berwick had moved back to the house quite recently and there was one aspect of it that Lady Berwick did not like. In the late eighteenth century the park had been redesigned according to a Red Book produced by Humphry Repton but it seems that Lady Berwick, the daughter of a Swiss clockmaker, found his spacious landscape 'bleak and charmless'.[17] Teresa loved gardening – an interest that had been encouraged by her friendship with Sir William Eden, Gertrude Jekyll's brother-in-law, and she was familiar with a number of distinguished formal Italian gardens, including Bernard Berenson's villa, I Tatti, in Florence where she stayed in 1917. When Cecil Pinsent, designer of the gardens at I Tatti, came to stay at Attingham in 1925, he was asked to advise on the laying out of a parterre in front of the house's portico. It seems that his scheme involved 'rather fussy, box-edged beds, surrounded by hedges and columns of yew' and that the design was not successfully related to Repton's sweeping parkland.[18]

Lady Berwick asked Colvin to prepare two schemes, one to replace Pinsent's formal garden in front of the house and on the slope that led down to the river and one for a new wild, riverside garden. In addition to any other failings it may have had, Colvin felt that the existing parterre did not relate well to the house, nor did the lines 'run out from the house towards the river – as a sort of invitation to walk that way'.[19] To replace it, she proposed two 'knots' on the flat piece of ground near the house, and a separate treatment of a double row of topiary designs for the remaining area to the north, between the existing design and the wing of the house. A wide flight of steps would lead to the sloping ground and on the slope itself she proposed a 'simple arrangement

of rose beds, shrubs and flowering trees'. She considered this was the only way of carrying out a formal treatment without the expense of levelling, although admitted she would have preferred to terrace the slope right down to the river. For the wild garden she only drew a sketch plan but felt this was adequate. She proposed a few broad groups of planting with mown grass paths going round them and the rest left rough with 'bulbs and things' in the grass. Cost seemed to be a source of great anxiety to Lady Berwick and in the end it was only the proposal for the 'Wild Garden' that was carried out. Colvin sent an old Swanley friend, Miss Bindley, to carry out the planting the following spring. In 1947 Lord Berwick gave Attingham Park to the National Trust and in 1976 Pinsent's formal gardens were grassed over, but some of Colvin's planting appears to have survived. In his *Gardens of the National Trust*, Graham Stuart Thomas mentions the 'Red Oaks, Dogwoods, Sumach and American Thorns' that contribute autumn colour near the water.[20]

In 1930 Colvin received a commission from Lady Bunbury at Naunton Hall, Suffolk (No. 170). Again she used one of her photographs of this garden to illustrate her 1952 'Gardens to Enjoy' article, captioning it 'Shallow terraces, rising by gentle degrees, make easy a transition between the house (from whose window the picture is seen) and the higher ground behind'. She also points out that the 'background of tall trees is the making of this picture: without them the succession of horizontal lines might have become oppressive'.[21] She had already used the same photograph to illustrate an article on herbaceous borders in autumn 1936, pointing out the 'Retaining walls and steps in a combination of brick and stone form the low terraces which are designed to give borders on three different levels'.[22] The layout is conventional, almost Arts and Crafts in style,

OPPOSITE ABOVE The horizontal lines of the shallow terraces at Naunton Hall contrast successfully with the vertical lines of the trees behind.
OPPOSITE BELOW An inviting pathway at Naunton Hall.

but, as Colvin herself commented, the horizontal lines of the terraces are well balanced by the vertical lines of the trees behind and also by the planting within. The planting plans for other borders which appear in the same article include some of her favourite sculptural and foliage plants: *Euphorbia characias* subsp. *wulfenii*, bergenia and *Epimedium* × *rubrum*. In the view along the pathway, the simplicity of the lawn with the tree with its trunk cleared is balanced by a herbaceous border

with good contrasting foliage and, in the background, rows of clipped lavender soften the hard landscaping beyond. Colvin displayed two photographs of her work at Naunton Hall at the Chelsea Flower Show in 1953.

In 1931 Colvin started work on a design for Miss Nora Kennedy, one of two sisters who commissioned her. Both lived near Tewkesbury, and both houses were in elevated positions with magnificent views. Her own pictures and a number of family photographs of Sarn

OPPOSITE An intriguingly coloured photograph of flower borders at Sarn Hill Grange with far-reaching views into the countryside beyond.
LEFT Steps leading down to a semicircular rose garden hedged with yew and with views to the countryside beyond.
BELOW Massed irises line the edges of a walk through trees.

Hill Grange show elaborate double herbaceous borders extending in terraces below the house and steps leading down to a semicircular rose garden bounded with yew hedging – broken at the apex to allow views out to the landscape beyond.[23] Elsewhere, a walk through trees is underplanted with a mass of irises. No plans of the garden at Sarn Hill Grange survive but three of Colvin's plans for Mrs Maxwell, Miss Kennedy's sister, at Conderton have recently been discovered.[24] These consist of what is presumably her first plan of 'proposed alterations' dated 6 November 1933, a revised treatment for the east end of the terrace dated 2 October 1934, and finally a further revised treatment for this troublesome end of terrace together with a proposed forecourt treatment dated 23 July 1936. Dotted lines on the first plan show some rather minimal existing features – a couple of long, narrow beds, a deodar cedar, and a path that curves away from the front of the house towards a group of elm trees.

Close to the house, Colvin echoes its symmetrical façade with a simple architectural design with paved paths in grass leading from a small paved court. The main vista extends straight out from the house to the

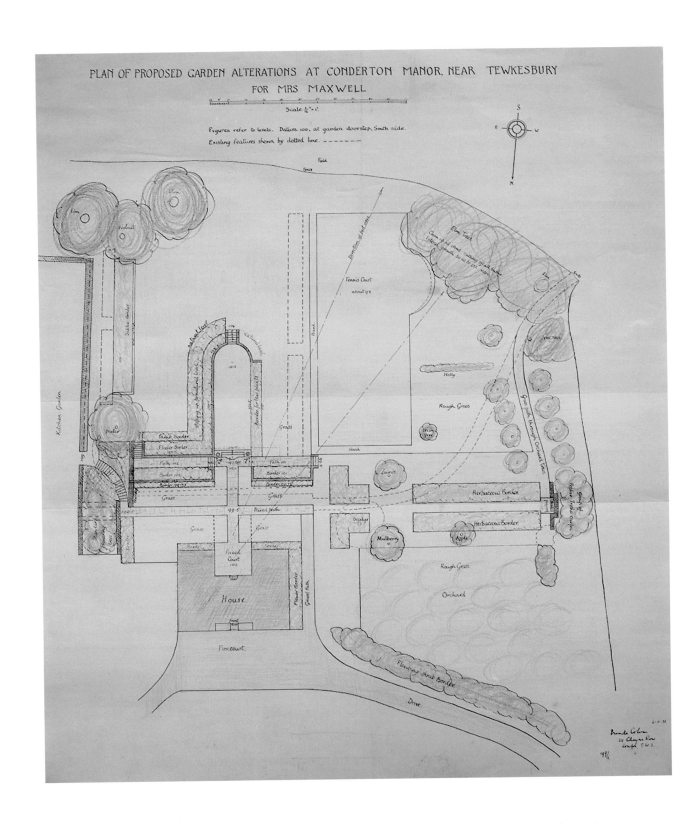

ABOVE Colvin's first plan (dated 6 November 1933) for garden alterations at Conderton Manor shows the more formal arrangement close to the house graduating into rough grass. Lines indicate the 'direction of best view' to the south and the elm trees are marked up to have 'all bushy lateral growth' removed to reveal the view.

south, through a narrow enclosed area with a shrub border to the left, and low planting in the direction of the view to the right. This area ends in steps up through a semicircle offering clear views of the north Cotswolds. Interestingly, Colvin's main plan also points out that the best view from the house is to be had not from the key axis of her design but at an angle to it, framed by elm trees that she specifies should have their stems cleaned by 'cutting off all bushy lateral growth so as to see view' (see p.91). At right angles to the main path from the house, another path heads west between double herbaceous borders towards a group of poplars and, to the east where the ground rises up and blocks any views, to what was originally planned to be an area of standard flowering trees on one side with the path ending in a curved flight of steps leading up to the kitchen garden. This was the end of the terrace that was redesigned. In Colvin's second suggestion the steps are moved to go up beside the house and a sloping border for trees and shrubs is proposed. In the final plan two small garden houses with a fountain and pool in the centre are suggested for this space but this scheme was never carried out. This plan also shows a formal arrangement for the front of the house, again echoing the outline of the façade. One puzzling oddity on the first plan is a dahlia border in front of the kitchen garden which seems totally at odds with Colvin's emphasis on planting for continuous interest by using contrasting foliage and not depending simply on colour. Perhaps this was a special request from her client at Conderton.

Moving away from the house, Colvin's style typically becomes more relaxed. There is rough grass in the orchard that borders the drive, almost certainly planted with bulbs, and a flowering shrub border at its edge. A mown grass path meanders through the trees to the west of the garden and the obligatory grass tennis court is made less conspicuous by being sunk down below banks of grass. The retention of a number of established trees – a deodar cedar near the house, elms and a walnut further away – will have helped the garden to feel established from the start.

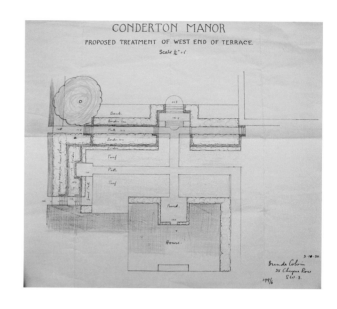

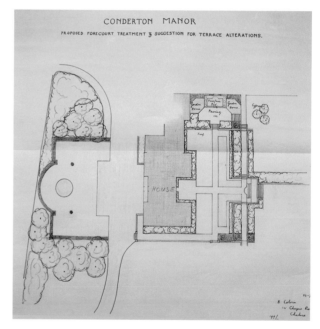

TOP Colvin's revised treatment for the east end of the terrace (mistakenly headed 'West End'), submitted in October 1934.

ABOVE Colvin's proposal from July 1936 for a simple formal forecourt and further terrace alterations.

LEFT Looking west along the main axis in front of Conderton Manor – the original paved court to the right has now been glazed over with a conservatory.
BELOW The view of the north Cotswolds through the elms.
OPPOSITE ABOVE Colvin's photograph from 1936 shows the maturing planting.
OPPOSITE BELOW The existing deodar cedar at the back of the flower border was saved, as can be seen in this photograph Colvin took in the summer of 1936.

In her turn, Mrs Maxwell at Conderton recommended Colvin to the Holland-Martins from whom she was renting the manor. The Holland-Martins, a banking family, lived at Overbury Court where they employed a number of well known designers over the years, including Russell Page and Geoffrey Jellicoe as well as Colvin, but it is not clear exactly what each of them contributed to its garden.

These larger gardens all reveal Colvin's skill at handling the typical elements required by garden owners in the 1920s and 1930s – from the planting of the herbaceous borders and rose gardens to the hard landscaping and siting of tennis courts – but they also display her talent for incorporating the wider landscape into her gardens and for a softer, more natural style of gardening in appropriate areas further away from the house. Even her angular, formal designs are transformed by her skilful planting which softens their hard edges. Time and again she retained existing trees but cleared their trunks to allow views of the countryside beyond the

garden, and wild 'meadow' areas, planted with masses of spring bulbs, are a regular feature. And she took practical considerations into account – paved edging to herbaceous borders, for example, allowed for easier maintenance and also allowed for that softer planting to billow over the edges without spoiling the grass.

A few years earlier, in 1931, Colvin had begun work on her design for the garden at Gangbridge, St Mary Bourne in Hampshire, and this certainly included all these elements. It was going to be a longer than average project because it was for her parents and, in addition to the more formal photographs of it, there are many family snapshots of the house and garden and its occupants in Colvin's photographs.[25] Four years later she wrote about it in *Landscape and Garden*. She explains that existing features had played a large part in the making of the garden, in particular some well established trees, an old wall which partly enclosed the garden and an orchard beyond. Her description of the initial changes gives us a tantalising glimpse of her parents:

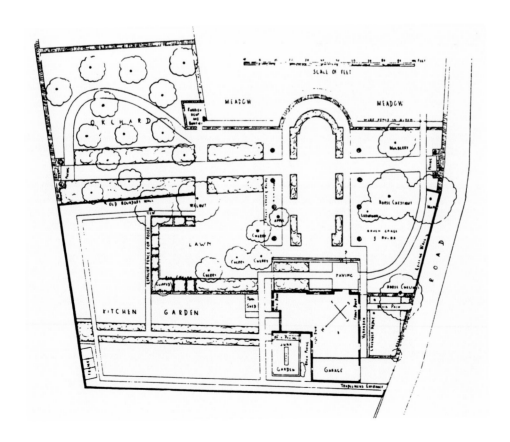

LEFT Colvin's plan of the layout for Gangbridge, her parents' house in Hampshire.

RIGHT The paved terrace in front of the house with the base of the clipped yew column marking the corner of the kitchen garden just visible behind the flowering cherry.

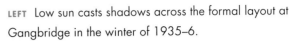

LEFT Low sun casts shadows across the formal layout at Gangbridge in the winter of 1935–6.

BELOW LEFT Colvin's father, her nieces Julia and Hilary, and her sister-in-law Madeline enjoy the garden in 1938.

BELOW RIGHT Hilary and Julia play by the circular pond in 1938.

OPPOSITE ABOVE Flower borders flourish among existing trees, seen here five years after Colvin's parents moved to Gangbridge.

OPPOSITE BELOW Colvin's parents in a shady spot under a hawthorn.

Some previous owners had evidently used the present garden door…as a front door, feeling perhaps that the 'carriage sweep' would be a better social asset than the modest hand-gate and footpath to the old front door. The present owners feel that privacy, and as much flower garden as space permits, are of greater value, especially as the house stands so near the road.[26]

Clearly her parents were as interested in plants as she was. In his manuscript memoir her father recalled a visit to Vevey in Switzerland in 1930 and noted that 'a marvellous show of narcissus on the hills in spring' had been 'one of the points which stood out'.[27]

In place of the gravel sweep at Gangbridge, Colvin laid out a paved terrace planted with low evergreen and aromatic plants and a lawn with some simple formal rose beds. A view from the garden of meadow and cows with trees beyond was preserved by the creation of a ha-ha beyond the existing low lonicera hedge, and the young planting of a formal layout looking out over the meadow can be seen in Colvin's own photographs. A small circular pond was a later addition to this section of the garden and, judging by the number of photographs of it, seems to have been a favourite spot for her parents and her brother's two children.

The orchard had previously been outside the boundary but she brought it into touch with the rest of the garden by creating a wide grass walk that ran the entire width of the property. Although this did not run quite parallel to the house, she considered it deceived the eye 'in actuality'. The orchard trees were carefully pruned and seemed 'to welcome the change and embrace the vista with gnarled charm'. Under these trees she planted foxgloves, anemones, honesty, Solomon's seal and

phloxes, and in the orchard itself there was 'a growing collection of native plants, most effective of which is the wild musk mallow'. Two large yew trees, 'beautiful as they were', limited the space available for vegetables and so one was cut back almost to the trunk. After three years it had regrown and thereafter was kept trimmed as a tall, narrow column with a square base, a punctuation point for the corner of the border between the kitchen garden and the lawn. To the north of the house she created a small sunk garden – 'partly with the object of keeping the house dry as the kitchen garden slopes to the south-west'. The pool in it was lined with blue glass tiles, but it had a practical function, too: 'it receives rain that falls on the roof, and so is a useful reserve of soft water for the garden.'[28] Colvin's parents must have taken great pleasure from seeing the garden develop and they enjoyed almost ten years together there until the death of her father in August 1940.[29]

In 1935 Colvin set to work on another family garden – this time the design was a wedding present for her brother Hugh who had just moved to a new home, Oakley Hall at Ugley in Essex. Colvin's early photographs here show a sizeable but dingy house overgrown with creeper, the entrance drive coming straight along the front of the house with four steps up to the front door. Showing the same ability to make a radical but effective change as she had done with the access road at Steeple Manor, here she decided to divert the drive around the back of the house and create a parking area and a new main entrance door at the side. At the front of the house, an attractive raised, brick-faced terrace made a much more pleasing entrance to the garden, with any cars now safely out of sight at the rear of the house.

Leading away from the house, she created two broad axial paths. The first ran through an elaborate rose garden. Colvin's planting plan shows a background, planted against trellis, of climbing roses, honeysuckle, *Vitis vinifera* 'Purpurea', *Parthenocissus henryana* and a number of different clematis designed to give colour through the seasons. Standard roses – 'François Juranville' and 'General MacArthur' – are grown in box-edged squares at both ends of the double rose borders

which are made up of nine-foot box-edged bays each containing its own rose variety.[30] The roses may have been the now derided hybrid teas, but Colvin's choice of varieties was good, almost all of them highly scented. One, 'Angèle Pernet', is still described by rose expert Peter Beales as 'a beautiful rose of exquisite form'; another, 'Etoile de Hollande', as 'superbly fragrant'.[31] Parallel to the rose garden, a wider path ran between two borders. The one backing on to the rose garden trellis was a traditionally planted herbaceous border but the other, blending in to the garden beyond had a more natural feel with honesty, violas, valerians, thrift and wallflowers backed by a sweeping planting of mixed phloxes and Michaelmas daisies with *Artemisia lactiflora* as a punctuation mark at the end closest to the house. Colvin's brother's family stayed at Ugley until 1955 and their successors were there for the next 40 years. Perhaps because of such long-lasting ownership, the bones of this garden have survived until today.

Another garden that has stood the test of time is that of Savages House in Bishop's Tachbrook near Leamington Spa which Colvin designed for Mrs Hickson in 1935.[32] Some 46 years later, still in the same ownership, it was described as being 'much as Miss Colvin left it',[33] and many elements of her design remain even today. At the garden end of the entrance drive Colvin planted some double white cherries one of which has developed into a very fine specimen. As

OPPOSITE Colvin's photograph of Oakley Hall before her alterations were carried out.

LEFT With the drive moved to the back of the house, this terrace made an attractive entrance to the garden.

BELOW The wide herbaceous border backing on to the rose garden trellis on the right, in a photograph from 1940.

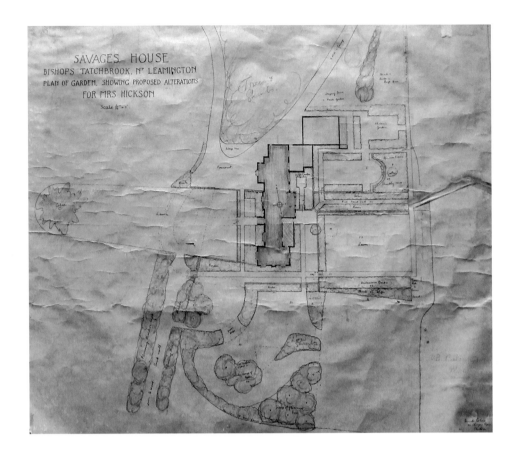

SAVAGES HOUSE
BISHOPS TATCHBROOK, Nᵣ LEAMINGTON
PLAN OF GARDEN, SHOWING PROPOSED ALTERATIONS
FOR MRS HICKSON

LEFT Colvin's plan for Savage's House, designed in 1935.

OPPOSITE ABOVE Colvin displayed this photograph of her woodland walk at Woldingham at the Chelsea Flower Show in 1953.

OPPOSITE BELOW A path runs between the clean trunks of a glade of silver birches at the New Castle at Zywiec in Poland.

can be seen on Colvin's plan,[34] the drive stops short of the older section of the house which therefore had an uninterrupted view over a lawn to the west with box hedges on each side to a cedar planted on a raised area at the far end. A wide 'sunk walk' with flowering shrubs and trees alongside it runs south from the main lawn and steps lead up to a raised lawn area at the southern end of the house with two old mulberries, survivors from an earlier garden, and two blue cedars that Colvin planted. These are still there today, now about 20 metres tall. The outer boundary of this area is a tall holly hedge with a brick path. There are more brick paths around the house and the garden on the east side of the house has a more formal layout, with clipped hedges, rose beds and a children's garden. Among the trees Colvin planted were a *Magnolia grandiflora* on the house and a tulip tree as well as the cedars. One area that did change was a woodland wild garden to the southwest, the character of which was completely

changed following the loss and removal of 25 elms, mostly large trees.

Colvin's love of natural planting, seen in the relaxed feel of the orchard at her parents' Gangbridge and the woodland garden at Savage's House, was echoed in a woodland walk at Melville in Woldingham in Surrey,[35] with trimmed tree trunks and spring bulbs, and again in the silver birch grove that was part of the extensive work that she completed for Archduke Charles Albert Habsburg at his summer palace, the New Castle, at Zywiec in Poland. This was job No. 249 in Colvin's notebook in 1936 and came through *Good Gardening*, branded 'The Garden Lover's Magazine', to which she contributed a number of articles.[36]

In August that year Colvin made her first long journey to Zywiec, not far from Cracow in southern Poland. Even today, the advice offered is that travelling to Poland by car is only for the intrepid and yet Colvin made several trips, one through snowstorms in her Wolseley (see p.29).[37]

At least she had experienced travel in Bulgaria when she joined her parents in the early 1920s as well as visiting several other western European countries. She made further trips to Zywiec in spring 1937 and 1938 and her last visit was in 1939, as war was brewing. The German invasion of Poland, one of the immediate causes of the Second World War, took place on 1 September 1939 – Colvin can only have missed this by a short time. One photograph in her album from the previous year is of what she terms a 'frontier incident' with her travelling companion, known only as 'M.P.T.', and a Nazi guard. The German border police could not believe that the two women could be travelling alone. They were convinced that they must have menfolk with them who were not present and were therefore presumably spying. Repeatedly they asked, '*Wo sind die Männer?*' [Where are the men?] This roll of film was saved but others were confiscated by the Nazis.[38]

Arriving at Zywiec, Colvin would have found a sizeable nineteenth-century English-landscape-style park of about 26 hectares with many trees, a canal and a Chinese-style summer house situated on an island. She was commissioned to make extensive additions and alterations to the garden. She travelled there each spring for the next three years to prepare designs for the next year's work and give instructions. She used to explain that it was somewhat problematic that the head gardener spoke no English and she spoke no Polish. The paths in the garden were of sand, however, so, if there was a query, the gardener would draw out the problem with a stick in the sand. Colvin, with the tip of her parasol, would draw the answer alongside the query.[39]

Photographs from her first visit show haymaking on the site of the new English garden and the site for the water garden, as well as a portrait of a group of Polish garden workers, most of them women, the archduchess being driven through the estate, and a rare photograph of Colvin herself about to get into a pony cart. The next spring's pictures show work on one of Colvin's new layouts taking place, turning a formal arrival area into a quiet courtyard, as well as preparations for work on the island with its pagoda-style summer house, and studies of the lake and water garden, and the glade of silver birches (see previous page). A year later the new courtyard with its wellhead designed by Colvin is completed although looking a little bare compared with the next year when the planting has begun to make an impact. By this time, work was in progress on a pergola leading to a sunken circular pool in the English garden which is seen completed the following year. On her final

TOP ROW The entrance drive to the New Castle at Zywiec (left); the summer house on the island (right).
MIDDLE ROW Haymaking on the site of the new English garden that Colvin was commissioned to create at Zywiec (left); a group of barefoot Polish women gardeners move a trellis (right).
BOTTOM ROW The archduchess travels in a pony cart through the hayricks at Zywiec (left); 'Self in pony cart' is Colvin's caption to this photograph taken in August 1936 outside the New Castle (right).

LEFT ABOVE Work on laying out the new courtyard at the front of the castle in 1937.

LEFT CENTRE Work in progress on the pergola and pool in 1938.

LEFT BELOW The water garden seen during Colvin's final visit to Zywiec.

RIGHT ABOVE In the spring of 1938, the new courtyard is complete with a wellhead designed by Colvin.

RIGHT BELOW By spring 1939, the new courtyard is looking more established.

ABOVE The pergola and sunken pool in the English garden, photographed on Colvin's last visit in 1939. LEFT Before she left Zywiec for the last time, Colvin took this photograph of the garden workers.

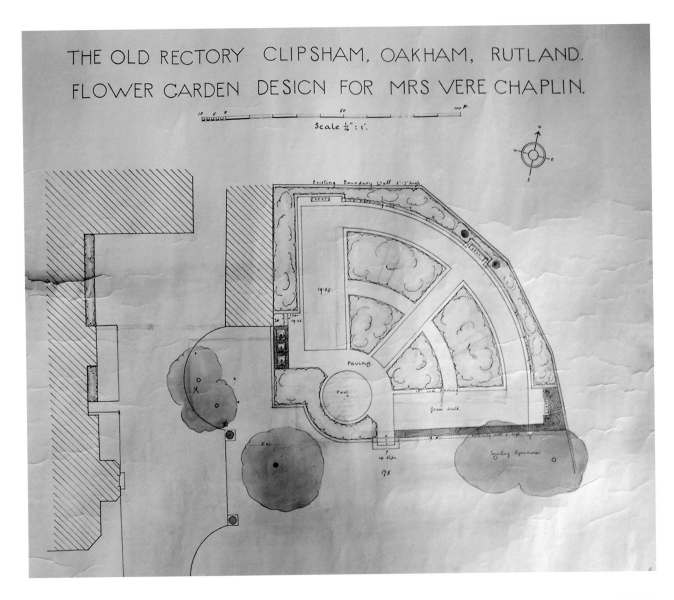

THE OLD RECTORY CLIPSHAM, OAKHAM, RUTLAND.
FLOWER GARDEN DESIGN FOR MRS VERE CHAPLIN.

Scale 1/16": 1'.

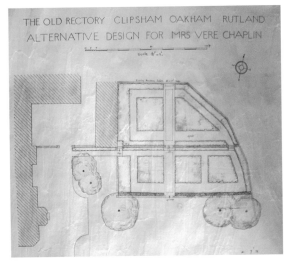

THE OLD RECTORY CLIPSHAM OAKHAM RUTLAND
ALTERNATIVE DESIGN FOR MRS VERE CHAPLIN

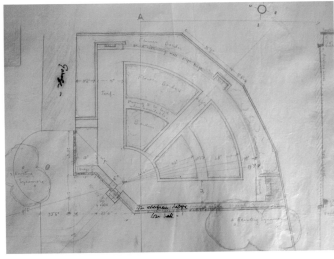

visit Colvin took pictures of the water garden and a farewell photograph shows ten garden workers posing on one of the bridges leading to the island.

In the course of her visits to Zywiec, Colvin struck up a friendship with the Habsburg children's English governess, Nelly Ryan, and they corresponded over the years, with Ryan sending a number of picture postcards of the castle to Colvin. On one, dated July 1939, poignantly, she had written, 'I sit in the evenings beside the calm circle of your pool wondering what will become of us.'[40]

One of the last gardens Colvin worked on before the war – and, in fact, during the war as well – was that belonging to Mrs Vere Chaplin: The Old Rectory at Clipsham in Rutland (No. 282). Margaret Chaplin was the elder daughter of Mark Fenwick who had commissioned Sir Edwin Lutyens to design his garden at Abbotswood, near Stow-on-the-Wold, and was himself a passionate gardener, ultimately awarded the Royal Horticultural Society's Victoria Medal of Honour. According to her daughter Molly Wheatley, Mrs Chaplin was a woman who would not have been easy to deal with, a woman with strong ideas. How much of a personality clash there was between the two women is not known but Colvin submitted her first plan dated 11 July 1938 and then, perhaps at her client's request, an alternative design some ten days later. The area for the garden was an irregular shape on

OPPOSITE ABOVE Colvin's first plan for a flower garden at The Old Rectory, Clipsham, drawn in July 1938.

OPPOSITE BELOW LEFT Colvin's second suggestion for the flower garden, a less successful plan.

OPPOSITE BELOW RIGHT Colvin's final plan of 1943, according to which the flower garden was finally built.

ABOVE LEFT Rounded steps lead up to the central path with a garden seat as its focal point.

ABOVE RIGHT The curving paths lead the eye on round the garden.

BELOW Tucked away in a raised corner a little distance from the house, the flower garden is a sheltered, secret haven.

sloping ground a little distance from the house. Colvin proposed to raise its level, putting in a wall and steps – the wall would have the added advantage of protecting the garden from the prevailing southwesterly winds. The design that was chosen – four beds like wedges of cheese with a large raised bed all around the back – made the best of the asymmetrical shape available and manages to make the space seem much larger than it is. Wherever you look, there is another corner to tempt you further on and wherever you are, you get the views and the curves of the beds. The alternative plan divides the plot into four unequal quarters with squared-off beds and fits the space much less well. Between the 1938 plan and its execution, the pool sited at the apex of the quarter-circle was lost and its place taken by the steps – Colvin's plan for this was submitted in October 1943. This plan necessitated the loss of an existing tree which Colvin had possibly been trying to preserve. It

shows the design virtually as it was carried out. The grass paths are edged with runnels and the spaces between the flower borders are marked up 'Paving to be laid when available'. Mrs Chaplin's daughter Molly and her husband moved to Clipsham after the house had been rented out for some years. They found the bones of the garden still intact but, much as the owners of Steeple Manor, had to replant. It is a secret oasis, rather like an eighteenth-century flower garden hidden away from the parkland and the house, waiting to be explored and enjoyed, and a surprising survival of Colvin's pre-war garden work.[41]

Writing in 1979, disillusioned with private garden work, Colvin said she had heard that Château Zywiec 'was over-run by German troops and later became a Russian barracks, so regard it as typical of what happens to private garden work'.[42] Surprisingly, although the gardens at Zywiec were neglected they have largely survived – neither the Germans nor the Russians who followed them had ever bothered to make any changes. Today the gardens are enjoyed by the town's inhabitants and the summer house on the island is used as a café.

Of her other work Colvin thought that Steeple Manor and Conderton Manor might have survived 'more or less as intended'[43] and elements of these two certainly have. The others she listed have not fared so well. Colvin's own photographs show her work at Boldre Hill, West Stowell and Sarn Hill Grange but little remains today of these or of Little Holland Hall in Clacton (now a nursing home), Merley House at Wimborne (a 30-acre holiday park and business centre) and Berkley House in Frome (now in multiple occupation).

Of course there were many, many other gardens – just under 300 entries in her notebook to 1939 – that Colvin worked on in the years before the Second World War. Again evidence for a few of these comes from accounts by visitors or from Colvin's own photographs,[44] as in the following two examples. In 1926 she was employed by Viscount Boyne at Burwarton House, Bridgnorth (No. 88 in the notebook). According to Ron Sidwell's survey of West Midland gardens in 1981, she may have worked with others here, to extend the terrace on the south side of the house and create an enclosed rose garden behind yew hedges with peepholes.[45] Colvin's own photographs of her work at Old House, Haywards Heath, show a terrace in front of the house with steps up to a wide expanse of lawn surrounded by lushly planted herbaceous borders edged with paving.[46] To the side, a more formal double border of rose beds leads to a garden seat. This commission – No. 222 – is from 1935 for Mrs Burgoyne on a recommendation through Swanley.

After the war Colvin designed some significant private gardens, which are discussed later, but generally there was less scope for this type of work. The world had changed and the emphasis had moved out to the wider landscape. In general garden design had a low priority among gardeners who were struggling to rescue their gardens from wartime neglect. There was little money for professional fees and owners concentrated on labour-saving ideas and low-maintenance planting. As garden designer John Brookes puts it:

We still had rationing in the 1950s whereas on the Continent they were roaring away on the Marshall Plan, and the private clients didn't really come through until the late 60s. We were all so busy doing new town work.[47]

Many of Colvin's pre-war gardens were quite conventional in layout but, as we have seen, they reveal her growing concern with planting structure, her extensive knowledge of and developing originality in her use of plant form, size, texture and colour, her move where appropriate towards a more natural style, and her search for good architectural groupings. Increasingly, too, she was moving towards sustainable practice in the modern sense, as well as the Robinsonian, as can be seen in her use of native plants and, at her parents' home, the reservoir of rainwater. Many of her clients would still have favoured the nostalgically romantic Arts and Crafts style but increasingly Colvin was convinced that the garden should be thought of as an extension to the house – a place to live in. Her international contacts meant she was aware of modern gardens in mainland Europe and Scandinavia and she was also increasingly conscious of the need to reduce the amount of maintenance required. These factors made her knowledge of plants and her developing skill in planting design all the more important.

An enthusiasm for plants

'The planting is intended to give continuous calm enjoyment at all seasons, rather than to dazzle the eye in the height of summer....But it is difficult to reconcile simplicity with one's enthusiasm for plants.'[1]

I N THE FIRST TWO DECADES of her career as a garden designer Colvin had demonstrated her skill at creating thoughtful, elegant gardens for her clients. She had proved herself to be an able, professional woman working in what was still to a large extent a man's world. She had travelled widely, both for her work and for pleasure, at home and abroad. In the sphere of planting, she was equally able and, in the course of her long career, was to become an extremely knowledgeable and skilful plantsman – a term she would have approved of as she had a strong dislike of the politically correct use of 'woman' or 'person'.

Her deep interest in plants, no doubt initially sparked by the 'wealth of wild flowers and the almond blossom orchards' and the gardens of the Shalimar that she had experienced during her childhood in Kashmir, meant that the role of planting in garden design – and in the wider landscape – was a topic close to her heart and one she was to write about extensively. And her enthusiasm and thirst for knowledge about plants never waned. On one occasion, late in her life, when a young work experience student came back to the office bearing an armful of wild grasses she had discovered while out on a photography assignment, Colvin ended the day sat on the floor with her, wildflower guide at her side, determined to identify each and every one of them.[2]

A number of photographs that Colvin took in the 1930s and 1940s have survived as negatives with small contact prints stored in two albums. Naturally, there are family photographs – her parents, her nieces – but the vast majority reveal the profound, almost all-pervading significance to her of landscape, gardens and plants. In addition to pictures of the gardens she had designed and others she visited, the earlier photographs include some of the spectacular countryside seen during camping holidays in Pembrokeshire, drifts of crocuses and daffodils in London parks, weeping willows in spring at Wisley, and alpine flowers from a holiday in the Tyrol. There are pictures taken in Paris and its surrounding area when she visited the International Conference of Garden Design in June 1937. Here she saw 'sunlit fountains playing dramatic roles on a green stage' in the classic seventeenth-century gardens of Vaux-le-Vicomte and 'pleached walls' at the

RIGHT Colvin's design for the river walk at Buscot Old Parsonage in Berkshire created an impressive vista with the sculptural foliage of giant hogweed to the right and the broad leaves of gunnera in the distance on the river bank.

ABOVE The spectacular
landscape of Pembrokeshire
in August 1937 during
a camping holiday that
Colvin took near Dale,
accompanied by one of
her collies.
RIGHT Weeping willows
coming into leaf at Wisley
in spring 1938.

RIGHT Colvin's 1937 photograph of the surrounding green walls and colonnades reflected in a pool at the Château de Champs near Paris.

BELOW LEFT Gardeners hard at work maintaining the strict straight lines and neat edges in André Vera's own garden in St Germain, Paris, photographed by Colvin in 1937.

BELOW RIGHT Lemons in pots border a path at La Pietra, Mr Acton's villa in the via Bolognese, Florence (June 1938).

Château de Champs,[3] Le Nôtre's Terrasse at St Germain and two gardens designed by the Modernist André Vera (see above and p.43). The following year she travelled to Alassio and Florence, and visited the Boboli Gardens, 'Mr Acton's Villa' and the Villa Medici, and took many pictures of these gardens and their layouts as well as close-ups of plants and planting combinations, such as the contrasting shapes and colours of wispy olive trees and spiky architectural agaves, and a typical arrangement of lemon trees in terracotta pots. She was continually observing and learning from the gardens and landscapes she saw around her.

Initially Colvin had gone to college at Swanley to study general horticulture but she had switched to the garden design course because of her growing interest in ornamental plants. While a student, she had met the two people most closely associated with the strong reaction against Victorian artificiality in planting – William Robinson and Gertrude Jekyll. In 1870 Robinson had published his book, *The Wild Garden*. In it he did not insist, as is often thought, on native-plant gardening but recommended the use of any wild or introduced plant that would thrive in a given situation. It was a philosophy of low-maintenance gardening, where self-sustaining plant associations would flourish together, as opposed to the labour-intensive bedding-out schemes of Victorian gardens. *The Wild Garden* also contained ideas for managing the transition between the garden proper and the surrounding landscape – ideas that Robinson's disciple Gertrude Jekyll was to elaborate. His idea of naturalising spring bulbs such as crocuses, snowdrops, narcissi, anemones and bluebells in grass was innovative, as were his suggestions for woodland planting.

Jekyll had first met William Robinson in 1875 and he later advised her on the planting of her new garden at Munstead Wood. In her own enthusiastic writing about wild flowers and woodland gardens and in her free style of planting, Jekyll furthered Robinson's ideas and took them to a wider audience. She was attempting to reform the Victorian style of gardening and maintained that it was not the fault of the plant that that style of gardening did not work. If visitors were surprised to see her planting geraniums [pelargoniums] on her terrace, she would point out that 'bedding plants are only passive agents in their own misuse and that a geranium was a geranium long before it was a bedding plant'.[4]

Later Colvin wrote of how it was this revolt against formality headed by Robinson that had led to a widespread, mistaken belief 'that garden design consists of growing beautiful plants in suitable conditions and in their natural form'. Robinson himself had been a skilful planter: he 'had instinctively much feeling for constructive design – he used his material well'.[5] According to landscape architect Sylvia Crowe, who had visited Robinson's Gravetye Manor as a child, he had a 'style that appealed…in particular the sculptural feel, using the plants in a sculptural way. His informality had composition.'[6] Unfortunately, in Colvin's view, the same could not be said of his followers who 'were content to grow interesting collections of flowering plants without troubling further about design'.[7]

It was the lack of design in these plant collectors' gardens that had aroused the new champions of the formal style – the architectural profession. The fresh attack was led by the pugnacious architect Sir Reginald Blomfield with his 1892 book *The Formal Garden in England*, with support from artist Inigo Thomas and architects Inigo Triggs and Sir Edwin Lutyens. In his book Blomfield suggested that a house should have a proper architectural setting and he concentrated more on design than plants, being of the dismissive view that 'horticulture stands to garden design much as building does to architecture'. Holding the middle ground was John Dando Sedding with his *Garden Craft, Old and New* (1891) which encouraged both an architectural

framework but also freedom in the planting. Both Blomfield and Sedding may have been Robinson's arch-enemies but both, like him, condemned the worst excesses of bedding out.

In Colvin's view, Jekyll had bridged the two camps, both in her books and in her planting work in many of Lutyens's gardens, but their unique partnership by which she gave his gardens 'an interior decoration harmonizing with his own intention' was not duplicated and only served to strengthen the architects' view that construction and planting were separate, unrelated subjects. Meanwhile, followers of the Robinson school 'failed to realize that if brick and stone are banished, plants must be used structurally'.[8]

As Colvin began her studies, then, planting style was evolving from the Arts and Crafts influence that had continued after the First World War, although Robinson's influence remained dominant with wild and woodland gardens, rock gardens and herbaceous borders forming a unified, natural style, but often in a strongly structured axial layout. Colvin's teacher Madeline Agar had already been working as a professional landscape gardener and so would have been well qualified to teach about the technicalities of garden design. Whether she was as knowledgeable about planting design is less clear.

In her *Garden Design* book, published in 1913, Agar had provided only limited advice on planting.[9] The book began with a brief history of garden styles and then gave practical guidance on preparing a design, the structural elements such as paths and terraces, and how best to organise the component parts of a garden. In her chapter on planting, while acknowledging that carpet bedding had 'fallen in esteem', she still advocated it as suitable for the more formal areas near to the house. Her advice on the mixed herbaceous border was that, whether planting for colour contrast or a sequence of colour, 'groups must be bold – never less than three plants together – and dove-tailed into one another'. The planting of borders, she considered, required 'an extensive experience with plants…so as to have something in bloom at all seasons'. She also noted that although, 'Roughly speaking, the tallest plants are put at the back…to rigidly keep to graded heights would give a sameness to the elevation, and groups of high plants should be brought forward in some places.' Then, apart from a page of purely practical advice on the mechanics of drawing up planting plans, the rest of the chapter on planting was devoted to general advice on shrubberies and tree planting, hedges and boundaries and how to achieve privacy by judicious planting. If Agar's teaching about planting at Swanley a few years later reflected the limited, traditional approach of her book, it is all the more remarkable that Colvin was to develop such a sophisticated planting philosophy.

According to Colvin plants were not just the 'interior decoration of a structure already assembled, because they are an important part of the structure itself'.[10] Whether in a small garden or the wider landscape, the plants linked the main features of the design together. As she emphasised in her criticism of Robinson's less skilful followers, it was the need for the structural use of plants that was vital:

> Planting for the landscape architect includes all plants….That includes grass, trees, woodland and farm crops as well as the shrubs and other ornamental plants of park and garden….Many of the most satisfying compositions are those where plants are used both collectively as part of the structure and individually as punctuation, highlights, or 'eye catchers' in prominent positions.[11]

Plants should be used structurally in even the smallest project – each separate section of a little garden could be given its individual three-dimensional proportions by the use of trees and shrubs. She declared herself 'not really pleased' when, just as planting of one of her designs was about to begin, her client had announced brightly: 'We think the garden looks so nice as it is that we have decided not to have any of the shrubs planted.' Colvin's sarcastic, but unspoken response was, 'A nice splash of geraniums and dahlias would show up the ground plan so much better and all could be seen at a glance'. Of course, what the client had failed to understand was that:

> One of the purposes of planting design is to prevent everything from being seen at a glance. Rather to concentrate appreciation on one theme at a time and to refine our delight by timing each view to appear in sequence.[12]

Such structural planting could be seen in the formal gardens of more southern climates which made architectural use of plants: 'Green passages connect the various open gardens, and the contrast of light and

RIGHT Objects in shadow frame a sunlit scene in Colvin's photograph taken in the Boboli Gardens, Florence in 1938 – a good example of the contrast of light and shade.

be used in association with gothic architecture, and that upright or tall, pointed trees go better with the classic style'. The synthesis of natural and architectural forms was vital if our town planning was to develop real beauty:

It is not merely a question of relationship of forms – colour and texture relationships are also involved. Extreme contrasts or delicate harmonies may both serve the designer's purpose…but a mere huddle of chance textures is often worse than useless.[17]

dark, of the open and the enclosed, of compression and release – becomes all the more dramatic for being so closely allied to architectural feeling.'[13] This contrast of light and shadow played a vital part in Colvin's planting design: the bright maze at West Stowell highlighted by the shady woodland area beyond, the sunlit field seen beyond the filtered light of the pond garden at Boldre Hill, the narrow, shady walks at Stair House leading out to the bright light and wide horizon of the clifftop. As she expressed it, 'A brilliantly lit group seen against deep shadow, or a shaded group seen against the light, stirs the emotions beyond our understanding.'[14]

The plant material should also contrast with the building, as she told a meeting of the Institute of Landscape Architects:

Low buildings are set off by tall trees and very tall buildings by low planting. You remember Repton's principle of round-headed trees with gothic architecture and perpendicular trees with classical architecture.…Foliage usually does contrast, in form, colour, and texture with those of architectural material: with very few exceptions I should say the stronger the contrast the better.[15]

Colvin considered that Repton was probably the first person to analyse the relationship between architectural forms and plant forms and included an illustration of 'Repton's rule' in both editions of her *Land and Landscape*[16], showing how 'round-headed trees should

Colvin was fond of the strongly architectural shapes of topiary which she felt had always been used in the cottage garden 'as a humble conciliation between art and nature'.[18] She considered topiary or green architecture could be effectively used where house and garden met, as could plants whose striking, sculptural quality would contrast with the architectural forms – plants with 'bold foliage and intriguing shape'.[19] Of her own house, Little Peacocks, at Filkins in the Cotswolds, she wrote:

It contains two ancient clipped yews. They are, I believe, the bases (or perches) of the clipped topiary peacocks which gave the house its name, but which my predecessors got tired of and chopped off. I do not blame them and am glad not to have had to make the decision myself.

OPPOSITE ABOVE Contrast of light and shade between the sunny maze at West Stowell and the dark woodland behind.

OPPOSITE BELOW Sunlight filters through the trees on to the water garden at Boldre Hill, contrasting with the bright field beyond.

ABOVE This drawing by Richard Westmacott in the second edition of Colvin's *Land and Landscape* illustrates 'Repton's rule' showing how round-headed trees are better adapted to gothic architecture and upright ones to the classic style.

In this particular instance, though, she 'grudged' the yews (which she referred to as 'the bowler hats') the space they occupied because they made the ground underneath too dry and shady for successful planting. There are, however, a number of photographs of elaborate topiary work in cottage gardens in her albums and she included one in the second edition of her book *Land and Landscape* captioned: 'Clipped yews in cottage gardens prove generations of devoted care, giving a sense of duration in history…'[20]

She considered that clipped hedges, topiary work and pleached trees could be used as architecturally as brick and stone and yet they were definitely part of the garden and helped introduce the house into its surroundings:

> clipped architectural or 'abstract' asymmetric shapes could be very happily used in connection with modern architecture. At a time when architects are bringing the garden into the house, and opening the house out to the garden in a series of carefully-graded stages…the use of green architecture would provide one more step in the series, and opportunities for rich variety.[21]

As an illustration, Colvin used a photograph of the hornbeam stilt hedge at Hidcote in Gloucestershire where the 'stems are columns supporting walls of foliage – green in summer and brown in winter'.[22] She had included a stilt hedge herself in one of her earliest

LEFT ABOVE The art of green sculpture seen in its one 'invulnerable stronghold' – the cottage garden where the native evergreens were trimmed into what Colvin described in the second edition of *Land and Landscape* as 'huge and gloriously non-functional ornaments'.

LEFT CENTRE The 'bowler hats', the remains of the topiary peacocks after which Colvin's house in the Cotswolds was named.

LEFT BELOW Colvin felt that topiary in a cottage garden provided evidence of generations of devoted care.

LEFT Green architecture such as this hornbeam stilt hedge at Hidcote – a carpet of turf between arcades of hornbeam – could help introduce the house into its setting, as Colvin's photograph demonstrates.

BELOW The stilt hedge at Steeple Manor, Dorset, in 1948, twenty-four years after Colvin first worked there.

designs, Steeple Manor. The narrow clipped yew on a pedestal in her parents' garden at Gangbridge was a very formal abstract shape (see p.63) that provided a striking contrast to the soft, relaxed foliage of the trees around it. In contemporary garden design the use of such 'green architecture' has become commonplace, as has the grouping of strongly architectural plants, but in the 1920s Colvin was developing her innovative ideas on such planting and was 'struggling to work out compatible species for such compositions'.[23]

In the 1920s and 1930s the Modern movement was making its mark on gardens, more so in Europe than in Britain. In Belgium, for example, Jean Caneel-Claes was making small gardens with smooth white concrete paving and sculptural plants – such as acanthus, fatsia, phormium, ornamental rhubarb and *Viburnum davidii* – plants that Colvin used right from the start of her career and plants that Henri Correvon had labelled *'formes architecturales'*, those that could provide the necessary contrast to the stark materials of the hard landscaping. In garden designer John Brookes's view, 'Modernist designers sought out plants of form and shape that worked visually with their designs, did not smother them.…Planting as such was not important – individual plants as sculptures were.'[24]

In the vanguard, in the water garden at Boldre Hill, for example, Colvin used a phormium, the handsome foliage plant *Rodgersia pinnata*, and, for a wild touch, the statuesque cow parsnip (*Heracleum sphondylium*). Later at The Old Parsonage, Buscot, she used a sizeable clump of giant hogweed (which she referred to as giant hemlock, *Heracleum mantegazzianum*), and some of the very architectural 'ornamental rhubarb' (*Gunnera manicata*) (see pp.79 and 202 for photographs of this riverside garden). In 'Planting as a Medium of Design', Colvin said of giant hogweed that its 'huge lacey

LEFT Colvin's photograph of *Acanthus spinosus* planted against a wall at Filkins.

RIGHT The exciting but neglected 'purple black hoods glowering over pale throats of dusty pink' of *Acanthus spinosus*.

blooms…crown the sculpture of the leaves as a welcome and almost unexpected gift'. She felt 'the sculpture of a gunnera plant or a giant hemlock [seen] against an evergreen group in shadow or against the shade cast by taller trees' would 'give delight beyond expectation'.[25]

In general, though, Colvin felt the British neglected those sculptural plants that were available to them:

> For instance, acanthus, whose leaves inspired the ornament on the Corinthian order….Its leaves are still as fine as they used to be in ancient Greece, and in late summer it produces flowering spikes no less exciting than the foliage, with purple black hoods glowering over pale throats of dusty pink.

Sadly, she doubted whether this colour scheme would appeal to 'those who deck their pergolas with Dorothy Perkins and American Pillar roses' although in her view it was 'fit for a poet's eye'.[26]

In a number of her earlier gardens, Colvin's sensitivity to the sculptural quality in plants extended to trees: 'she could see in any tree a potential beauty of shape to be achieved by careful removal of superfluous limbs'.[27] There are many examples of trimmed tree trunks in her work, including those at Steeple Manor, Boldre Hill and Naunton Hall, and the woodland walk at Woldingham and the silver birch grove at Zywiec. She was also able to imagine the potential view to be had through heavy trees. This meant that, rather than removing a tree to reveal a hidden view, she would simply mark up the lower branches to be trimmed away. In the resulting composition distant space could be seen through foreground shade. One example was at Conderton Manor, where she identified that the problem was:

> Shall we cut down elms to obtain view of Bredon Hill? Tests proved that it was the lower skirts of the trees and border in front of them…By trimming frills off lower branches & moving border elsewhere, a view of Bredon was obtained magnificently framed in the stems and upper branches of trees – whose shape in itself was improved by trimming.[28]

Trees were structural too in that, along with boundaries and other existing features, they were the point of departure and the foundation on which a new garden would be based. 'Trees may limit us in the sense that we cannot plant underneath them,' she advised amateur gardeners in *Good Gardening* magazine,

> but they give reason to the direction of the paths and the shape of the lawn. We can build up to them in such a way that they appear to have been planted there on purpose as part of the design – thus lending their age to the new garden and giving it an invaluable feeling of maturity.[29]

In her own designs, she retained existing trees wherever possible for these reasons and also made use of trees beyond the garden's boundary as eye-catchers or simply to extend the sense of space.

Her interest in the treatment of the ground below trees and in the use of bulbs in rough grass echoed Robinson's innovative naturalising of spring bulbs – and was displayed in many of her gardens, again including Steeple Manor, Naunton Hall, Woldingham and the New Castle at Zywiec and many later designs.

In contrast to the natural simplicity of such treatments, Colvin felt that in England there was too much emphasis on getting an effect with a 'mass of colour', with the result that 'the more permanent use of plant form is neglected'. In this she did not see eye to eye with her father who would sometimes tease, 'Oh, come on, Brenda, let's have some colour – it's all greenery-yallery!' In the first of many articles she contributed to the Institute of Landscape Architects' journal, writing about the growing popularity of grey-leaved plants used as a foil to bright colours in the herbaceous border, Colvin credited Gertrude Jekyll with being one of the first to highlight the use of grey and silver foliage in this way.[30] Her notes for a series of lectures given in 1940 note that:

> The amateur tendency is to regard Flower colour as if it was the…only thing to aim at in Gdn Design. Hence poor results. In imagination the flowers are seen permanently – but not in real life.

The professional designer had to face up to this and understand the significance of the much greater proportional importance of plant form.

To impress the point on her students, she calculated that the proportion of the importance of plant form to flower was 7:1, but that had to be multiplied by 12 for the months of the year 'to get a just proportion of value', therefore 'the true proportion of plant form : flower colour is 84:1'.[31] In real life, 'although we can have some plants in bloom all the time, or all the plants in bloom some of the time, we cannot have all the plants in bloom all the time'.[32] Whatever colour schemes were arranged, their success depended largely on 'the sculptural value of the foliage which is their enduring base'.[33] In fact

she suggested that it would be an excellent training in appreciation of plant form and texture for students to be confined to studies in green, the equivalent of 'sepia studies' in painting. The garden designer Anthony du Gard Pasley, who joined Colvin in 1951 as 'perhaps the last, articled pupil on God's earth who actually paid to be a pupil', remembers being made to design borders of vegetables so that he could appreciate form and texture without the distraction of flowers.[34]

Colvin had realised from the start that contrasts in foliage texture and colour were important and recalled that her visit to Munstead Wood as a student had shown her clearly how plants, foliage and colour could be used to create particular effects.[35] She enjoyed combinations of pale greys and dark greens – willow-leaved pear with 'billows of *Senecio greyii*[36] grouped with Arbutus' – or the effects of greens on their own – 'a tall tulip tree in full sunlight, seen against the shadows and the dark rigidity of hemlock spruces'.[37] Equally, the stems of trees in shadow seen against a sunlit lawn or sunlit stems against dense woodland beyond were extremely effective, and the leaves of a pale green tree, well placed, 'may bring drifts of sunlight down to view in a dim courtyard'.[38] Among herbaceous plants, the contrasts of form and texture were almost infinite:

> there are tall spire-shaped plants…tall stalky plants with blobs at the top…low feathery foliage with flat soup plates held aloft…round-headed shimmery plants…and round-headed solid plants…close grey carpeting plants and bright green spiky carpeting plants…plants with sword-like perpendicular lines such as Iris and montbretia, that group well with round leaves…and with mat-surface plants…woolly white plants such as stachys that are such an excellent foil for any bright colour growing near them.[39]

RIGHT At Conderton Manor in Worcestershire, Bredon Hill can be seen through the tree trunks – before the lower branches were trimmed, it had been thought that the opening up of this view would necessitate felling the trees.

She was very conscious, too, of the need to provide planting that would be pleasing throughout the year and would reflect seasonal change. Much of this philosophy seems unsurprising today but was new and refreshing when Colvin was expressing it. As her professional partner Hal Moggridge puts it, 'In a way, in a debased form, her planting style appears in every supermarket today – simple masses of plants with interesting texture and colour.'

In spite of this emphasis on foliage, Colvin used and appreciated flower colour and considered it had an important place in design. During a mild winter in the 1970s, she recorded 54 different species – excluding the roses – in flower in her own garden on Christmas Day.[40] As an enthusiast herself, she appreciated the difficulty for gardeners, even for beginners, of finding space for all their favourite plants but, as she wrote in *Good Gardening*, 'Unless we are content to let the garden look like a stamp album, we must plant for general effect'. Ultimately it is plants that give 'good value over a long period' that are required: 'It is not only the flowering period to which I refer, but the length of time during which the whole plant looks shapely and tidy.' She also warned against repeating the same kind of planting through the garden.

Far more variety and interest can be had by giving each section of the garden a completely different treatment, so that as you come from one section to another, there is a subtle change of mood…it is a good plan to change from a brilliant section of border with many bright colours, to a quieter area where green is the prevailing colour.[41]

Her skill in the use of foliage was matched by her skill in placing flowering plants in relation to the fall of light, making a small cluster of pale blooms stand out bright in sunlight against the dark foliage of shrubs or evergreens. Reiterating Gertrude Jekyll's theory, she also pointed out that a group of strong colours tends to seem closer to the observer than a group of softer tones: 'Soft blues and lilac give an impression of distance, and, therefore, it is a good plan to plant the far end of a border with these colours.'[42]

Not that she was in favour of pastels in all circumstances. Anticipating the attitude of 'gardener provocateur' Christopher Lloyd, who was to consider 'good taste' a swear word and who would look with disdain on 'the brigade that wants colours in pastel shades', she did not follow fashion.[43] Writing in 1936 she commented that to sing the praises of magenta 'in this, the age of its unpopularity' was 'as idle an occupation as that of the topiary expert who wanted the late Mr Robinson to have a pair of peacocks in clipped yew guarding the entrance to his drive'. Nevertheless she went on to say:

LEFT Contrasts of form and texture in foliage in Colvin's own garden, Little Peacocks at Filkins in the Cotswolds.

One of the most lovely colour scheme borders I ever saw was carried out entirely in magenta....But this, I know, is dangerous ground. Let us return to 'safer' colours. Yet pause to consider the use of the word 'safe' in connection with colour. How often one hears it said 'Pink and blue are always quite safe together' – what a confession it is of inability to see for one's self; since 'safe' can only apply to the verdict of public opinion.[44]

Nevertheless the flowers were just temporary incidents in the garden composition, to be controlled in position and colour. The use of pots was another way in which a greater degree of control was made possible: the pot itself could be a feature in the design and a succession of bloom could be ensured for certain focal points.[45]

After the war 'the passing of the old-fashioned gardener' brought 'a demand for easy maintenance through preservation of wild growth, reduction and simplification of lawn areas, avoidance of clipped hedges, limitation of flower beds'.[46] The gardens Colvin designed – and her recommended planting – increasingly reflected this need for labour-saving gardening. In 1950, in her chapter for the *Studio Annual* called 'Gardens to Enjoy', she emphasised the one fundamental principle common to all garden styles:

Our appreciation of plants depends on their setting and grouping. The relationship of each group to its neighbours, to its background and all its surroundings is of far greater consequence than the individual beauty of any single plant or flower.

She considered that 'modern conditions' – especially our need for seclusion and harmony away from the 'restlessness and rush of our working lives' – meant that garden design should move in the direction of greater simplicity. She commented that:

Working in the garden is in itself a relaxation to many of us, but the ideal is to have as little essential work as possible. Most of us like to have some gardening to do, with a little pottering – and lots of lounging according to the climate.

To approach this ideal she proposed shade-giving trees, good groupings of flowering shrubs, a relatively small area of sunlit lawn and a few flower beds near the house. For non-gardeners, she suggested mown grass paths through orchard trees with almost wild planting: bulbs, bluebells and forget-me-nots.[47]

She also hoped that such signs of a changing attitude in small private gardens would be reflected in the treatment of public gardens. 'Some "sweet disorder" must be tolerated if it saves labour' and she wrote of the search that was on for

a system of planting which shall eliminate much of the repetitive and tedious tasks, leaving scope for those more creative jobs we all enjoy....Permanent ground cover planting is one of the directions of this research....For the designer, this use of plants as accompaniment or secondary theme, looking after the ground around primary groups, becomes an element of beauty and promise.[48]

Colvin's increasingly ecological approach to plants and planting marks her out as a true descendant of Robinson, and as a precursor of the American garden style of Wolfgang Oehme and James van Sweden of the 1980s, using native prairie plants and grasses, and the more recent new German and Dutch-style perennial planting. Her use in the 1920s of flowering perennials in grass with mown paths through them as seen at Steeple Manor is very much in the style of Dutch designer Piet Oudolf. At Boldre Hill, her pond garden included native plants such as comfrey, stinking iris, royal ferns, solomon's seal and that strikingly tall daisy, elecampane, as well as foxgloves and honesty to be grown from seed. And there was that 'growing collection of native plants' that she nurtured in the orchard at her parents' house, Gangbridge.

An important reference source for Colvin was A.G. Tansley's *The British Islands and Their Vegetation*, published in 1939. Her copy of the book is still on the shelf at Colvin & Moggridge, the firm she established in Gloucestershire. Tansley was one of the most influential founders of the discipline of ecology and he showed how vegetation is affected by soil, climate, the presence of wild and domesticated animals, previous land management, and contemporary human activities. Noting how certain groups of plants show a preference for certain soils and rocks, Colvin felt it was vital that the landscape designer should study these natural plant communities in order to appreciate the native character of any particular region's landscape:

> Nothing is easier than to introduce foreign plants of outstanding beauty and to grow them where we will…to spread these recklessly over the countryside is to overlay the existing subtle variations of our land and to lead in the end to a deathly monotony.[49]

Again she was a forerunner – she was writing this in 1947 and it was not until 1983, two years after her death, that the charity Common Ground was formed and used the term 'local distinctiveness' to define these regional variations and today it is still campaigning to preserve them.

Tansley's book was to become an influential guide for landscape architects but very few of Colvin's contemporaries had the same concern for the ecological approach that it proposed. For example, Geoffrey Jellicoe was completely uninterested in the natural world and in fact used to boast that he did not know any plants at all. In the early days, until his wife Susan took over the role, he often relied on Colvin to do planting plans for him. His Moss Garden at Sutton Place was destined to fail because its airy situation was totally unsuited to growing moss – Colvin would have known that.

Her own garden at Little Peacocks was in a limestone district, so she planted lime-loving plants such as clematis and viburnums, roses and all the berrying trees and shrubs. She much preferred 'the enthusiastic growth of those which enjoy the conditions I can offer to the slow survival of rebellious, resentful specimens in need of constant coddling and attention'. Here she attempted to follow her own rules on planting. She describes her aims – and to what degree she felt she had succeeded:

> The planting is intended to give continuous calm enjoyment at all seasons, rather than dazzle the eye in the height of summer. The ground is well covered with low plants chosen for beauty of foliage: many are evergreen and there are masses of spring bulbs. In and over the ground-cover plants are many flowering shrubs, roses, viburnums, hydrangeas, tree paeonies, etc., to provide flower all through the year.…
>
> I have tried to get a feeling of quiet space in this small area, enclosed as it is by grey stone walls and farm buildings. I try, too, to engender a sense of anticipation and interest by the progression from one interesting plant group to the next in a rhythm, giving definite contrasts without loss of unity. But it is difficult to reconcile simplicity with one's enthusiasm for plants in so small a garden, and I probably let the plants jostle one another too much.[50]

Undoubtedly she struggled between her eagerness to grow plants and her eagerness on the other hand to do lean designs which could be more easily maintained. For clients, because of the maintenance implications, it was important to produce reasonably uncomplicated schemes which did not have too many plants in them.

Colvin's personal pleasure in plants is obvious in the way she describes her own garden, and in much of her writing. She loved the delicacy of some flowers: describing the tiny ground-covering *Raoulia australis* when flowering 'as though some careless person passing by had spilt pecks of gold dust on a silver carpet';[51] and we have already seen her enthusiastic description of the acanthus. Of the whitebeam, she writes: 'a tree which has beauty of flower, leaf and berry, but whose most beautiful stage of all is before any of these appear…Like little silver candles on the naked twigs, [the leaf buds] stand upright and sparkle in the sun.'[52]

Beyond her personal enthusiasm for them, plants played a vital role in Colvin's whole design philosophy. To associate her, as some have done, merely with groundcover

planting is an error – the main characteristic of her planting is its great range and diversity. The key, in her view, was to avoid thinking of plants only as 'decorative touches to designs conceived in other materials', they were the foundation of the structure itself.[53] The influence of her ideas spread as she communicated them to other landscape architects, town planners and architects through her evening talks to the institute and her lectures during the 1930s and 1940s at the Regent Street Polytechnic, at Swanley Horticultural College, at Studley Horticultural and Agricultural College, and at the Architectural Association, and in the 1950s her 'crits' for a part-time course in landscape architecture that Peter Youngman ran for gardeners, architects and planners at University College, London. While it is generally acknowledged that she was not a charismatic lecturer, nonetheless her ideas and the passion with which she expressed them impressed her audiences. It was to become a time, too, of post-war

planning and reconstruction when people were ready to listen to what she had to say. She wrote extensively about planting for the institute's journals as well as for the more populist *Good Gardening* magazine and, in the 1960s, she contributed a number of inspiring articles as a member of the *Observer's* new team of specialist writers, appointed to 'help amateur gardeners with their expert knowledge'.[54] And her *Land and Landscape*, first published in 1947 with a second edition published in 1970, became 'a standard work on good landscape practice'.[55]

If Colvin's skill in handling plants in her designs was outstanding, it was certainly matched by her knowledge of trees and her ability to use them to best effect, both in her garden and her landscape work.

ABOVE Colvin's own general view of her garden at Little Peacocks in 1959 with its quiet sense of enclosure.

Trees in town and country

'Trees play an all-important role in British landscape. For the landscape architect they are a material of design, used not only for their beauty but also for their functional value as shelter, screens, backcloth.... They define and separate the open spaces, thus serving as do the walls and pillars of a building.'[1]

I N 1953 Colvin was asked – 'almost in the 18th century tradition', as she put it – to carry out a report on the tree planting at the Compton Beauchamp estate in Wiltshire. Her client, editor of *The Observer* and philanthropist David Astor, for whom she also designed three private gardens, had recently purchased the property.[2] She found that existing plantations and shelter belts were neglected, giving little protection and having little or no timber value. There were, however, some 'striking overgrown hedges…valuable as shelter'. She proposed planting of new trees and shelter belts, and renovation of existing woods, spinneys and shelter belts, to be carried out in three phases. For her, the 'great beauty of shelter belts on the downland is the emphasis they give to contours and to mild undulations, bringing out land sculpture otherwise unseen'. She also suggested ways of persuading tenant farmers to restore field boundaries with hedges and hedgerow trees. When the tendency around the country was for the destruction of hedgerows, the value of such estate plantings was enormous.[3]

Writing David Astor's obituary in December 2001, Hal Moggridge noted how, on Colvin's advice, Astor had planted 'long new shelter belts across the back of the Berkshire Downs between White Horse Hill and Ashdown House, as noble in scale as eighteenth-century landscape works'. In the 1970s Astor also, in an 'extraordinary public-spirited action in the landscape', reorganised the surroundings of Uffington Castle and the White Horse. He 'hated the cars parked all over the hills beneath these monuments' and 'dreamt that visitors should be able to experience these ancient artefacts in a landscape completely detached from more practical aspects of life'.[4] Colvin & Moggridge, with Colvin taking the role of background adviser, designed a car park and the hilltop was restored to grassland. Having reorganised White Horse Hill, Astor donated it all to the National Trust to conserve it for the public in perpetuity.

OPPOSITE ABOVE Colvin's study shows how the preservation of mature trees enhanced the modern Impington Country College, Cambridge, designed by Walter Gropius and his partner Maxwell Fry and opened in 1939.

OPPOSITE BELOW A picture of elm trees from Colvin's own photograph album.

RIGHT S.R. Badmin's illustration of the ash tree from *Trees for Town and Country,* showing detail of leaf, seeds and twigs.

OPPOSITE The photograph of an ash from *Trees for Town and Country,* showing the tree's typical outline.

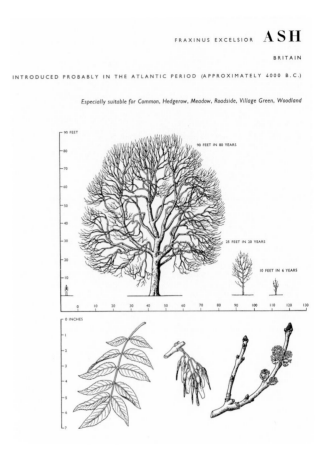

FRAXINUS EXCELSIOR **ASH**

BRITAIN

INTRODUCED PROBABLY IN THE ATLANTIC PERIOD (APPROXIMATELY 4000 B.C.)

Especially suitable for Common, Hedgerow, Meadow, Roadside, Village Green, Woodland

At Compton Beauchamp, Colvin showed her sensitivity to the vital role trees played in the wider landscape, just as she was sensitive to their use on the smaller scale of garden design. In 1947 she had her first book published: *Trees for Town and Country*.[5] The book was prepared during the war years with Colvin writing the text, assisted by town planner Jacqueline Tyrwhitt, and it was illustrated with line drawings by S.R. Badmin. Idealistically, the book's jacket said it:

> looked forward to a renaissance of tree-planting which could make as bold and beautiful an impress upon the English landscape as the stately avenues of large trees in the spacious grounds of country houses, the dense islands of woodland planted as game preserves, and the network of tree-studded hedgerows of our 18th century ancestors.

Local authorities, town planners, architects, preservation societies and the general public took the book up with enthusiasm, and by 1949 it had already gone to a third edition. It was the standard reference work for many years, with a final edition published in 1972. A few years after its publication, Colvin was sat at a dinner next to an extremely bombastic architect who was holding forth to her. She asked him whether he used landscape architects at all. No, was his response, he didn't need anything like that. In fact, he said, he had a very good little book he used. It was called *Trees for Town and Country*. Did she know of it? She pulled herself up to her very considerable height and said, 'Well, actually, I wrote it.'[6]

In the book 60 trees suitable for general cultivation in Britain are described, not in botanical terms, but 'as material for use in landscape composition'.[7] It was unusual in that it illustrated tree height and spread at different stages of growth as well as giving clear details of leaf, flower, fruit and twigs to help in identification. Badmin felt the success of his drawings was largely due to Colvin's contribution:

> I learnt a lot from Brenda Colvin. She taught me what to look for in trees – the angle of branches, for instance. Every specimen has its angle of growth. It is quite incredible. I did the trees in winter and also in three stages of growth, at planting and after about 25 or thirty years. An architect could see how a tree would develop and end up.[8]

Each species was also shown in a black-and-white photograph and accompanied by notes on cultivation and an indication of uses for which it was considered especially suitable. The list of uses was: coast, common, clipped hedges, hedgerow trees, lawns, meadow, roadside,

benefits they confer that we really experience the full spell of their beauty.[10]

Under this spell herself, in her many articles and talks on trees Colvin always stressed the huge range of benefits they offered, far beyond their simple ornamental appearance. 'Trees must never be regarded just as a remedy for something ugly,' she insisted:[11]

Apart from their health value in purifying the atmosphere, trees provide the vertical scale of design in open country. They can define the various divisions of space without necessarily enclosing them, while at the same time serving as screens, protecting areas from wind, cold, dust, smoke, or noise; or they can be used to frame and emphasise pleasant views and vistas. The shade of trees is useful both for man and beast, and it can relieve the eye from the glare reflected by roads and buildings on sunny days. The outlines of trees serve to connect buildings with the surrounding land forms and…admit man-made edifices to membership of the landscape.[12]

town, streets, village green, waterside, windscreens and woodland. Even in 1992, by which time a number of much more modern, glossy colour guides to trees had been published, garden writer Mary Keen felt it was still the best book on tree size and suitability, the only book that gave 'an idea of the inhuman scale of some forest trees, showing trees at various stages in their life dwarfing a six-foot man'.[9]

Colvin's passion for trees is evident in her introduction to the book:

Land forms and vegetation are the main materials both of natural landscape and of landscape designed as a setting for human buildings and human life. Trees form the most prominent component of this setting and serve many more important functions in the total design than that of ornamental appearance. Indeed it is only when we make full use of all the

One of the biggest factors in considering trees as promoters of health and well-being was their use for wind shelter. Colvin was convinced it contributed to 'human health, resistance to disease, and efficiency; one need only consider how difficult it [is] to do mental arithmetic in a high wind to realise the effect on efficiency.'[13] In a sheltered area, people would spend more time in the open air, more windows would be opened to sun and air, and less spent on fuel. She took a close look at the problem of wind shelter at a symposium on 'Landscape Architecture in the New Towns' held in May 1950. In her talk she used the example of the new town at East Kilbride where she was consultant to the development corporation. There she confessed she had found her 'previous partiality for hardwoods was soon blown away by the wind, in favour of a high proportion of Conifers'.[14]

Shelter belts were definitely needed for the citizens-to-be of this new town being built on a bleak windswept

LEFT Planted by schoolchildren – a practice begun by Colvin – this tree belt adjacent to Hunter Primary School, East Kilbride, between the school's playing fields and the surrounding Calderwood neighbourhood homes, was photographed in 2005.

RIGHT Colvin used this photograph of beech trunks on Edgehill in Warwickshire to illustrate how the repetition of the similar yet different stems of one species enhances a composition. Here, the curve, following the line of the footpath, invites further exploration and anticipation.

site, but they were also necessary for the sake of all the other planting in parks, housing estates and open spaces there. She outlined a number of very practical reasons why felled areas and derelict woodland were to be reused: visually they would form a good backdrop for the new buildings; they were mostly on land less suitable for building; because of tree stumps and roots in the ground, they were not coveted by farmer or architect; they were enclosed by hedges which would shelter the new trees; and, lastly, the soil contained the woodland organisms favourable to tree growth. To ensure continuity, she proposed a main forest belt and a few other broad shelter belts to be planted with timber trees with carefully planned felling schemes. A large number of these trees would be conifers – best for the climate and because of the demand for soft wood. 'They will provide dark green massive outlines, curving up the hills and crowning the crests.' To offset these, she hoped to see 'part of the Calder Glen treated as a Nature Reserve'. It was in various stages of reversion to mixed forest where the natural ecology could be studied. Today Calderglen Park is a popular country park with more than eight miles of nature trails along the River Calder, including waterfalls and important Site of Special Scientfic Interest geological features along the way. For the more open ornamental planting in the town she chose pale-leaved deciduous trees – birch, beech, Norway maple, wild cherry and mountain ash grouped on greens, roadsides and other open spaces. One small park was chosen for the first 'Schools Planting Day, when 130 children took part in a ceremonial planting...in order to encourage an appreciation of the town's landscape in the rising generation.'[15] This idea of Colvin's was continued for many years with a scheme under which every child planted a tree in neighbourhood nurseries.[16]

More generally Colvin considered the grouping of trees was of key importance: 'most of the purposes for which trees are planted call for groupings...bold groups planted to form a sculptural unity of a single species, or else of several species that contrast strongly in outline, give far more pleasing effects than carelessly mixed groups, or than numerous unrelated individual trees.'[17] Grouping was nature's way: 'experience teaches that appreciation even of the individual depends on its context, and that good relationships between the individuals in a group, or between one group and another, please the eye better than plants which are merely "displayed".' Trees of a single species were better grouped together 'for the sake of rhythm in the stem pattern and for the sense of unity in the canopy.'[18] In the second edition of her book *Land and Landscape*, she included a picture of a row of beeches: 'The repetition of

stems of one species gives a rhythm to the composition. Each is a different individual shape, yet they share a common character.'[19] Another particularly striking example she cited was a belt of scarlet willows on a river bank near Salisbury: 'It brightens the valley scenery in winter for the whole neighbourhood…no mixture could have been half so effective as the broad massing of a single species.' Yet she recognised that some mixtures worked well too: nearby were some 'yew woods on the chalk downs whose beauty is enhanced by the sprinkling of whitebeams along the fringe'.[20]

Colvin's belief in the importance of plant form in relation to architecture was especially true of trees. Writing in 1934, she said,

In all ages certain plant forms have been appreciated for their architectural value. The massive forms of clipped evergreens, the upright columns of the cypress and the smooth carpet of turf; the tracery of deciduous trees in winter and their heavy rounded heads in summer….All these are used to enrich great buildings and to bring them into harmony with surrounding nature.[21]

In garden design, then, trees 'inevitably play the most important part in the general scheme: their tall irregular outlines seen against the sky behind a house are an admirable foil to the straight lines of masonry and seem to give it countenance.'[22] Because 'shadow design' was an important part of a garden's landscape, 'trees on or near a lawn need careful placing, not simply with regard to their effect as frame or background, but also with regard to the position of their shadow at various times of the day.' In English gardens, in particular, lawns and trees complemented each other: 'Lawn alone…is almost valueless without its complement of trees.'[23] In French gardens, she considered that trees were used collectively – planted for mass effect, to form a frame and setting for open parterres, and to give height, background and shade, but never for their individual character. By contrast, in England,

the tradition of freedom and the love of natural forms is so strong that even our formal gardens are planted informally and the trees are allowed to have individuality, delighting us by their characteristic habit and shape….Take an English garden one knows well and visualize it in imagination – there is always some well-loved tree presiding over the lawn, under which we have sat and talked or happily dozed so often in the past. It commands our affection and respect as if it were a member of the family.[24]

At her parents' house in Hampshire it was the well established trees already there, including a walnut, a chestnut, some yews and cherries, that were ruling factors in her design. In her own garden at Filkins she retained existing trees, including a horse chestnut and an old Blenheim Orange apple tree that partly shaded a paved seating area.

In most instances, though, the new housing estates did not have the good fortune to inherit such beauties. In connection with them – or any other new building – Colvin felt the most important function of trees in

design terms was 'to supply large vertical masses to counteract an extent of rather low building'.[25] If the horizon consisted of large trees, then there was less need for planting in front of the houses for decoration. The widespread use of small ornamental cherries and similar trees in front of rows of housing was a mistake: 'not so much because the avenue principle is

OPPOSITE Colvin's own photograph of yews and white-beams on Box Hill in Surrey in spring 1946, a successful mix of colours. With the beechwoods on the skyline, three phases of natural reversion to forest can be seen.

BELOW A view of Colvin's own garden at Little Peacocks in Filkins in 1974 showing the Blenheim apple tree to the right and the overhanging branches of the horse chestnut to the left, both existing trees that she retained.

inappropriate, but because the trees are the same size as the houses and their spacing is equally monotonous'; consequently they failed to provide a skyline and merely accentuated the lack of variety and the low horizon.[26] A single large tree or an important group well positioned with some space around it 'may compose far better with a town street than an avenue'. Where new housing was to be built on land that already had mature trees, however, their beauty could be borrowed for the new layout.[27]

The same principle applied to industrial or other larger scale building. An example Colvin used in *Land and Landscape* was the W.H. Smith warehouse at Swindon where an existing tree 'lends maturity and frames a view of the new buildings'. The future outline of Colvin's additional planting of newly planted, quick-growing species is indicated on the picture by white dots. On the far side of the building, mature and semi-

mature trees were planted to provide quicker effect in the early years.[28]

Trees could also be used to mark boundaries and define open spaces in a design. On housing estates this could simply mean hedges separating garden from garden. In a lecture given at the Housing Centre in May 1947, sympathetic to the residents of new estates, Colvin said she had often noticed that where there were no hedges between back gardens, the tenants almost gave up the hope of keeping their gardens well because of all the rubbish that blew between them. They had no seclusion either. They would also benefit from a screen of trees between housing and industrial areas or railways which would give them protection from dust, smoke and noise.

One of the worst difficulties in the post-war period, Colvin felt, was that so much of the land used for

building was high land on the ridge above a valley. She used the example of High Wycombe where one of the finest skylines in the country had been spoilt by housing development. In her view the high ridge of ground should have been the site for the biggest trees with the houses built just below, so the trees formed a skyline for them. It was important to remember that 'trees are at home on hills, and grow most happily there'.[29] If trees and shrubs and other plants were to fulfil their proper function, then they had to be provided from the outset as an element of the design – they should be considered almost on the same basis as buildings.

At East Kilbride Colvin encouraged the growth of natural self-sown scrub in some areas, and the Calder Glen was a part of this. She realised that such self-sown plantings were far more likely to succeed and give natural-looking spinneys and woodland than any

new plantings would do. Increasingly she stressed the importance of what she called 'ecological planting'. Unlike the gardener who could adapt the site to their choice of tree, the landscape architect had to follow the tree's ecological requirements. Visually, such a choice was better suited to large-scale projects, maintenance would be less demanding and, ultimately, it would reflect and help to conserve 'the wonderful diversity of character in the wider landscape which is founded on the ecological facts of our land'.[30] She recognised that sometimes concessions had to be made to popular taste, but felt that a 'graduation from pop planting near the buildings to classic ecological truth on the fringes' was a reasonable compromise.

Compromise was needed too in one particular aspect of Colvin's work at Aldershot where, early in 1963, she was appointed landscape consultant to the planning group set up to organise the rebuild of 1,500 acres (600 hectares) of the military town. Here, in landscape terms, a regimented tarmac-dominated town, built in the nineteenth century on a grid pattern, was to be changed into a green town based on integration into the existing landform. The army's brief was to provide opportunities 'for the soldier to enjoy a full life in his off-duty hours in his home and in attractive surroundings comparable with those of well paid workers in industry'.[31] Some of Colvin's staff were surprised when she said that she had been asked to produce areas where soldiers and their girlfriends could disappear and do what soldiers and their girlfriends do, but in fact it was not such a surprising interpretation: she always worked on a very human level with a keen appreciation of people's needs.[32] Her landscape report considered that:

> Extensive use of woodland planting [was] necessary in the Military Town area to ensure the fullest use and proper maintenance of space not required for other specific use....Visually the woodlands are an important landscape feature, giving character to the site. They provide strong visual links between the units and the general layout in scale with the area of the town....It is proposed to use the characteristic vegetation in the surrounding woods...to relate the town to the region and to preserve its overall unity.[33]

The army, however, were not too keen on some of the rather 'untidy' new planting and so Colvin had to make different categories of landscape. One of these was rough woodlands, but by putting fences around these areas and letting the army mow round the outside of the fence, there was a clear demarcation between the neatly maintained areas and the area inside that could be left wild. As a result many areas of woodland were

made, at low cost, just by being fenced. They regenerated naturally, mostly with oak, sweet chestnut, ash and birch, which grew happily in the local gravelly soil.

Colvin's extensive knowledge of tree growth and cultivation meant that she was able to promote such simple, economic ways of encouraging trees. In addition to the protection of self-sown scrub, and the use of tree saplings 'capable of fine maturity' found in hedgerows and disused waste ground, she recommended that old established trees at risk of damage, because of changed drainage levels or other interference as a result of development, should be matched with understudy planting. Large nursery-grown trees could be added for short-term effect.

Such mixed systems of planting could work well but the difficulty of ensuring long-term maintenance had led to failures in the past, as Colvin knew only too well. She quoted the example of Madeline Agar's 1920s war memorial garden on Wimbledon Common. As a long-term objective Agar had planned concentric rings of English oak with undisturbed ground between them, but for short-term public use had superimposed over the long-term plan an additional scheme of winding paths with flowering trees and shrubs for immediate effect. Colvin noted with regret that it had been 'before

LEFT Dense woodland being created in Aldershot by natural regeneration was conserved from excessive maintenance by surrounding fencing which also provided a neat edge.

OPPOSITE Colvin pointed out that much fine timber – elms in this photograph of hers – grows in the hedgerows. She feared that mechanised hedge clipping threatened the future of all hedgerow trees.

the days of semi-mature tree planting: the small oaks were sacrificed as soon as they began to threaten the lilacs and laburnums, although sensitive thinning could have preserved both until the oaks, nearing maturity, could have proved the long-term value of [Agar's] choice.'

Colvin sums up the reasons for ecological planting, especially in the case of trees, as conservation, appearance, diversity and economy (capital cost and long-term maintenance). In landscape, 'conservation' meant the design and maintenance of a self-perpetuating environment – 'in perpetual balance as it exists in nature'. A successful visual appearance could be achieved by working with natural forces, that is, on an ecological basis. The third reason was the need for 'broad scale diversity'. Finally, with an objective of a self-perpetuating environment, economy would reinforce and strengthen the reasons for ecological planting in the long term because long-term landscape maintenance far outweighed capital cost.[34]

Her approach was always conservationist, recognising the huge importance of the preservation of trees and hedges throughout the country. In the late 1940s and 1950s, anticipating the now widely used phrase 'green corridor', she spoke of

the green network binding buildings and roads to the landscape beyond.…The agricultural pattern beyond the towns gives continuity of this green network wherever the hedges and hedgerow trees have been retained. The sight of trees and hedges being rooted out for the sake of the tractor over large areas of arable land is, for me, like seeing the breakdown of the cell walls in living plant tissue.[35]

In 1974 she emphasised the conservation value of the 'continuity of a web or network of vegetation, connecting town and country, from coast to coast… the broad national implications of conservation are identical with fine landscape quality: they should go together.'[36] The importance of 'green networks' is still being emphasised today, with town planners recently being advised, following a 'Wild About Gardens' survey, that they should make biodiversity a core consideration within urban and suburban regeneration plans.

The use of native species was just one element in this conservationist approach but Colvin did not belong to the 'native species only' school. She chose trees on a pragmatic basis to solve particular problems and so would use exotics where necessary to achieve her landscape objectives. In many sites, such as parks and gardens in towns or close to human habitation, she felt it was appropriate to follow visual and aesthetic standards unlimited by ecology. But, in the wider and more open landscape, far more satisfactory results could be achieved by limiting new planting to the native plants associated with the site: 'Such restraint…brings its own reward in the resulting sense of unity and of harmony: that "oneness" with nature itself, giving simplicity which is calm, enduring and full of deep repose.'[37]

Colvin's expertise on trees and forestry meant that she was included as one of the members of the Institute of Landscape Architects' Forestry Committee, set up in July 1943.[38] Their report, published in the October 1944 *Wartime Journal*, is as relevant today as it was when it was published. It supported the need for afforestation on poor land, particularly in highland Britain, 'provided that good landscape principles are followed, just as the scenery in lowland Britain owes so much to the landscape planting of the 18th century, so we of this generation… have the power to create a new and hitherto undreamt of scenery.'[39] Colvin was adamant that the Forestry Commission's responsibility should be 'not only for the timber production but also for the maintenance of the landscape quality' of the land they acquired.

Where the Commission failed in this responsibility, Colvin felt she had a duty to criticise and she certainly had the knowledge to do so. In the first edition of *Land and Landscape*, she was critical of 'Closely planted forest plots of rigid geometrical outline, imposed on the hillside without regard to contours and other existing features' – these looked 'wrong' in the landscape, regardless of what trees were grown.[40] Nevertheless, going in the face of the widespread criticism of coniferous afforestation at that time, she considered that commercial forestry could be beneficial. Good design could balance what might seem conflicting interests: the need for timber production, the need to raise the agricultural yields of highland districts and the recreational value of these areas. Additional benefits from forestry were the prevention of soil erosion, the conservation of water supply, the maintenance or creation of soil fertility, and the maintenance of biological balance. The ILA's report summarised it:

'Losses on the departmental swings would be more than compensated by gains on the national roundabouts.'[41] While acknowledging that the Forestry Commission had been doing much to improve the landscape in its areas in the second edition of her book in 1970, she expressed concern that the commission was now putting an even greater emphasis on commercial timber production and not paying sufficient attention to the other land uses which could be integrated with forestry.

In 1960, as an acknowledged expert, Colvin was invited by the Royal Horticultural Society to speak on 'Trees in Towns and Their Treatment for Landscape Effect'. Analysing the difference between tree planting in urban and rural areas, she listed three factors: 'the competition for space, light and air is keener in town'; 'horticultural conditions tend to be more difficult'; and, because there was some difference in the purpose of tree planting, 'a tree's appearance and its relationship to its surroundings is all the more important.' She felt that the 'value of trees as visual elements of the townscape' could hardly be overrated. 'Their power of bringing natural beauty into the town, and of relating architecture and other man-made features to nature should be used to the fullest possible extent.' Noting the skill of photographers in using existing trees to enhance their pictures of buildings by framing or providing a background for them, she emphasised that 'the need for important tree groups should be realized at the outset, and the street pattern deliberately planned to include them.' It seemed there was a social divide, she noted sarcastically: 'Why is it that people living in old houses like trees and shade more than those who move to new estates? And why is

OPPOSITE ABOVE Colvin felt that within a conifer forest, the open spaces, rides and footpaths matter most from the landscape point of view. Here, a wide ride, planted with hardwoods, conceals the conifer plantations.

OPPOSITE BELOW Colvin was critical of unbroken conifer plantations such as this which give 'a prickly skyline' and, unrelieved by lighter colours, have a depressing effect in our climate.

it that the higher the [council] rates, the more shade we can endure?'

Of the horticultural difficulties, she felt that drought probably accounted for most of the losses of newly planted town trees, but vandalism was the other great hazard and difficult to control. Generously she considered that much of the damage by children was 'due to the effect of novelty, and as that wears off and the trees become a normal part of life they are allowed to grow.' Using landscape architect Peter Shepheard's expressive phrase, 'the law of diminishing vandalism', she felt that the cost of replacing damaged trees should be allowed for in all estimates. She ended her talk with a plea to hybridists and horticulturists for the one type of tree as yet unavailable: 'a lime-tolerant tree looking like *Quercus ilex* but growing as fast as a poplar, and willing to transplant at 18 feet high. Its flowers should be as lovely and freely born as a rose and its roots should abhor drains and foundations.'[42] That tree has still to be bred.

As with plants and landscape, Colvin's lifelong interest in trees is confirmed by her surviving photographs which include a large number of pictures of individual trees and of trees in the wider landscape.

TOP A filling station serving a parkway in Westchester County, New York, is set back from the road in woodland, photographed by Colvin in 1931.
CENTRE Colvin gave this photograph her own critical caption in her album of contact prints.
BELOW One of many photographs of roadside trees taken by Colvin – here, 'well-grouped trees' beside an existing road.

Some of the photographs were marked up with her own critical comments, rather in the style of Clough Williams-Ellis's illustrations in *England and the Octopus*, including that one of a 'Ghastly garage' (see p.38 right) that she used in *Land and Landscape*, comparing it unfavourably with a much more agreeable filling station serving a parkway in Westchester County, New York, set back from the road in a wooded location.[43] Another roadside shot is captioned 'ill judged tree planting, existing trees adequate'. Some of the later photographs show the advantageous use of existing mature trees in the grounds of new buildings as at Impington Country College in Cambridgeshire (see p.97 top), and a road with 'well-grouped trees'; earlier ones include a set of 'roadside trees' photographed in July 1939. There are pictures, too, of a caravan tour of Norfolk that she made with Sylvia Crowe in 1946 (see p.123), a year

after Crowe had joined her in her Baker Street office. These included some of conifer plantations and one of an attractive open glade with old hardwoods preserved inside a recently planted conifer forest.

Colvin's awareness of the values of the landscape and of the use of trees within it was to stand her in good stead in the 1940s and 1950s as she worked to promote the profession of landscape architecture through the institute and through her influential role as a member of many of the committees making preparations for post-war reconstruction.

BELOW Colvin photographed this open glade with old hardwoods preserved inside recent plantations of conifers near Thetford on her caravan trip to Norfolk with Sylvia Crowe in 1946.

ABOVE A group photograph taken at St Peter's Hall, Oxford, after a joint meeting of the Institute of Landscape Architects and the Town Planning Institute in 1934. Fellows of the ILA present are (front row, left to right) George Dillistone (2nd), Richard Sudell (3rd), Geoffrey Jellicoe (4th); (second row, sitting) T.F. Thomson (1st), Edward White (3rd), Mrs Edward White (4th), E. Prentice Mawson (5th), Dr Thomas Adams (6th), Gilbert H. Jenkins (8th), J.W.R. Adams (10th); (third row) Brenda Colvin (2nd), R.V. Giffard Woolley (4th), L. Milner White (8th); (fourth row) Madeline Agar (1st), Walter S. Chamberlain (2nd).

Working for splendour

'We are now in for a new and splendid age, or else for chaos, and we cannot plan for chaos; so let us work for splendour, especially as by doing so we promote its likelihood.'

CLOUGH WILLIAMS-ELLIS, 1942[1]

ONE OF SYLVIA CROWE'S happier memories of the war years was of the Institute of Landscape Architects' council meetings: 'one got away from the grind of seeing things through and thought about the future. One's creative energies had had a stopper put on them and they came bubbling up.' Lord Reith, then Minister of Public Works and Buildings and recently elected the institute's first honorary fellow, was there in his admiral's uniform, alongside Geoffrey Jellicoe and Colvin. Other regulars at these wartime meetings were Jacqueline Tyrwhitt, Marjory Allen and town planner James Adams. At this time, according to Crowe, 'Brenda…was a marvellous leader and her influence can't be overestimated. She had both vision and steadfastness of purpose and would never give up anything as hopeless if she thought it was the right thing. She was absolutely first class.'[2]

In the first ten years of its life, the institute consisted of only a small number of practitioners and by 1939 there were still fewer than a hundred members.[3] At this stage, despite its solid-sounding name, the institute did not even have a home of its own but was 'housed' in various people's offices. Those belonging to the institute may have considered and discussed questions of planning and landscape design, but the reality was that the vast majority of the work available was still in garden and park design. As Colvin was to recall, they had little idea of how the organisation might develop or how its work and influence could expand. They knew, however, that they needed to communicate and share information. They also recognised that a better educational system and greater public recognition were needed. Nevertheless, as Colvin put it, their 'sights were still set low'.[4]

Given this situation Crowe's words about Colvin's leadership qualities were perceptive. In Colvin, right from the start the institute had been fortunate in finding a staunch supporter who was not afraid to speak out to defend what she believed in. Just as she had insisted on her rights when a student at Swanley, in the course of her involvement with the institute she was to draw on her strong personality to fight many battles on its behalf. From the moment of her first meeting with Richard Sudell in early 1929, prior to what she later referred to as 'that inconspicuous little gathering in a corner'[5] of the Chelsea Flower Show, Colvin was determined to do what she could to help create an independent landscape profession in a country that had previously been

dominated by gifted laymen. For her 'unstinted efforts' in this, above all, Geoffrey Jellicoe considered her place in history assured.[6]

She was to encounter many difficulties – prejudice against women taking leading roles, the confusion of war and all that that would bring to stop natural progress, political struggle with other organisations, and, most frustrating of all, great reluctance to include landscape architects right from the start of the planning process. For 47 years from its foundation Colvin was a vital, dedicated fellow of the institute, re-elected without a break to serve on the council, a clear indication of her standing among her peers. She was elected honorary secretary from July 1939 until 1948, vice-president in 1949 and, finally, against the general acceptance of male rather than female leadership in those days, was voted president in April 1951.

When the institute's secretary Gwen Browne wrote to congratulate her on her election, rather surprisingly she also expressed her doubts about women as presidents. Colvin responded to this with great honesty: 'As to the [president] position I feel distinctly alarmed at the thought myself and all the more so on hearing that you have strong views against women p.s which I didn't realize before.'[7] Her 'alarm' at taking on the role is understandable – she was the first woman to be president of any of the environmental or engineering professions. In her presidential address, she referred to her 'sense of anxiety in taking on this heavy responsibility at such a difficult time', especially when she was following after such able and distinguished former presidents. The newsworthy story that the institute had elected a woman president for the first time during Festival of Britain year was syndicated to at least nine newspapers. Nevertheless Colvin was willingly accepted by her peers. An article in the institute's journal, not attributed but almost certainly

LEFT Brenda Colvin photographed on her election as president of the Institute of Landscape Architects in 1951 at the age of 53.

by the editor Richard Sudell, introduced the new president as a person who had 'probably done more than anyone in the profession to foster a recognition of the organic basis of landscape architecture'. The institute's progress, the writer continued, 'owes a great deal to her energy and devotion'.[8]

In the earlier years of the war, however, although there were some meetings of the council and of sub-committees, Colvin's work on behalf of the institute was a little less intense. Characteristically, though, she was not idle and as well as carrying on with the very small amount of garden design work available through her own practice she became involved in a number of other fields where her leadership qualities were to develop and become invaluable. One of these was the Women's Farm and Garden Association (WFGA). A voluntary association, the WFGA had been established in 1899 by a small group of women, mostly farmers or landowners in their own right, who were concerned about the lack of opportunities for training, employment and advancement for women working on the land. Madeline Agar had been a member of the association's committee since 1907 and no doubt encouraged Colvin's involvement. The association had had a number of financial and organisational problems in the years immediately before the war, but Colvin was one of an active group of members who helped to get it back on its feet. In October 1940 she was staying with Lady Bruce Richmond at Netherhampton House, Salisbury, where she had done some garden design work in 1935.[9] Writing from there to the institute's treasurer, Mr Hughes, on another matter, Colvin explained:

I have taken on a job for the Women's Farm and Garden Association – organising a training scheme for women gardeners in wartime. It is being tried out in this neighbourhood first but one hopes that it will extend soon to a much wider area, as I think it is really needed....I feel very cut off from all my usual activities and have heard nothing of the Institute for ages...the WFGA is flooded with demands for women gardeners to replace men called up.[10]

The scheme, she explained, was for girls interested in gardening and horticulture who could not afford college training. They were apprenticed to head gardeners of private gardens. They did 'garden boy and under gardener work in exchange for keep and tuition'. By December she was writing on WFGA headed paper from Woodyates Manor near Salisbury, home of the association's president Lady Lucas, where a 'probation centre' for the young women trainees had been set up.

In the course of her long career, starting at a time when women were undervalued and under-represented, Colvin was bound to be sympathetic to the cause of the advancement of women but this certainly did not mean that she was in favour of militant feminism. She was to set out her views on the subject forcefully in a letter written in 1973, when she was in her seventies:

> I resist segregation of *any* sort and see no necessity for special women's organisations, as it seems to me that we exert a far greater influence in mixed bodies than is possible from opposing organisations.... It is no use women crying for positions until they prove ability in sufficient numbers and sufficiently wide fields in their own spheres and develop a less biased attitude about the problem ....By addressing your letter to 'dear woman Landscape Architect' you yourself make a distinction. Do I assume you would not write to 'dear man Landscape Architect'? I feel the same about your use of the word 'Chairperson'. Are you and your fellowesses all huwoman beings? As chairman of a group of human beings regardless of their sex, colour, age, nationality, religion or political views I am glad not to have to distinguish precisely as to the status of each.[11]

Although this impatience is understandable from a woman who had worked hard and had successfully made her own way in a man's world, such a fierce reaction seems surprising today, especially when language has changed quite considerably in the intervening thirty or so years. In some ways, too, her reaction is contradictory to the work she did on behalf of the *Women's* Farm and Garden

Association and her concern throughout her career for the welfare and education of women. Writing to the head gardener at The Manor House, Sutton Courtenay in the early 1960s, she refers to the employment of 'Griffiths' daughter, who wishes to train as a gardener'. It was agreed that she should be taken on as an apprentice for a year at the rate of pay suggested by the WFGA and that she 'should receive instruction in the work and not [be] allowed to spend all her time on weeding etc.'[12] There was no reason why a young woman should just be given menial tasks and not proper training. And no reason why she should not receive a fair wage.

Before taking on the WFGA work, Colvin had also been involved with the Auxiliary Fire Service (AFS) which was formed from volunteers, many of them women, to assist the regular fire brigades, and she also trained as an Air Raid Protection (ARP) warden. A few of her photographs show that she was at an AFS and ARP camp in August 1939. They also show AFS exercises being undertaken in London, a group of volunteers trying out their anti-gas clothing, and snow scenes captured during four days' leave in the first, snowy winter of the war. Later Colvin spent time on duty fire-watching and occupied herself by working on her book, *Land and Landscape*, which she developed from lectures she had given at the Architectural Association. At some point she also worked with the Land Army.[13]

Colvin's busy wartime life was hit by personal sorrow early on, in August 1940, when her father died. Shortly after she and her mother spent some time at her brother Hugh's house at Ugley in Essex. Photographs of a family group with a dog, her two nieces playing and of sunny days in the garden belie the sadness. Colvin shared her mother's fondness for border collies and owned several over the years. At one point, when she was with the Land Army, she told the story of how the farmer she

OPPOSITE ABOVE One of Colvin's photographs of an AFS and ARP exercise in the early days of the war.
OPPOSITE BELOW Some of Colvin's fellow Air Raid Wardens try on their anti-gas clothing.

was billeted with told her one day that her dogs would have to go. Surprised, she asked whether they had been worrying his sheep. The farmer said not, but that he had been puzzled by the fact that the sheep were losing condition so badly. Eventually he found that her dogs kept rounding the flock up in a corner of the field and would not let them move all day.[14] Thereafter the dogs spent more time at her brother's house. The loss of her father was followed less than four years later by her mother's death in May 1944.

In the summers of 1943 and 1944 Colvin once again put into practice her belief in the importance of education for young women by travelling to Warwickshire where she taught surveying and plan drawing to the degree and diploma students at Studley Horticultural and Agricultural College for Women. Her ability to fit in there was appreciated by those with whom she worked. Mary Kaye, one of the junior members of staff then, remembers how at weekends they were given rations for their evening meal which they used to have in their study bedrooms. They were given 'bread, butter, cheese, fruit and an egg' and used to gather together to make scrambled eggs and anything else they could find on their small coal-fired stoves. Colvin, who would have been a useful person to have around at that time of rationing as she was a good cook and interested in using wild ingredients, joined in with the weekend cooking and her company was always welcome.[15]

Colvin also played an important educational role on behalf of the institute, even in its early days. As she wrote in the journal's 'Quarterly Notes' in the spring of 1934, the institute had established a standard of qualification for its members and one of its chief aims was 'to maintain such a standard at the highest possible level and to arrange that education up to that standard [was] available for all those entering the profession'. As well as contributing numerous articles to the journal in its various forms,[16] Colvin gave lectures to its own members and to other organisations such as the Architectural Association School of Architecture and the Regent Street Polytechnic School of Architecture where she lectured on landscape architecture to qualified architects and engineers who were working for the Town Planning Institute's exam. In 1945 an evening course, organised by the School of Planning and Regional Reconstruction, was continuing under her leadership at the London Polytechnic. Although, according to those who heard her, she was not especially charismatic as a lecturer, she was a commonsense and forceful speaker and, through her lectures and her writing, she had a direct influence on many post-war architects and town planners who adopted much of her philosophy and tried to place buildings in the landscape along the lines she was recommending.

Also in 1945 Colvin contributed to a small book published by the Architectural Press – *Bombed Churches as War Memorials*. This was produced in response to a proposal first advocated in the *Architectural Review* that 'a few of our bomb-damaged churches should be preserved in their ruined condition, as permanent memorials of this war'.[17] The architect Hugh Casson opened the book with an article expanding on the proposal and this was followed by a planting plan from Colvin for Christ Church, Newgate Street. Introduced as 'an expert landscape architect', she offered a considered, enchanting design that aimed to give 'as long a season as possible of flower colour and foliage beauty', with one area devoted to the 'veterans of 1940', the self-sown flowers of the Blitz.[18] A small book, but still further evidence of the expertise that a landscape architect could offer.

At the start of the war, with virtually no landscape work in progress, Geoffrey Jellicoe took the institute under his wing and ran it from his office. There were to be several moves. His first office in John Street was destroyed by a land mine in December 1940, then he was briefly in Kingsway and finally at 12 Gower Street, by chance exactly opposite Richard Sudell's office where the organisation had started its life. In Gower Street, Jellicoe recalled, there was a 'period of doodlebugs when the secretary, Mrs Gwendolen Browne, might have been observed performing her duties in a steel helmet'.[19] Embattled though it was, and with the council frozen for the duration, the institute set itself three clear wartime objectives. The first was to create an appreciation of landscape in the powers-that-be – to move the institute away from its image as a 'domestic garden society';[20] the second was to draw into the institute any lay or professional people known to be sympathetic; and the third was, in Geoffrey Jellicoe's words, 'to initiate an educational system that would transfer a stage army into a real one'.[21]

In the years just after the war, when it was a virtual impossibility to get any course in landscape architecture established, the institute worked hard to produce practitioners known to be qualified. It aimed, too, to establish its own examinations but with the disruption of the war, although a provisional syllabus of education was produced in September 1941, the first institute examination was not held until June 1946. The syllabus included obvious subjects such as history, design, plants and soils, but also – and this was new – ecology. That, according to Peter Youngman, was 'largely due to the influence of Brenda Colvin, Sylvia Crowe and Brian Hackett'.[22] For many years Colvin contributed questions to the examinations on geology, ecology and advanced theory and practice of landscape design, and marked the resulting papers, and she also supplied booklists for students.[23]

Eventually, in 1948, the institute's persistence in promoting an educational system was rewarded by two lectureships in landscape being sponsored by industry: Peter Youngman at London University and Brian Hackett at Durham. On her election as president in 1951, however, Colvin was still frustrated that 'Education in landscape architecture is still incomplete and hard to come by in this country' and it was as late as 1967 before

two university professorships in landscape architecture were created: Brian Hackett at Durham and Arnold Weddle at Sheffield.

In addition to her many other activities during the war, Colvin was pursuing Clough Williams-Ellis's 'work for splendour' through her close involvement with the production of the institute's papers for the various wartime committees preparing major reports for the government. She brought to this work her personal, spiritual vision of landscape architecture as an all-embracing discipline, far greater than garden design and linked to preservation and development. She expressed it clearly in an article entitled 'Landscape as an Expression of Social Evolution', submitted to the institute's second *Wartime Journal* in 1942:

We have seen a period when building and other new developments have been carried out almost without regard to their landscape appearance: when it was thought that any concession to that aspect was of sentimental value only, a luxury which might or might not be applied when the project was complete. We have seen the results of such thinking, and we know that they reflect unhealthy social conditions. We are learning that it is necessary to plan for the spiritual needs of humanity, as well as the more obvious material requirements, from the outset; and it has been noticed that landscape values often serve to emphasise these less obvious needs, as in the case of wide streets and open spaces in towns: but the full implication of this fact has yet to be studied and applied.

If the world is a stage, then landscape is the scenery....It is the setting for national and individual lives; and in so far as it is the result of human activities, it becomes a measure of underlying social structures.[24]

Speaking at a conference on the Landscape Architecture in the County of London Plan in November 1943, again she emphasised the key role that she believed landscape architecture had to play. It was necessary to regard the landscape problem as one of the essential sides of planning:

It was not enough to apply ornament when the architect and the engineer had completed their work. Landscape architecture had to do with the siting and the treatment of contours; the whole effect had to be thought of from the very start.[25]

Fortunately Colvin was able to bring her influence to bear on the planning for post-war reconstruction which began immediately after the great blitzes of 1940 when Churchill instructed Lord Reith as Minister of Public Works and Buildings to 'undertake the organisation of Physical Reconstruction after the war'.[26] A series of reports were prepared: Barlow (1940), Scott (1942), Uthwatt (1942), Beveridge (1942-3) and New Towns (1946) and it was Reith who piloted the New Towns legislation and established the guidelines for their planning. He was influenced in his ideas by town planners and architects within Whitehall but also by Colvin and Geoffrey Jellicoe. It was their contact with him that had led to his becoming the institute's first honorary fellow and a member of Council.[27]

Colvin and James Adams (planning officer for Kent and son of institute president, Thomas Adams) were the 'prime movers' preparing evidence for the institute's report to the New Towns Committee in 1946 and 'absolutely crucial in terms of influence on a budding profession'.[28] Geoffrey Jellicoe also had some input, as did Sylvia Crowe, although her driving duties with the Auxiliary Territorial Service meant she did not have much free time and could only occasionally make the journey to London to attend meetings. Covering the large issues of planning (site selection, relationship to the surrounding countryside, green belts and so on) as well as design details (home frontages and private gardens, children's playgrounds), this influential policy statement set out ideas which were then new. With regard to siting, the new town should be

so sited in relation to the existing topographical features that it lies naturally within the landscape, the trees and contours forming a background to the buildings, and the flow of the land…giving reason

to the direction of streets, terraces and parkways. The framework of hills and trees will thus form the skyline, except where the architect plans a fine building or group of buildings as a focal feature in the landscape. The topographical formation then becomes the very skeleton of the plan with ribs of high ground and woods…

The report recommended planting on the higher contours to emphasise

the background value of even slight elevations…and only by the allocation of land for this purpose from the first can the effective placing of the plant masses be accomplished. These green wedges, with their planting ecologically related to the countryside will serve to anchor the town firmly to its background.[29]

Colvin, Adams and Crowe also submitted evidence to the National Parks Committee, although they complained that they were given insufficient time to prepare it.[30] They agreed with the report that had been prepared for the ministry that if the parks were too few or too small the concentration of visitors would lead to damage, but they drew attention to five additional points that are still relevant to the management of the countryside today. First, that the establishment of National Parks should not delay the provision of Regional Parks nor the safeguarding of other areas of important landscape or recreational value. Second, in the case of the National Parks, care should be taken to avoid excessive holiday use that, by destroying vegetation and disturbing biological balance, would wholly alter the character. Development in surrounding areas also needed to be approached cautiously. Third, they recommended improvement to the existing network of footpaths to make it a nationwide system. Fourth, given the need for special knowledge and experience in regard to siting, no less than any subsequent planting that might be needed, they urged that qualified landscape architects should be included among the recommended planners. Lastly, they emphasised that the interests of nature conservation and of landscape were complementary: 'Each type of habitat represents a unique type of landscape and since variety is threatened in these days of change, by the tendency to over-all "sameness," this Institute warmly supports all efforts to preserve wild life as far as possible.'

Initially, as this report pointed out with reference to the National Parks, the value of landscape architects working closely with planners, architects and engineers was not recognised, in spite of the Reith Committee's recommendation, and even by the 1950s their lack of involvement was still a cause for concern. Echoing Colvin's earlier plea that they should not be asked just to 'apply ornament', the landscape architect Frank Clark, who worked on the new town at Stevenage, complained,

It really is time that we should be recognised not as exterior decorators who will, amiably or not, supply the necessary horticultural information when called upon to do so, but as professionals whose training fits them…to give opinions both on the determination of land use and on the art of three dimensional or visual planning.[31]

Colvin also chaired an institute committee and prepared their report on *Roads in the Landscape* which appeared in the journal in October 1946. In general terms, this recognised the importance of roads 'giving pleasure in addition to their other purposes' both for user satisfaction and as a way of enhancing safety. It called on designers to consider the landscape of the road 'as an integral part of the countryside from two points of view – that of the traveller who sees the road in perspective, and usually at speed … and that of the observer viewing the road from surrounding land or from the air.' It advocated the 'fitted highway, gently winding in response to existing forms' as 'best suited to modern needs in this country'.

Colvin's influence was not confined to planning issues, however, and she served on a wide range of other committees both during and after the war, as is revealed by papers in her membership file at the institute. In June 1941 she was acting as landscape consultant to Geoffrey Jellicoe for Ministry of Supply housing schemes and was shortly to work as landscape consultant in Regional Planning, especially in regard to forestry and roadside planting. A letter to Jellicoe in January 1942 mentions that a 'note on plant material came before the "Planning and Amenities Group" of the RIBA [Royal Institute of British Architects] Reconstruction Committee at a December meeting and was quite well received'. In March that year Jellicoe wrote to her referring to her 'Garden Space' report for the Regional Planning people which he considered 'first class', and in 1943 she was on a Hill Sheep Farming committee. In autumn 1946 and spring 1947 she was included on a Ministry of Housing subcommittee on the appearance of local authority housing, and her own photographs of different styles of housing and gardens reveal the extent to which she travelled.[32]

Her opinion on the treatment of roads was sought at an institute meeting with the Roads Beautifying Association in January 1947 and a meeting with the Town Planning Institute committee on roadside rests in February, and in March her name was given to the Ministry of Transport to give practical day-to-day advice on the planting and amenity treatment of trunk roads. In April that year she attended an institute 'Brains Trust' with the Royal Horticultural Society on post-war gardens. Between 1949 and 1954 she was the institute's representative on the Council for the Preservation of Rural England Joint Committee on the Landscape Treatment of Roads and in 1955 she served on the government's newly established advisory committee on the landscape treatment of trunk roads.[33] Patently her opinion on many areas of landscape design and planning was highly sought after and valued.

And, of course, there was the institute's forestry committee on which she served and whose report was published in 1944. Sylvia Crowe, who became a much praised consultant to the Forestry Commission, must have been greatly influenced by this report whose headings, in her own words, 'show a wide grasp of the many landscape factors involved in forestry', including 'Recreation and amenity', 'Employment', 'Biological balance' and 'Landscape', areas of concern not previously given adequate consideration.[34] In 1946

ABOVE Sylvia Crowe beside the caravan with Dan the dog on a trip the two women took to north Norfolk in 1946. The car is a *c.*1937 Hillman Minx.

Colvin and Crowe travelled together on a caravan tour of north Norfolk and Colvin's photographs of this trip, including several of conifer plantations and mixed woodland (see pp.109 and 111), reveal that a good part of their trip would have been spent in discussion of different types of landscape and forestry. Eventually, though, it was Crowe who was appointed advisor to the Forestry Commission in 1964, a post she held for ten years. But behind this appointment lies an intriguing tale. It was widely rumoured by those who worked for Colvin and Crowe that, on the strength of her work for the institute's forestry committee, the commission had intended to appoint Colvin rather than Crowe.[35] If true, the confusion probably arose because at the time the two women shared their office premises. Nevertheless, although Colvin's work on behalf of the commission would certainly have been at least as good as Crowe's, it is likely that with her more brusque manner she might have handled the diplomatic side of dealing with forestry staff less well.

Different in temperament they may have been, but both women were actively involved with the institute and both believed strongly in the future of their profession, a profession to be promoted for its service to the community rather than the advancement of its members. In her presidential address Colvin considered that the institute's 'members must necessarily be ready to give it service and help for the sake of what it may become rather than for anything which it might be able to do for them now' – a perfect description of her own selfless approach. She concluded her speech with her predecessor Thomas Sharp's words, 'Our work is of far greater importance than our personal share in it'. In her view:

The more genuinely convinced we are of this and the more willing we are to forego personal advantage for the sake of what we believe to be in the true interests of landscape…the greater will be our hope of advancing that work….Let this age aim at leaving a landscape for the future to enjoy.[36]

At one point both she and Crowe were 'ardent advocates' of a sort of Hippocratic oath to be sworn by new members on admission, with concern for the landscape taking priority over the interests of the client as one of its main components. As Peter Youngman put it, 'The Institute's more limited and prosaic code of conduct, though accepted as more realistic, was always something of a disappointment' to them.[37]

Colvin and Crowe saw eye to eye too on the question of maintaining the institute's independence. Initially the institute had little support from other professional bodies, but in 1946 the Royal Institute of British Architects (RIBA) thought landscape architects should be absorbed within their orbit 'as an inferior branch of architecture'.[38] Then the Town Planning Institute (TPI) followed suit.[39] This possibility had already been raised in 1934 at the TPI annual conference and summer school at St Peter's Hall, Oxford, which several institute fellows including Colvin had attended (see photograph p.112).[40] For a while there was a real possibility that landscape architects might have to find a home in one or other of the rival institutes, or perhaps both, and that the Institute of Landscape Architects (ILA) would be disbanded. It was Colvin and Crowe's forceful opposition that led to the ILA's rejection of this proposal. It was a difficult decision: most of the institute's members were architects and/or town planners, so they were not always easily persuaded that landscape architecture was a third, different profession. Indeed it was Gilbert Jenkins, himself a member of the ILA, who had proposed the amalgamation with the TPI in 1934. Nevertheless, in Geoffrey Jellicoe's words, it was 'thanks largely to those two Furies ("the friendly ones" to the Greeks)…the warm embrace of the RIBA had been resisted.'[41]

In 1973, at the age of 75, Colvin chaired a committee which led to the inclusion of landscape managers as professional members of the institute – from her own experience she had learnt that design and aftercare were so closely related that they should be represented together in the same professional body. In 1978 following this decision to broaden the membership to include those whose professional work involved landscape management and landscape sciences, the institute's name changed to the Landscape Institute. In 1997 the institute was granted a royal charter.

But Colvin's influence was not just felt in the United Kingdom. She was also closely involved with the establishment of the International Federation of Landscape Architects (IFLA). According to Jellicoe, at the ILA's annual general meeting in 1946, 'Margery [sic] Allen…leapt to her feet and cried "Let's have an international conference". And we did.'[42] In fact, several years earlier, before 1939, Colvin had already discussed the possibility of an international federation with a small group of landscape architects, notably from France and Belgium.[43] The first international conference and exhibition was called by the institute and was held at County Hall in London in August 1948, and many eminent people attended, including Lord Silkin, the minister concerned with planning. 'We then went on to Cambridge to continue our international meeting,' Sylvia Crowe remembered. 'The delegates from different countries all said "we have got to have an International Federation of Landscape Architects", and so it was founded at Jesus College.'[44] Each of the nations present appointed a delegate who became the IFLA foundation member. Britain emerged with three: Jellicoe who chaired the meeting was elected president, Crowe attended as chairman of the conference committee and was elected honorary secretary, and Colvin was the chosen ILA delegate.

For many years she was, in Crowe's words, 'unfailing in her attendance as the ILA delegate, and her sound advice was internationally valued'.[45] Attendance also meant that Colvin travelled to and experienced the developing styles of landscape architecture in different countries. She reported on IFLA visits to Sweden in *Country Life* in 1952 and to Israel and Warsaw in the

This photograph of IFLA delegates in Stockholm in 1952 accompanied Colvin's report on the visit in *Country Life.*

institute's journal in 1962 and 1963.[46] On the last trip she and Susan and Geoffrey Jellicoe 'decided to go unofficially to Moscow before the IFLA meeting…to see what was happening in the way of landscape design in the USSR and also to find out whether the Russian landscape architects were interested in IFLA. This they undoubtedly were.' The three met a number of architects and associated professionals and found that an 'enthusiastic recognition of the value of landscape has been given freer rein and official support in recent years'. In general she appreciated the opportunity provided by these visits to exchange ideas with landscape architects who worked in other parts of the world and to learn from what she saw. The contrast between Scandinavian and Spanish gardens revealed the 'value of strong differences in national garden design', each beautifully

adapted to national character and local conditions; in Israel she was alarmed at the dangers inherent in the speed of development where 'Vast areas of ploughed land unprotected by shelter planting, grazing strips, or rotational cropping brought to mind the history of erosion and dust bowls in other lands'.

In 1976, when the institute was debating its membership of and subscriptions to the IFLA, Colvin, Crowe and Jellicoe wrote a joint letter to the institute's journal in support of the international federation, not for profit or prestige or even technical knowledge, but because they considered it 'essential for us to break out of insularity into a very much wider world than that of our daily experience'. They saw the federation as 'a power for peace' and reminded people that the declared aims of the founders were 'first, to promote understanding and knowledge throughout a war-shattered world through the common language of landscape; second, to raise universally the prestige of landscape in the public mind; and third, to enable member countries to keep abreast of world ideas'.[47]

Since their wartime work together on behalf of the institute, Colvin, Crowe and Jellicoe had been close colleagues and friends. In 1945 Colvin generously offered 'house-room' to Crowe in her office at 28 Baker Street in London. Crowe was just setting up in practice at that time, with work 'pushed' to her by Geoffrey Jellicoe.[48] There were only two rooms in this office, occupied by them and their assistant Carol Møller, who joined them in 1947, and their Polish secretary Wanda Zaluska.[49] In 1952 the two moved to 182 Gloucester Place, just a few streets away (see p.207 for a photograph of the office garden there, designed by Colvin). Although they shared the office, their assistant and secretary, they remained independent practitioners. Anthony du Gard Pasley, who worked for them both, described them as

> sharing an office in an odd way. The practices were totally different but they shared me and they shared the secretary and they shared the premises but the practices had nothing to do with one another. So when one was short of work and the other was busy, I'd be working for that one.[50]

As Geoffrey Jellicoe noted, before schools of landscape design were created, Colvin's office was one of the very few that were in a position to take in students. Later, when students were leaving school and seeking practical experience, her office was foremost in 'taking on the idealistic but immature assistant'.[51] Among those who worked there were Anthony du Gard Pasley, John Brookes, Barbara Oakeley, Carol Møller, Sally Race, Ivor Cunningham, Michael Laurie, Janet Jack, Diana Ford and Wendy Powell. Barry Newland, who worked there in 1956/7, recalls his time there:

> It was a nice office to work in and I thought Brenda Colvin a lovely person, who, having said that, stood no nonsense. Some may have considered her intimidating but, as a youngster of 18, I didn't. A tall, somewhat gaunt figure, she wouldn't tolerate sloppy speech and I was at the receiving end of her wrath (justifiably) on more than one occasion. She

was, I discovered, a good teacher and her wealth of experience…was of tremendous benefit to me….I recall the office library which sowed the seeds of my love of books! As the office junior, my tasks were varied, ranging from tea making, errand running, taking BC's dog for walks in Regent's Park when she was up and washing off the Gloucestershire mud from her Vauxhall car, watering the office garden as well as draughting and survey duties. It was a very civilised working environment.[52]

In 1965 following an illness, helped greatly by Tim Rowell, one of her assistants, Colvin moved her office to the Cotswolds – to Little Peacocks, the house she had bought in 1954 in the village of Filkins near Lechlade. There, with semi-retirement in mind, she had a temporary office built to house her two or three staff and finish off the jobs she was doing. But at this point, as she was entering her 70s, the practice was expanding enormously in scope and scale and she decided to set up a partnership. This was a completely new departure for her – she had never had a partner before and had been free to run her business exactly as she chose. And, of course, in her own rather pessimistic way, she had always considered her business was running on a shoestring and likely to fail at any moment. A partnership would mean real commitment. She decided that she could not just accept anyone, that she needed someone with qualifications so she approached her old friends Susan and Geoffrey Jellicoe and they suggested Hal Moggridge, a young landscape architect they knew. They invited him to a supper party they were holding. Moggridge was somewhat surprised to be invited to this evening for founding members of the institute and, unsuspecting, found himself sat next to Colvin throughout the whole evening. Shortly after she telephoned him to ask him to visit her at Filkins as she was considering asking him to become her partner. This 'final inspection' did not start

RIGHT The 'temporary' office in the garden of Little Peacocks in Filkins, built in 1965 and still in use today.

well – following a car accident on the way Moggridge arrived late and in a damaged car. Nevertheless the two agreed on a three-month trial period and, after about a month, it was clear to them both that the plan was going to work.[53] Finally, at Easter 1969, the partnership of Colvin & Moggridge was founded.

The practice continues to this day and Colvin's principles are still followed there. Writing in 1986, echoing Colvin's own attitude, partners Hal Moggridge and Chris Carter expressed the view that:

> a landscape architect stands between the short-term interests of the client and the long-term duties towards society and, indeed, towards the whole planet….For this reason it is open to anyone working at Colvin & Moggridge to refuse to work on a particular job which is repugnant to their personal values. Occasionally the staff may as a group resolve that an offered job is not acceptable to the practice on ethical grounds.[54]

Throughout the time that she was campaigning for recognition of the importance of design for the wider landscape, Colvin was also developing her own ideas through garden design. She believed that 'each garden went to the heart of the matter of landscape architecture, posing in miniature the problems to be solved in the largest project',[55] and that work on any landscape should be guided by the principles of garden design. As her practice expanded after the war she began to take on larger scale commissions in the public sphere of new towns, power stations, reservoirs, land reclamation schemes and universities.

LANDSCAPE MASTER PLAN

Scale 1:5000

1974

N

Farnborough

KEY

A landscape worth living in

'A vast combined operation is needed to prevent the destruction
of any small country's dwindling charm and to ensure for its people,
in the future, a landscape worth living in.'[1]

A S A NOVICE TEACHER running a part-time course for planning students in the 1950s, landscape architect Peter Youngman occasionally invited Brenda Colvin to come and do criticisms of his students' work, sometimes on site. One particular 'crit' made a profound impression on him. 'I can still picture her clearly', he recalled much later, 'at a scheme based on an inadequate survey of a London square. She was horrified that both they and I had assumed that the site was flat.' She taught them 'one fundamental lesson' – that ground form was 'the basis of all landscape design'. Of course she was right: there were 'changes of level, small but distinct; enough to produce error if overlooked, enough to lead to interesting design if appreciated'.[2] Youngman considered that this was 'One of her main lessons – you're starting off with the topography of the land. Everything relates back to that and flows from that – ecologically and geologically. Topography is your starting point.'[3] And, even more important than this lesson, he felt, were her 'professional philosophy and values expounded in [her book] *Land and Landscape*',[4] which did so much to promote the cause of fine landscape that she believed in so strongly.

The first edition of this 'timely'[5] book was published in 1947. Based on Colvin's wartime lectures and drafted while she was fire-watching in London during the war, it is a practical book that reviews the state of the British landscape and looks at the principles and materials of landscape design, the treatment of industrial landscapes, the nature of soils and the history of gardens. Running through it, however, is a more philosophical, pioneering note, reflecting the sentiment of the epigraph from G.M. Trevelyan that she chose for the title page: 'Without vision the people perish, and without a sight of the beauty of nature the spiritual power of the British people will be atrophied'. A dominant theme of the book is mankind's ecological relationship to

LEFT In 1963 Colvin was appointed overall landscape consultant for Aldershot Military Town. It was a huge commission. The Landscape Master Plan of 1974 shows the proposed structural landscape, some two kilometres wide and four kilometres north to south. In dark green, the plan shows 'dense deciduous woodland with shrub layer: established and maintained by forestry methods'; some areas are darker 'with conifers'; in mid green, 'open woodland, standard trees in rough grass, avenues' with mid green dots showing 'small scale ornamental landscape around buildings'; pale green represents 'grass including sportsfields'; and black indicates water – the Basingstoke canal and the new lake.

the landscape and the means by which our impact on it can be changed from a hostile force to one of conscious, cooperative design. Colvin starts Chapter One, 'Nature and Man', forcefully with words that are astonishingly relevant today:

> The control which modern man is able to exert over his environment is so great that we easily overlook the power of the environment over man. Perhaps we just assume that any environment, modified and conditioned by human activity, must inevitably be suited to human life. We know that this is not so, really, and that man can ruin his surroundings and make them unsuitable for future generations, just as he can make war and leave unsolved political problems leading to more war; but we continue to act as if we did not know it, and we have not properly mastered the methods which the elementary knowledge should lead us to apply.
>
> We should think of this planet, Earth, as a single organism, in which humanity is involved. The sense of superior individuality which we enjoy is illusory.[6]

At the time, Sylvia Crowe predicted that the book, in which 'all the varied subjects which go to make up landscape architecture are, for the first time, woven together', was 'likely to become a classic in its subject… In the sentence, "Landscape is the expression of the underlying relationship of land and life", Brenda Colvin sums up a philosophy which will find an echo in all who have a feeling for the wider implications of landscape architecture.'[7] The book has since been widely recognised as a 'pioneering' study and one that had 'an enormous influence in spreading a wider view of landscape'.[8] In 1980 Geoffrey Jellicoe was still able to write that the book, by then in its second edition, was 'known and read throughout the English speaking world, respected in Europe and translated into Japanese', and that it had 'become a standard work on good landscape practice'.[9]

Unfortunately, even in the 'brave new world' of post-war reconstruction, the crucial need for a meaningful contribution from landscape architects was not always recognised. On her election as president of the Institute of Landscape Architects in 1951, Colvin lamented this omission:

> It is perhaps…surprising, but certainly no less regrettable, that unsightly erections for the development of atomic energy or other forms of power should be built often with utter disregard for the surrounding landscape. It seems as if, in his grasp for power, man has to create ugliness and to despoil his own heritage of natural beauty: and the fact that this is done with scarcely a tremor of conscience, and with so little attempt to give the areas thus taken over some positive new landscape of character is, I think, rather a sinister reflection on this age…It is not that the buildings concerned in these developments are incapable of being absorbed into the landscape: in some cases…they are fine in themselves and present grand possibilities.[10]

But it was not just in her writing and lectures or in her role as adviser on many committees that Colvin was to have a significant influence on landscape philosophy. The post-war years brought her many important commissions and were undoubtedly her most creative period, a time in which she planned and created a series of influential large-scale landscapes.

Some of her early commissions, however, were particularly frustrating. When she was appointed landscape consultant at East Kilbride, Scotland's first new town, in 1950, the first master plan for the town had already been prepared and published by town planners in the Scottish Office and, in what was a rather 'traditional' design office, even many of the younger architects felt they played 'subservient roles' to the town planners and engineers.[11]

In October 1945, after the election of the new Labour Government led by Prime Minister Clement Attlee, a New Towns Committee had been set up under the chairmanship of Lord Reith. A total of fourteen New Towns were designated between 1946 and 1950, eight of them for Greater London.[12] The other six were Corby (Northamptonshire), Newton Aycliffe and Peterlee in the north-east, East Kilbride and Glenrothes in Scotland, and Cwmbran in Wales. These towns were developed partly to relieve the post-war housing shortage but they also had explicit social ambitions. The Reith Committee that reported to Lewis Silkin, the new Minister of Town and Country Planning, in 1946 placed particular emphasis on the need for a strong sense of community, highlighting the potential benefits of the neighbourhood unit.

In the post-war years the landscape architects who were involved in the development of the New Towns strove to ensure they were consulted over the earliest and most fundamental stages of design. But they were not always successful. The evidence prepared by Brenda Colvin and James Adams with Sylvia Crowe on behalf of the Institute of Landscape Architects (ILA) for Reith's committee in 1946 was wide-ranging, covering the larger issues of planning as well as the details of design, and emphasised the value of landscape architects working closely with planners, architects and engineers from the earliest stages.

Even though they were hardly involved with the initial master planning, the work of Colvin at East Kilbride,[13] Sylvia Crowe at Harlow (with Frederick Gibberd) and Frank Clark at Stevenage demonstrated the value of their contribution and they described their work in a symposium that was reported in the ILA's journal in July 1950.[14]

Speaking first at the symposium, Clark emphasised the importance of 'the technique of collaboration'. He had found the necessary teamwork at Stevenage 'extremely stimulating' and especially appreciated the input of the social scientist. He emphasised the importance of the landscape survey which should be 'one of the first… which should be undertaken and not the last, as is now the practice'. He complained that 'since the landscape architect is, if appointed at all, the last member of the planning team to be briefed', it was often too late to avoid various 'offences' against the landscape. He concluded with a plea that they should not be called in just as 'exterior decorators…but as professionals', trained to give their views on both land use and on the 'art of three dimensional or visual planning'.

On the question of green space, Clark was controversial, making the point that it was necessary to be 'temperate' in the use of green space 'for fear that we may inadvertently substitute suburbanism for urbanism and urbanity'. Sylvia Crowe reiterated this point with her criticism of 'small scattered spaces' which were 'dead landscape'. 'No one uses the odd grass corner', she said, 'except to throw bus tickets on it, no one wants to sit exposed midway between a bus route and a terrace of houses'. It was better, in her view, to have large wedges of open space occupying the valleys and linking with the countryside.

Colvin's site at East Kilbride, to the southeast of Glasgow, was much bleaker and more windswept than Stevenage or Harlow, and 'local character and climate both pointed to a rather higher population density than in places further south'. She had to work on a massive scale there, creating 'a continuous forest belt round the south and west of the built-up area'. As we have seen, the local conditions also meant that, to provide the new citizens and the town's new plantings with shelter, she found that, contrary to her previous preference for hardwoods, she needed to plant a high proportion of conifers. These were offset with a nature reserve of mixed forest at Calder Glen and the planting of roadside cuttings and embankments with native deciduous trees. Some green corridors were left for agriculture or for wild scrub in order to preserve wildlife, and twenty or so small brooks or burns that existed on the boggy site were all preserved. And Colvin's idea of a 'Schools Planting Day' was continued for many years with schoolchildren planting trees in neighbourhood nurseries (see p.100), thereby becoming involved with the landscape around them. Almost the first impression given by the town until recently was 'the use of major areas of now mature tree planting, creating a constant punctuation and framing of the built environment'.[15] Unfortunately East Kilbride is now being 'regenerated' with every area subject to change and development and most of the green space being lost to urban development and housing.[16]

Colvin cared greatly about the effect of her work on people and was very conscious of the needs of East Kilbride's inhabitants. As was often the case in the earlier post-war years, she was frustrated by the lack of consideration given to her proposals and, eventually, she was to resign from her post at East Kilbride because she objected to what the general manager, a retired Royal Engineer, was planning in areas that she felt were her responsibility and 'not for him as a layman to butt in'.[17] She had been invited to join the scheme too late to be able to influence the main through road for the town but was clear in her own mind that the roads here were not just for motorists – they were part of the landscape for those who lived or worked nearby. Accordingly, she managed to take the footpaths off the side of the main road and site them on existing levels above cuttings or below embankments, thereby keeping, as she put it, 'some sylvan quality separated from the roads'.[18] As a result the road fitted better into its context and the footpaths were more convenient, safer and quieter for pedestrians. A bonus was that the costs of road construction were considerably reduced.[19] These attractive, peaceful pedestrian walkways – so designed that none of them has a gradient greater than seven per cent – are constantly used, even today, and it is frequently quicker to walk somewhere in East Kilbride than it is to drive. And, because of the gently undulating topography, the pathways offer views both in and out, with plenty of opportunities to view one part of the town from another and to look out at the surrounding countryside.

In *Land and Landscape*, Colvin had made the point that unlike villages and towns that had grown slowly, New Towns, built at relative speed and without all the accumulated experience of living on the site,

> often lack that feeling of homeliness, intimacy and comfort....In order to win that mature charm, they must have a clear relationship with their natural surroundings, and that calls for special powers of imagination on the part of the town-planners... and great sensitiveness to the indications of the land forms and the local climate.[20]

At East Kilbride, she showed that sensitivity and, until recently, the town has been a vibrant and energetic one and on the whole its residents have revealed 'considerable loyalty and pride of place'.[21]

Colvin, Crowe and Clark were the pioneers in the field of New Towns and they influenced those such as Peter Youngman, who worked on New Town master plans after them. Youngman felt that 'their example made our roles expected and accepted. In the second wave of new towns there was no cause to echo Clark's complaint [that they should not be regarded as exterior decorators].'[22]

In contrast to the situation Colvin encountered at East Kilbride, the rebuilding of Aldershot Military Town in the 1960s appeared to offer a clear opportunity for landscape advice to be 'embodied in the master plan' and promised to be a project where it would be 'incumbent on the architects developing each area of the town to adhere to the landscape principles laid down'.[23] This was the intention expressed by David Woods, the Building Design Partnership associate in charge of the rebuild, in a letter he sent to Colvin in November 1962 inviting her to become the landscape consultant to the building of what was in effect a New Town.

The scope of this commission was huge, consisting of the substantial reconstruction of the 1,500-acre (600-hectare) tarmac-dominated military town. Built in the nineteenth century on a grid pattern, Colvin noted how it had been imposed on the landscape 'with little regard to hill and vale or of the echoing line of ridge and canal'.[24] By contrast, the local geography provided a natural basis for her plan (see p.128). Aldershot Military Town was to be changed into a green town integrated into the landform of the area, 'a community in a woodland setting'.[25] The Army's original directive was that opportunities should be provided 'for the soldier to enjoy a full life in his off-duty hours in his home and in attractive surroundings comparable with those of well paid workers in industry'.[26] In Colvin's words, her brief was to create a working environment that the recruits – as opposed to conscripts – would find encouraging.

She was appointed overall landscape consultant in early 1963 and also undertook several commissions for individual areas, five by 1966, and eleven more as well as several 'landscape development areas' (parts of the town's landscape not included in specific rebuilds) by the end of 1967. It was Colvin's idea that there should be these separately funded development areas and a landscape

committee to coordinate all landscape matters. This was vital to the success of the landscape project because so much of the town was outside functional sites and therefore outside normal funding sources. In a note of his first impressions in 1970, Hal Moggridge called it 'a very enlightened idea' because it meant that the military town could be considered as a whole, 'without undesigned fragments of land or ill considered edges of schemes'.[27] Colvin retained full control of the Aldershot commission until June 1975 when she became ill with shingles but the job remained on Colvin & Moggridge's books until about 1990.

OPPOSITE The 'tarmac town' that Colvin found at Aldershot is seen in this contact print of a photograph that she took in June 1965.

ABOVE A new path was created alongside the Basingstoke Canal in Aldershot Military Town; beyond the distant fence line is dense deciduous woodland; barracks are situated on the far side of the canal.

RIGHT An overall view of Aldershot Military Town in 1974 from high ground towards the south. New barracks and new tree planting are visible centre and right.

In the first year she made many visits to Aldershot, dealing with numerous points of detail, while working up her strategic ideas. She realised that on the thin, infertile Bagshot gravels two fundamentally different types of landscape were necessary. Wild vegetation was re-created by fencing off areas and regenerating the thick scrub woodland native to the area, while the Army's need for military precision was met by trim grass with well-spaced trees. This neatness acted effectively as a contrast to the areas of 'wilderness' inside the fence line (see p.106). A bonus was that the natural regeneration of woodland proved so effective that the original budget was halved, in spite of inflation, without any loss of content.

But it was not all plain sailing – in August 1968 her notes for consideration at a meeting emphasised that the problems facing landscape architects at Aldershot seemed to 'stem from the low priority that landscape takes in general estimation, from architects and others who have had little previous experience of co-operation with landscape architects, and who therefore tend to regard the need for such co-operation as an extra complication to be side-tracked or overruled when convenient'.[28] Now in her seventies, Colvin's confidence in her ability and her passionate belief in the importance of the landscape meant that she had even less fear than ever about being outspoken when things did not go as she would have liked. It was rumoured that, if ever there was bad news to pass on to her, the architects would draw lots as to who should make the telephone call and receive the flak.[29] Maintenance – or the lack of it – was also a particularly sore point and the subject of several fierce letters and memos from Colvin. In fact on one occasion, what Hal Moggridge has described as her 'tetchy capacity for effective tactlessness' led her to criticise the brigadier in command for allowing her planting to be poorly maintained – in front of his shocked subordinates.[30] After extensive discussion, it was agreed that, as maintenance problems were most critical in the early years, there should be an experimental contract procedure to cover planting and subsequent maintenance for a three-year period. It had been intended that Aldershot would be an open town with free movement but, after the start of the IRA

bombing campaign in mainland England in the 1970s, much of that open aspect was lost in the name of security, although a great many wooded areas have survived.

One major element of Colvin's work at Aldershot was the Hill and Lake project. It was to be not only a lesson in landscape design but also, intriguingly, one in political processes. This imaginative plan had been included in the initial proposals in 1964 and work started on its more detailed design in December 1967. It was not a case of 'flights of fancy' but based on economic considerations.[31] The Lake was excavated initially to provide top soil but was also intended to serve for recreation and to enhance the quality of the landscape. The Hill, making positive

BELOW An early study for the structural landscape of Aldershot Military Town, in preparation for the landscape report of May 1964.

RIGHT Open woodland beside Duke's Park housing in Aldershot Military Town in 1972; the rough textures of heathland vegetation can be seen beneath the thinned birch and oak; in the foreground the road verge is mown to maintain a crisp character.

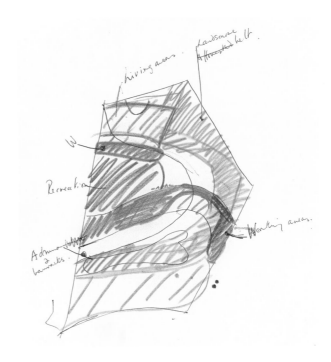

use of waste material from numerous sources throughout the military town in the course of its building, was to become an important landscape feature, appearing as 'an outlier of the existing ridge, well related to the character of the Hog's Back region'.[32] It arose from the need for a new waste tip once the old North Camp tip was closed. There were a number of areas in the Military Town where rubbish was being dumped and Colvin was very critical of this – she used 35 photographs to illustrate her report on illicit rubbish disposal. The Hill concept was to cover and seal layers of rubbish with layers of inert material (subsoil and gravel) excavated from the adjacent lake site which was located below the natural water table. Tipping at Hill and Lake was finally completed in May 1975 but not quite as Colvin had planned. That summer there had been a lot of flies and a local MP asked a question about the Hill in the House

ABOVE Colvin made use of natural regeneration of woodland at Aldershot. Here birch, rowan and sycamore (as well as oak and goat willow) regenerate on a scarified tarmac parade ground from which only the tarmac was removed.

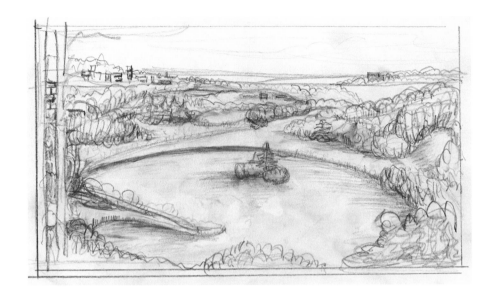

LEFT A sketch from the late 1960s of the proposed Aldershot Lake looking north from the proposed Hill. **BELOW** Layout plan and cross sections (1969) of the Hill and Lake proposed for the east centre of Aldershot Military Town. This feature, for recreation and nature conservation, solved an intractable rubbish disposal problem.

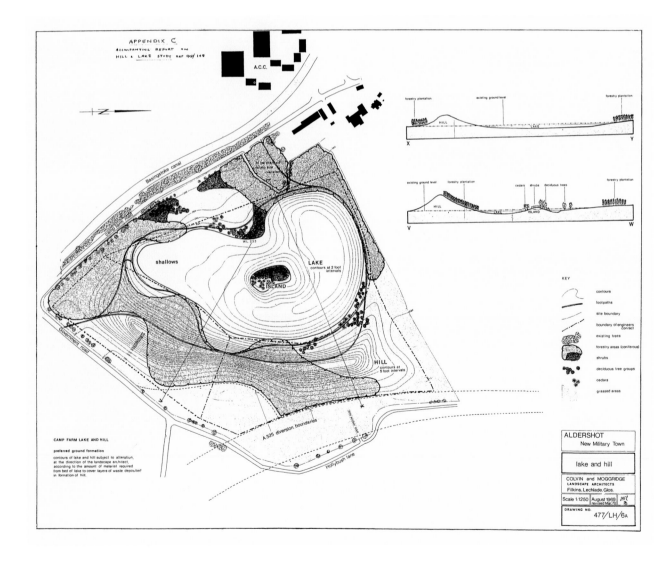

LEFT A set of contacts of the photographs Colvin took in June 1965 to show illicit rubbish disposal – in effect a series of 'before' photographs of the military town.
BELOW Aldershot Hill and Lake under construction in 1975, looking east.
BOTTOM View of the completed Aldershot Lake looking north from the Hill in 1986.

of Commons, three months before it was finished. As the Minister concerned responded with the statement that the Hill was now finished, following Parliamentary rules, work had to stop. As a result the top of the Hill is rather flat, whereas Colvin had intended it to have an irregular form. Aldershot Garrison Angling Club now enjoys the fishing rights to the Lake, an attractive place, home to much wildlife, with the native trees planted on the Hill providing a colourful backdrop.

One of the considerations governing Colvin's landscape plan for Aldershot was the need to segregate the motorist and pedestrian wherever possible, paying attention to their different needs:

> the motorist must have wider views but these must be well defined; where he is to be encouraged to stop and look at the views, car parking facilities should be provided…Pedestrians, with their much slower

rate of progress, need narrower and less well defined views which gradually unfold.[33]

In one example, the A325 dual carriageway and underpass, she kept the pedestrians away from the road on wooded footpaths, much as she had done at East Kilbride. In a typical combination of economy and design advantage, Colvin used soil excavated from the underpass to model contours linking the new road levels to their surroundings – the saving on transport of material contributed to the cost of the modelling.

Colvin's interest in the landscaping and planting of roads was longstanding. Although her hope, expressed in *Land and Landscape*, that pylons might one day join telegraph poles as 'forgotten curios of the twentieth century' has so far not materialised, her hopes for roads and their planting – 'a far more cheerful prospect' – seem closer to realisation. As a keen driver who had driven extensively both at home and abroad, she was naturally interested in and knowledgeable about what constituted a good road, and considered that people were 'becoming alive to the great possibilities of making beautiful roads'.[34]

Since the late 1930s roads had come very much to the fore in public discussion and their design was given much thought by planners as well as road engineers and landscape architects. By that time the motor car that had been seen as an eccentricity at the start of the century had become a necessity and, although there was a dramatic fall in car ownership during the war, afterwards it rose rapidly, especially following the end of petrol rationing in 1950. In 1921 there were 250,000 cars registered in the United Kingdom, by 1955 this figure had risen to almost 5,250,000.

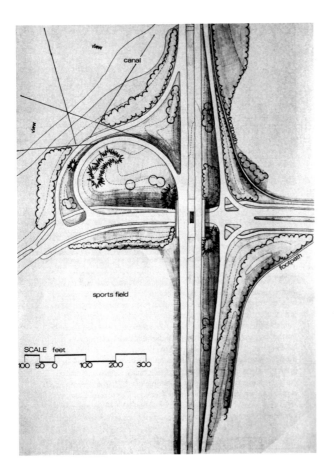

LEFT Soil excavated from the underpass on the A325 dual carriageway at Aldershot was used to shape flowing contours that linked the new road levels naturally to their context. The saving on transport of the surplus soil by using it on site made a useful contribution to the cost of the ground modelling.

Colvin's experience of the Westchester Parkway during her trip to America in 1931 had been significant in shaping her ideas on road design. There she had encountered what was termed the 'fitted highway' – roads sited and designed for their landscape value as well as for efficiency. The treatment of these roads illustrated 'the splendid results achieved by proper co-operation among the authorities concerned'. A few years later the ILA journal *Landscape and Garden* published a double-page spread entitled 'Modern Highways: American Examples'. In this, four photographs of the Westchester Parkway illustrated good practice: the footpath set below the roadway away from the traffic; natural woodland beside the road 'judiciously thinned and planted for landscape effects' (see p.39); and a filling station set back from the road with 'all the etceteras placed on the inside to avoid blocking traffic' (see p.110 top).[35] As well as the benefits in appearance, such roads also compared favourably in safety terms with those such as the early autobahns in Germany which were made on gradients and curves like those of a railway and which had proved to be dangerous because they made motoring 'a monotonous and dreary business, devoid of pleasure'.[36]

The holistic approach to designing roads, making them fit into the landscape, contrasted with the narrow horticultural concerns of groups such as the Roads Beautifying Association (RBA), the organisation that had been advising local councils on roadside planting since 1928. In his *Gardens in the Modern Landscape* (1938), landscape architect Christopher Tunnard had commented that roadside planting reflected the division between the formal and informal schools of design: the first

> prone to make of every byway a ceremonial avenue, with regimented tree planting lining thoroughfares along which no procession is ever destined to pass…. The second, more subtle yet all the more insidious in its power to blight, would follow the engineer along the arterial road, obscure the significance of his bold cuttings with a cover of arboreal growth, and emasculate the surrounding landscape with the products of the florist's window.

He went on to praise the work of the engineer 'whose activities are perhaps the greatest contribution made to the landscape in the last 100 years'.[37]

Colvin echoed his views – and those of Humphry Repton who had believed that well-designed roads could compose 'parkland into pictorial scenes, both in the view of the road and from it'[38] – in her own article on roadside planting in 1939. The object, she said, is 'not so much to "beautify" the road as to link it satisfactorily to the other existing features of the countryside: so to knit the highway into the landscape that it no longer appears as a naked scar cut across the face of the earth but becomes an integral component part of the whole'.[39] She accompanied this with a picture of a new road forging through an open landscape, captioned 'New roads open up new landscape. Why should it be hidden with unnecessary planting?' Her experience of motoring in the 1920s and 1930s meant that she appreciated the way in which roads in Europe were set into their landscape. She was to use a photograph of the sweeping Europa Bridge on the autobahn leading to the Brenner Pass in Austria on the cover of the second edition of *Land and Landscape* and, in that book, also used a photograph of a road crossing reservoirs in Germany, curving along the banks above the new high water level and responding 'to the shapes of mountain and water surface in a charming dialogue or counterpoint'.[40]

In Britain she felt most roadside planting showed 'an almost pathetic lack of vision'. The logic of much of it was based on the assumption that plantings of pretty flowering shrubs and trees would 'beautify' the roads. In a not very subtle attack on the activities of the RBA, she condemned the use of the word 'beautify'. She considered that most of the planting being done misunderstood the principles involved and was based on the assumption that

> since flowering trees and shrubs are pretty and excite our admiration, the more…we plant along the roads the more the roads will be 'beautified'. We find ourselves in sympathy with Polonius who condemned the word once and for all: 'That's an ill phrase, a vile phrase; "beautified" is a vile phrase.'[41]

What was needed was the use of 'massive tree forms in well-defined groups, properly related to the curves of the road and to the surrounding contours' (see 144, p.00). Where the country beyond was attractive the planting should not distract from the view. An open view to one side could contrast

> with a closed screen on the other, or for short lengths both sides may be screened as a change….Distant views often gain added charm when seen through a 'frame' formed by the stems, foliage and shade of trees, and therefore some careful planting of tall trees even on such open stretches of road can be very telling.

She also recognised that, for motorists, two factors affect their appreciation of landscape. The first is speed. At anything more than 30 mph, details of flower and leaf become irrelevant: as in garden design, 'form and mass, light and shadow are the materials we must make use of, and these are also the requirements from the point of view of the more distant observer'. Second, from the road most trees are seen in silhouette and it is therefore better to plant groups of one kind of tree or shrub. Colvin favoured the use of native trees and shrubs in country districts and forcefully defended the English countryside against the accusation of monotony:

> when the road passes from one geological formation to another, the designer has a grand opportunity for a dramatic, though logical, change of material. A new movement in the symphony begins…after the rugged and wild moorland effect of Scots pine, gorse, heather and birch on a high sandy stretch, we appreciate all the more…a run through a loamy valley where willows and poplars emphasize the lush character of the vegetation.

TOP Colvin used this photograph by Wilhelm Albrecht of the Europa Bridge in Austria on the cover of the second edition of *Land and Landscape*.
ABOVE Another picture from the second edition: an elegantly curving road crossing reservoirs near Mittenwald in Bavaria.

Her article ended with a plea for the use wherever possible of 'the enduring forest trees such as oak, beech, lime and chestnut'. She noted how we derive 'untold benefit' from the eighteenth-century planting of such trees. Just imagine, she goes on, how little of that would exist today 'if, at that time, cherries, crabs, and plums had enjoyed the vogue they have today'. On the approach to a town or village, however, the use of flowering trees and shrubs could usefully indicate a change from the rural landscape – and, in practical terms, in such a position the necessary maintenance could more easily be provided.

Many of the ideas and concerns expressed by Colvin in this article are reiterated in the 1946 'Roads in the Landscape' report of the ILA committee of which she was a key member.[42] Beyond the primary purpose of 'providing a system of efficient traffic channels', the report recognised the importance of the pleasure principle, not only from the point of view of user satisfaction but also as a means of enhancing safety:

> Roads beautifully adjusted to the local topography and treated as part of a fine landscape contribute to safety and efficiency of motoring through psychological processes militating against the boredom and fatigue of driving which is one of the factors leading to negligence and accidents.[43]

The committee urged designers to maintain and enhance the beauty of the landscape – the 'use and beauty of the roads should be inter-related inseparable functions' and provided a number of specific recommendations on general aims, siting, construction, boundaries and planting.

At the start of 1947 Colvin attended an ILA meeting with the RBA. Given her strong words about the 'vile' word 'beautified', it would have been an awkward encounter. The ILA committee's report had used more measured words but had also warned against the use of 'plants of incongruous appearance or plants which would require a garden standard of maintenance'.[44] Colvin returned to the subject in *Land and Landscape* where she argued that the problem of planting needed a 'more fundamental' approach. Landscape architects and engineers should ensure that modern dual carriageway roads were 'fitted' to the contours and existing features of the landscape so the road 'will seem to belong happily to its surroundings'.[45]

Landscape treatment and planting should be functional, keeping the driver 'alert and vigilant', cancelling 'the mechanical monotony of engine sound and road surface', preventing headlight glare, framing attractive views, screening eyesores. She felt the English had 'become too garden-city-minded' and that enthusiasm for planting the roadside (see p.110 centre) could 'overlay the native variety of our landscape with a monotony for which no amount of horticultural variety could compensate'.[46] The 'dramatic variations' of the English countryside would 'too easily be blurred and lost to the motorist by a lavish use of trees and shrubs of exotic or garden type'. Limiting the planting to what was found locally would 'make the most of natural landscape variety' and would require less maintenance, while the speed of modern motoring enabled the motorist to appreciate the beauty and regional variety of the nation's landscape. The speed of traffic should also influence the character of the planting. Moving at the speed of a horse, or slower, trees equally spaced give a pleasant rhythm of light and shade; at faster speeds that rhythm becomes a restless flicker that is tiring and distracting to the driver.

In addition to her persuasive written expression of the principles to be followed in the landscape design of roads and motorways, Colvin also brought her influence to bear on local and national government policy. From 1949 to 1954, she served as the ILA's representative on the Council for the Preservation of Rural England committee concerned with the landscape of roads, and in 1955 she was appointed to the government's newly established Advisory Committee on the Landscape Treatment of Trunk Roads. And, like many, she was critical of the early sections of Britain's first major motorway, the M1. In an article in October 1959, she criticised the 'hard sharp lines and clumsy angles' of the motorway's embankments and heavy concrete over-bridges designed by Sir Owen Williams and Partners. Unlike other contemporary light, clean-lined pre-stressed concrete bridges, in these reinforced concrete bridges the central supporting pillar spoilt 'the flow of open view under the arch, and the solid concrete parapet increases the apparent depth of the arch and the sense of its weight to an extent which is all the more oppressive because so frequent'.[47] She was also critical of the planting proposals for the motorway and noted that, without the influence of the Landscape Advisory Committee and the Royal Fine Art Commission, it might have 'had a ribbon of Forsythia and other garden shrubs on the central reserve…and subtopian decoration on side reserves and embankments'.[48] Under pressure from the Landscape Advisory Committee, the original planting plans had been modified and the motorway was spared the fussy distraction of colourful, ornamental species.

Of course, the Ministry of Transport's engineers did not always get it right and at the end of August 1970 Colvin joined what the *Guardian* referred to as 'the best-mannered demo of the year'. It was a walk over the disputed Chilterns section of the route for the M40 motorway. The protesters were increasingly frustrated and exasperated at the Ministry of Transport who would not listen seriously to their views. The ministry's highway engineers were sticking to the scheme they had first planned – which the county surveyor had tellingly referred to as 'the cheapest and best route' – a road dropping down from one of the highest points in the Chiltern escarpment in a vast and exposed cutting and then over a massive embankment from the foot of the slope to the Oxford plain. Against this plan were pitted the Royal Fine Art Commission, the Council for the Preservation of Rural England, the Ramblers' Association, the Chilterns Society, and an imposing list of eminent names including the artist John Piper, Dame Rebecca West, architect and town planner Lord Esher, the art historian Sir John Rothenstein – and Colvin. They backed the so-called Arup-Jellicoe route, a scheme produced just three weeks before the public inquiry opened by Geoffrey Jellicoe working with the civil engineering firm of Ove Arup. This scheme would have gone half a mile to the north, through densely wooded countryside whose quality was already downgraded by a cement works in the middle distance and ribbon development at the foot of the hills.

Colvin had already been called, with Jellicoe and Piper, as an expert witness at the public inquiry in

April 1969, but despite the extensive opposition, the ministry could not be made to see reason, mostly it is believed on the grounds that their route would save them about £500,000 – the price at that time of one kilometre of inter-urban motorway. The road cuts through what Peter Youngman referred to as 'a very critical bit of landscape. The old road comes winding up the hill on the other side and this one has cut a great big gash.'[49] In spite of the strength of the opposition, however, the ministry, 'concerned with engineering convenience, not the preservation of the countryside', built the M40 as proposed.[50]

The landscape treatment of roads was a subject of great importance to Colvin and most of the considerations she noted with regard to the treatment of roads are still valid and remain the main principles of good road design today.[51] And it was – and is – mostly from the roads as well as railways and footpaths that the vast majority of people experience the British landscape.

Of course, increasingly after the war the landscape that motorists encountered was undergoing major change and becoming home to some vast new industries, but in the 1960s, when she was working on some of these large-scale public landscapes, Colvin also took on four commissions for work in the more contemplative surroundings of universities. The most extensive and influential of these was at the University of East Anglia, but first, in 1960, she undertook a review of the trees and planting around the chapel and the president's house on the north side of the main quadrangle at Trinity College, Oxford. She proposed the removal of old and dying trees and their replacement by young specimens which would associate with the best of the old trees. She

RIGHT ABOVE The Chapel and the President's House on the north side of Trinity College, Oxford's main quadrangle where new specimen trees were chosen to associate well with the remaining mature trees.

RIGHT BELOW Contrasting foliage shapes including a large proportion of evergreen plants provide year-round interest in front of Trinity College Chapel.

redesigned the planting in front of the chapel, using low massed groups with a high proportion of evergreens for their winter effect, and permanent ground cover with extended seasonal interest that effectively softened the edges of the paths.[52]

In May 1961 Cruickshank & Seward, the Manchester-based architects appointed to build some new halls of residence at Queen's University, Belfast, wrote to the university's building committee proposing the appointment of Colvin as landscape architect for the Holyrood site where the halls were to be built. Her fees were to be 'at the rate of 20 guineas per day [approximately £320 today] or on the professional percentage scale, whichever should be less'. The senate duly invited her to advise on the laying out of the grounds and by December she had prepared her provisional proposals. She asked to present them in person – visits to Belfast gave her a chance to see her niece Hilary – and early in 1962 she outlined them to the halls of residence sub-committee 'with the aid of a plan and a model', neither of which has survived.[53] However, a photograph that Colvin used in the second edition of *Land and Landscape* shows the modern tower blocks in a very simple but effective landscape. Colvin captions it:

> Modern tower blocks tend to dominate their surroundings. Preservation of existing tree groups, and careful ground shaping with very broad simple treatment integrates them happily into the landscape. Close co-operation between architect and landscape architect is needed from the outset.[54]

Clearly in this instance Colvin had appreciated being invited to work with the architects at an early stage. The Queen's Elms halls of residence as they became known have recently been replaced by a number of 'self catered, purpose built, three-storey villas in a village setting',[55] and so little has survived of the 1960s landscape.

In contrast, Colvin's work at the University of Wales, Aberystwyth, is a rare survivor and is included in Cadw's Grade II* listing of the University of Wales site.[56] Barely a mile from the sea but some 200 feet above it, the site is 'fully exposed to salt-laden gales from the west and, in winter, to bitter winds from the east sweeping down from snow-covered hills on to the unprotected surface of the coastal belt'.[57] Landscaping of the site was going to be an integral part of its development and the architects, the Percy Thomas Partnership, were very aware of its importance in creating an attractive university environment. There was a strong Scandinavian influence on both buildings and layout that were designed and integrated in a way that was sensitive to the character of the site. All but two of the buildings were constructed after 1948. Not only was a great deal of planting carried out but a considerable amount of earth-moving was also undertaken.

From the earliest period of planting soon after 1959, prior to Colvin's arrival, shelter belts, mostly of pine, were created to keep out the salt-laden winds and these now protect and screen the site. Careful study was made of other coastal gardens, especially in the west and south and an extensive list prepared of plants that seemed likely to be suitable. In 1963 Colvin was commissioned by Sir Percy Thomas to lay out one particular area of the then bleak and barren Penglais campus. The earliest hall of residence, Pantycelyn Hall, lies at the west end of this campus, set slightly apart from and below the rest. A gentle slope rises away from the hall to the Edward Llwyd biology building to the southeast.

It is this sloping area that Colvin designed in 1963. She drew up two plans. The first, dated January 1963, gives the layout, with alterations to the existing contours of the site and an outline of tree and shrub planting. The main feature – the gently curving walk –

OPPOSITE Retention of existing trees and careful ground modelling helped to integrate the modern tower blocks of the halls of residence at Queen's University, Belfast.
LEFT The site at the Penglais Campus, Aberystwyth, in *c*.1963 as work begins on building.
BELOW Colvin's curving walk and her planting begin to take shape.

remains as she designed it. The second plan, dated June 1963, details the proposed planting. At its lower end the path is flanked by grass and there are three seats. For the 'Heath Garden' beside the path, Colvin suggested heathers, junipers, low-growing cotoneaster and hypericums, with taller heathers, Japanese maple and rose species on the upper part of the bank. Taller shrub planting to the back included a range of wind- and salt-hardy evergreens[58] with other tall evergreens

being allowed as temporary fillers between the choice slow-growers. These shrubs form dense banks and are in turn backed by pines and cypresses. Near the road, taller sections of planting where the view from the road could be obscured contrasted with lower sections that allowed views of the sea. Screening planting was also proposed round the car parks and sports areas. Colvin noted that her lists of plants were not meant to be exhaustive – additional planting could be included but the main tree groups should keep fairly closely to the list to 'preserve the simplicity of effect and to serve as shelter belts and background rather than as ornamental features in competition with the internal detailed planting'. In general terms, Colvin's suggested planting, well suited to the conditions of the site, has been adhered to in this garden-scale landscape.

Colvin's work at the University of East Anglia (UEA) on the outskirts of Norwich was on a much more extensive scale and was to have significant long-term benefit. The university had been founded in December 1961 and initially operated from a temporary site. Denys Lasdun & Partners were the architects for the first phase of permanent building, the first buildings of which were completed in 1966 on the Plain, the name adopted for the campus on the Yare valley slope. From the start, the vice-chancellor Frank Thistlethwaite was determined that UEA should be 'a stimulating environment' both in terms of its buildings and its landscape.[59] On the recommendation of Lasdun, who was later to comment

that the Plain was 'an exceptionally fine landscape of which the University is custodian',[60] Brenda Colvin was appointed landscape architect in early 1966. According to Colvin's friend, Lady Evershed, for whom she had worked in 1955, because Colvin was a 'perfectionist' she was 'sad at being brought in at such a late date'.[61] Nevertheless she set to work in characteristic detail, surveying trees, vegetation and the whole ecology of the 272-acre site. Her thoughtful and original landscape report of December 1967 has guided the subsequent development of UEA, a university particularly strong in biological and environmental studies.

To explain his layout, Lasdun supplied Colvin with detailed plans and two general illustrations that showed

BELOW The ground at the base of the residential ziggurats at the University of East Anglia was carefully recontoured to give the impression that the buildings have grown out of the ground.

the Draft II Development Plan of September 1963. There are three striking differences between these plans and the drawings in Colvin's 1967 report. First, she studied the whole of the university's land holding, including the land on the south side of the river, and not just the building land. Second she imagined the whole site in use, including a system of 'pedestrian ways' which would give access to the whole landscape. And third, she showed the Broad, a large body of water that crossed the site boundary into land owned by the City of Norwich. Colvin refers to a 'wide expanse of water as proposed in the report of 1965', so it seems the initial idea was Lasdun's; however its size and shape were to Colvin's design and it was certainly she who proposed that to offset the cost of construction, the useful natural materials on the site – the peat and the gravel – could be 'mined', given away to the firms prepared to remove them. This was a completely innovative and immensely practical solution.

The new use of this large site, 'introducing massive architectural elements and a vastly increased community', was self-evidently going to result in the creation of a new landscape. While Colvin hoped 'to preserve much of the character of the existing valley scenery', the university's needs involved 'overwhelming changes' which 'if accepted, foreseen and correctly planned in advance will enrich the landscape'.[62] The new buildings 'because of their scale and mass' would be the strongest element in the Plain but could co-exist happily with the river scenery to the south. The spaces between the buildings and the confined area to the north would 'present a completely new urban scene in contrast with the valley and the river'. This sharp contrast between two types of scene could be underlined and dramatised by suitable landscape treatment – the wide slope towards the river being simple with plain grass and trees and shrubs, the areas between buildings and those separated from the valley scene having more colourful planting and more elaborate detail design.

The site contained areas of varied ecological interest and Colvin recognised that its 'exceptionally rich heritage' would be of great value to the School of Biological Sciences. She felt it vital that 'all care should be taken to conserve as much as possible of these various natural habitats' which included the valley with its river and adjoining marshland that drained to a slow-flowing dyke; woodlands, both natural and planted; a willow spinney; a dell in the east illustrating all the phases of natural development from bare chalk to mature woodland; and a dell in the south showing the early stages of development from neglected farm hedgerow to natural deciduous woodland. Shelter and screen planting was needed in various areas and she suggested that the tree groups could be sited 'to form a kind of network… defining the open spaces of the site and linking these to existing woods and other landscape features'. The existing woodlands formed the basis of her design and their value in the overall landscape was 'paramount'; with the right treatment, some young plantations on the former golf course could become important features, lending maturity to the scene; and a mature group of Spanish chestnuts – 'a particularly fine feature' – would need protection during the construction of the new central buildings. She felt the old names of certain areas – 'Violet Wood', 'The Heronry' and 'Bluebell Wood' – suggested 'a rich foundation of wild life which, even if no longer existing, is of historic significance capable, perhaps, of re-instatement.'

Her suggestions for new planting followed her usual clear-sighted principles. Near the main buildings it would be used 'to promote the architectural character' with the canopy of the tree groups being kept well above eye level. Single specimen trees would be the exception but 'an occasional cedar or other important tree may become a feature'. Near the river and in the woodlands more naturalistic grouping was more suitable and, although planting would not be confined to indigenous species, the character of the existing landscape should govern the use of introduced species. She realised that the existence of the biological department prompted the inclusion of a wide variety of species of horticultural and botanical interest, but suggested that their grouping and placing should conform to the aesthetic needs of the site. And – an echo of her views on roadside planting – she urged that the 'tendency towards suburban character, which too easily arises with the need for horticultural interest, should be resisted; the broad park-like landscape should be emphasised throughout.'

Overall Colvin planned a 'continuous flow of space, with sight lines leading from the main buildings outwards and connecting the various areas'. Each area would have a distinctive character according to its use: open parkland between main buildings and marsh; marsh land and river walk; recreation grounds on both sides of the river; the dell and ground to the east of the site; space between buildings; approach roads; and an experimental garden. Essential to the final appearance of the landscape was 'carefully designed ground modelling, to adjust altered levels to the context'. A matter for cooperation between architects and landscape architect, this would be applied throughout the site, wherever new development involved change to existing contours and levels. The ground to the south of Lasdun's buildings, for example, was remodelled to make it 'fit the site sweetly' (see p.146).[63]

But it was this area that was also cause of a tremendous row between Lasdun and Colvin. He was adamant that there should be no paths on the south side of the buildings. Practical as ever, Colvin acknowledged that, although visually it might be best 'to eliminate hard surface paths in order to preserve the unbroken breadth of turf', in reality there had to be footpaths for the students in winter and they would need to be constructed for hard wear – and 'wide enough to allow for groups of three or four walking abreast, and for use by bicycle'. Temporary paths of 'stabilized turf' would make it possible to 'ensure that the final routes correspond with natural "desire lines" before the University is committed to what could become an increasing multiplicity of hard surface paths

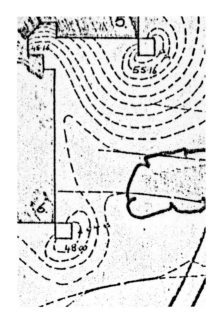

many of which might be unused.' Planting groups near path junctions would also keep wayward pedestrians to the right route. She ensured that the footpaths, when constructed, would be so positioned that they would not visually interrupt the general flow of open space.

As well as being highly practical and effective aesthetically, Colvin's proposals were particularly sensitive to the site's ecological demands, even though at the time she had disagreements with Lasdun and had to fight for the ecological base of her proposals for the valley beyond the buildings.[64] The willow spinney, for example, was 'derelict and past normal renovation', needing complete replanting. Colvin suggested negotiating with a cricket bat willow firm who had previously approached the architects. Rotational felling by them would preserve the spinney's landscape value while allowing for timber production. This was a good solution on all fronts: 'bat willow is a beautiful species at all stages of growth', commercial use of the plantation would provide variety and interest, and it was financially sound. Equally, the preservation of much of the marsh in its natural state would 'maintain the variety of landscape and provide biological interest rarely available within academic precincts'.

Also of great ecological interest was the Dell, a large hollow, possibly an old chalk pit, in the eastern area near Bluebell Road. Colvin considered it 'an exceptionally pleasing feature' worth conserving, but the architects, by then Fielden & Mawson, wanted to put excavated spoil from below buildings in it. Hal Moggridge had the idea of creating a ridge above the Dell instead, using the spoil and planting it with trees. At its southern end there was a small wood containing self-sown deciduous trees of mixed ages, while the other slopes showed earlier phases of natural regeneration. Colvin proposed conserving the majority of this for its special biological value.

OPPOSITE Part of a recontouring plan at the University of East Anglia; the path, bottom right, is recessed into the ground so that it barely shows in the landscape.

ABOVE A recent photograph of the Broad shows various habitats and Lasdun's buildings settled on to the carefully shaped open grassland in the background. The Broad has been made into a large lake since Colvin's original idea for a valley lake was accepted.

For the whole site she suggested a 'contrast of ground texture' that would 'not disturb the sense of unbroken expanse but…provide more seasonal colour variety and interest'. To achieve this she recommended that lawns in all the areas close to buildings should be of closely mown fine turf, but further away a change of texture to rough grass would form a 'pleasing contrast', would reduce maintenance costs and the main tree groups in these areas could be underplanted with bulbs. Colvin's landscape report also provided a meticulous, almost tree-by-tree survey covering pruning, removing, replacing and new planting and this lies behind the fine treescape that the university enjoys today. Although partly inherited from the old golf course and valley parkland, 'it was selected and shaped by Brenda Colvin'.[65]

Colvin herself was under no illusion about the role of man in creating landscape. She told Roy Campbell who acted as her host at UEA that 'most people think the landscape is normally green: it isn't, it is black'.[66] Although the university's council had approved her landscape in principle in 1968, she was frustrated that lack of funds delayed implementation of the plan. On occasion she stayed with the vice-chancellor, Frank Thistlethwaite, who became a personal friend, and the two of them worked to increase investment in the landscape. In November that year, seemingly writing to thank him and his wife for their hospitality, but in fact responding to his request for something with which to impress council, she expressed her views:

> the English landscape is very largely a man-made work of art, but I doubt if the general public realise that its quality depends on constant care, perhaps even more so than in the case of an Art Gallery or Library, since as a living asset it is subject to growth and decay.…Our generation benefits from their [earlier landowners'] forethought and generosity. We accept the privileges, too often with little thought of the related responsibilities to the future.…I feel that any landowner, more especially a University, has the responsibilities of ensuring for the future the benefits inherited from the past.[67]

In October 1968 UEA 'disengaged' from Lasdun's firm as architects and in January the following year Bernard Fielden of Fielden & Mawson was appointed consultant architect. The following spring he produced a report reconsidering the future of the university. This included a section written by Colvin which reviewed 'the landscape recommendations put forward in 1967, though the main principles still stand'. Her section was included in Fielden's report without any acknowledgement to its author. After 1970 Colvin & Moggridge's role was reduced as Fielden & Mawson employed their own landscape architect and, by the end of 1971, the practice felt 'excluded from the key strategic landscape considerations and disappointed by the meagre investment in landscape and…resigned the commission.'[68]

Today the university is proud of its landscape and in recent years has used a postcard of the Broad in a fund-raising drive. Its schools of biological sciences and environmental science are among the longest established and most experienced in the United Kingdom, undoubtedly encouraged in their development by the variety of habitats available as a direct result of Colvin's ecological approach. The campus and its grounds are open to the public and the site is visited by many thousands each year who enjoy the beauty of the parkland, the woods and the Broad.

Colvin's work also lives on in two much smaller public landscapes. First the garden she created on a bomb site at Seething Lane in the City of London. It was a commission from the Port of London Authority's head office in 1947.[69] It is now known as Seething Lane Garden or, occasionally, the Pepys Garden as it is on the site of the former Navy Office and official residence of the Clerk of the Acts, one Samuel Pepys, who moved there in July 1660.[70] It is said that during the Great Fire of 1666 on 4 September Samuel Pepys and Sir William Penn dug a pit in the Naval Office garden and buried their wine and Parmesan cheese for safety and then sat there 'gloomily discoursing upon the great tragedy'.[71] The garden is about a third of an acre in size and has a simple layout with a central lawn surrounded by paving and trees and shrubs around the outside. Contemporary photographs, including some of Colvin's own taken during its construction, show it as a sunny oasis, 'very bright with grass and flowers', surrounded by tall buildings.[72] Colvin exhibited plans and photographs of the garden at Chelsea in 1952 and still today it is a popular place with City workers for lunchtime and evening meetings and relaxation. A sign outside it reads: 'The Port of London Authority invite the public to use this garden …' and many take advantage of that invitation to enjoy the shade of the trees or sit in the sunshine.

Also displayed by Colvin at Chelsea (in 1958) and reviewed in the institute's journal was 'a crematorium landscape scheme…a series of glades leading from the crematorium out towards typical suburban housing'.[73] This commission had come from Salisbury District Council in 1956 and was followed by another three years later to design the Queen Elizabeth Gardens in a central part of the city. These opened to the public in the early 1960s to commemorate the coronation of Queen Elizabeth II on 2 June 1953, and have remained a

definite attraction for both locals and visitors ever since. The council had purchased the land as various plots over several decades from 1935, specifically to create a public garden there. On the western edge of the city centre, less than 300 yards from the High Street and Cathedral Close, the gardens occupy a roughly diamond-shaped plot of unfenced land of about 7½ acres (3 hectares) with roads to the north and the rivers Avon and Nadder on the southeastern and southwestern boundaries. Their creation would have involved some major landscape work. In part to discourage vandalism, Colvin aimed for great simplicity with her design depending on 'ground formation, trees and grass rather than more vulnerable features'.[74] To bring the river into view, she lowered the contours on the central sightline, and created tree groups on raised lateral mounds so that they framed the 'open vista across the water to the Cathedral spire'. On a sunny, gentle south-facing slope, the gardens still feature open grassy spaces edged by the natural rivers) and, as Colvin planned, plantings of poplars, willows, red oak, ash, alder and hawthorns frame the wonderful views of

RIGHT The Seething Lane garden designed for the Port of London Authority.

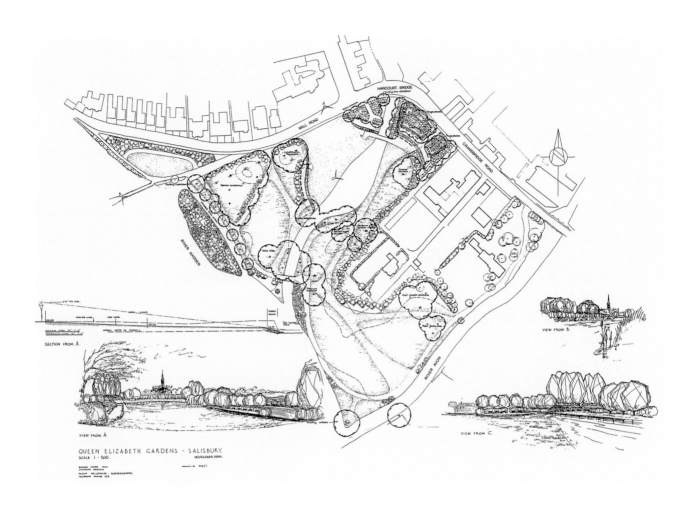

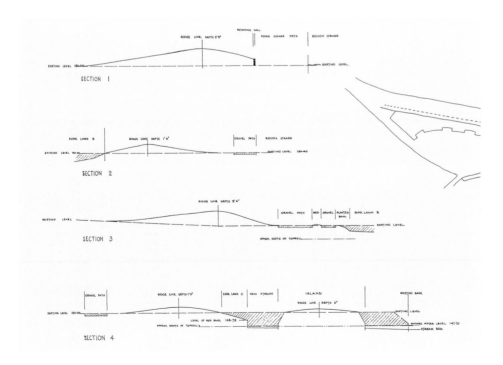

ABOVE Colvin's proposals for Queen Elizabeth Gardens, Salisbury (1959), including sketches of views from various positions.

LEFT Proposed cross-sections through Queen Elizabeth Gardens, showing the made-up levels.

the water meadows and the cathedral, the view from Long Bridge and the Town Path virtually unchanged since John Constable painted his now famous view of Salisbury Cathedral.

And it was to such great buildings of the past that Colvin believed landscape architecture should look when siting major industrial structures in the rural scene. They should, as in the past, contribute 'to the grandeur of the scene'.[75]

ABOVE The Queen Elizabeth Gardens in Salisbury remain a peaceful place, relying on simple planting of trees with grass and gently moulded ground.

LEFT Colvin's own photograph of the view of Salisbury Cathedral from the Queen Elizabeth Gardens.

ABOVE In 1959 Colvin was commissioned at Drakelow 'C' power station in Staffordshire. She found a 'doomed forgotten landscape lamenting lost glory' but felt it could become 'a fine landscape of the future'. She intended that the reflections of Drakelow cooling towers in the water surfaces of her nature reserve should 'contribute landscape quality to the area'.

Industry in the landscape

'Our power stations, oil refineries, factories and water-works must take
their place, in time, with the pyramids, castles and temples of the past.'[1]

ARLY IN 1962 Colvin was employed by the City of Birmingham Water Department to work
on a proposed reservoir, held by bunds or embankments against the hillside, at Trimpley in
Worcestershire. It was to be built in a bend of the River Severn on Eymore Farm land. In the
words of the department's policy statement it constituted 'a major change of the landscape of the
area and a threat to its existing calm and rural character'. It was to give Colvin a chance to put into
practice some innovative and creative thinking.

In *Land and Landscape* she had expressed the view that reservoirs, instead of being 'hideous
disfigurements of natural scenery' as many were, might instead become 'beautiful features'. She
considered their ugliness was the result of their having been designed with just one purpose in
mind and with a strict eye on economic efficiency for that purpose. If other values were considered,
especially those beyond immediate economics, the 'landscape criterion' could be applied, and
the schemes could enrich people's lives, not only by providing the necessary water, but also by
creating new beauty; they would serve the needs of visitors and holidaymakers as well as the local
inhabitants, so contributing to a better-balanced community and also to the general 'biological
balance' of plant and animal life.[2] Such an approach would affect the siting of the dam, and of
roads and footpaths in the neighbourhood, as well as the positioning and choice of trees and
other plants. It would influence the treatment of the contours near the water's edge.

In Hal Moggridge's view Colvin's work at Trimpley was, once again, an example of how she 'tended
to initiate new thinking and managed to influence the engineers in the way it was constructed'.[3] Many
of the elements of Colvin's design were pioneering and prevented it being just a simple engineering
structure. By the judicious addition of topsoil saved from the reservoir bed to the outer side of the
engineered bund or embankment that goes around three-quarters of the perimeter, she created a
landform which is well integrated into its setting. The soil added to the structural bank allowed
for tree planting and created an attractive, irregular landform. In the end the amount of planting
on the bund was reduced to a few clumps in order to display the flowing lines of the earthwork
as pastureland in a natural contrast to the surrounding woods. There was a practical reason for
gentle slopes, too: the water authority let some of the land for sheep grazing and the contours were
designed with this in mind.[4] An existing walk along the adjacent River Severn bank was enclosed
by the new embankment, the face of which was modelled as if it were a river terrace, and a path
along the top of the embankment offered views down to the river and across the reservoir to the
hills. Fishing and boating on the reservoir proved popular and a little gravel cove was created for

boats beside the club buildings in the former farmhouse. Colvin ensured that a group of existing trees around this were successfully preserved, and special care ensured the survival of a yew tree by the waterside – a curved platform built out beyond the rim of the reservoir was kept constantly irrigated during the construction work. Separate from the reservoir with its changing water levels, she created a pond as a small nature reserve by damming a stream, again with existing trees being preserved. This is now home to a wide variety of birdlife, including kingfishers, grey herons, ducks including goosanders, and even rare ospreys at the right time of the year. New tree species were largely local types – willow, alder and poplar on low levels, and oak, ash, pine, field maple, holly and beech on the higher contours.

Treatment of the rim exposed between high and low water depths was always a problem with reservoirs. Writing on the landscape of reservoirs in 1971, Colvin looked at how this problem could be resolved and noted how in tropical countries, where reservoirs fill only during the annual monsoon, the exposed rim would often be 'meticulously cultivated. Quick cash crops benefit from the deposited fertility and are harvested in haste before the approaching storm.' She recalled one ancient dam in Rajasthan that was 'crowned with temples, whose steps leading down to the sacred water are the stage for religious ceremony and pilgrimage, as well as for the daily laundry of the local inhabitants…. It is the non-use of the drawdown rim which so often causes problems.' At Trimpley Colvin concealed

LEFT Trimpley reservoir under construction in 1966. The River Severn from which water is drawn can be seen top right, with the engineered bunds and reservoir base in the centre. Existing protected trees, including a yew and a cedar beside the reservoir margin and a copse where a pond was created for a small nature reserve are seen bottom left.

RIGHT ABOVE The reservoir structural bund beside the River Severn (on the right), with a conserved mature tree and modulated profile as seen in early 1970.

RIGHT CENTRE The outer face of the structural bund with tree planting on added soil. The River Severn is on the left.

RIGHT BELOW The sailing club at Trimpley makes use of old farm buildings, with 30-40 boats parked in an adjacent hollowed-out cove surfaced with gravel. Cars are parked on grass reinforced with hardcore beneath unwashed ballast, as is the service access track around the reservoir rim (photo from early 1970).

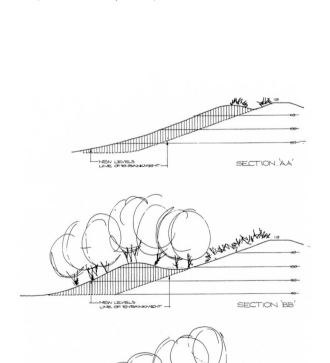

LEFT These bund cross-sections from the 1963 reservoir landscape proposals plan show soil added to the outer face to allow for planting and sweet profiles.

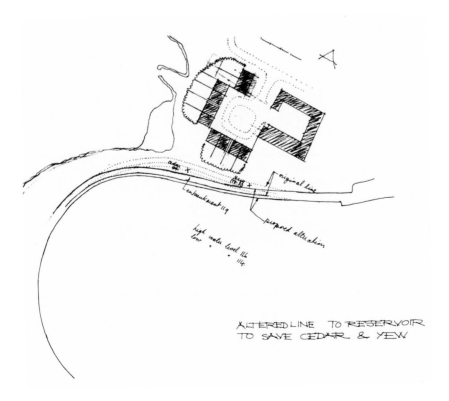

ALTERED LINE TO RESERVOIR
TO SAVE CEDAR & YEW

ABOVE This edge of Trimpley reservoir lies against the natural hillside with the yew and cedar that were kept by adopting Colvin's line for the margin which is up to 10 metres outside the engineers' original proposal, with a backfall to the cedar.

LEFT This sketch plan shows the line of the reservoir edge altered to save the cedar and yew, the pond formed as part of a small nature reserve, and the farm buildings used for the sailing club.

RIGHT The ornamental nature reserve pool at Trimpley with a sailing boat on the reservoir beyond. The pre-existing alder has had its canopy raised to let light on to the water and to enhance the view.

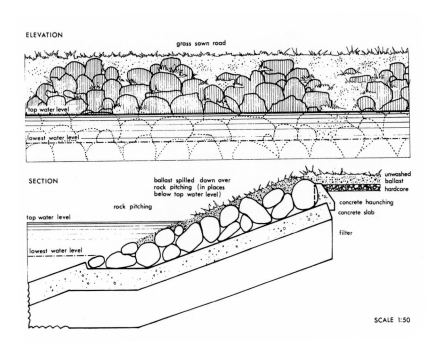

ELEVATION

grass sown road

top water level

lowest water level

SECTION

ballast spilled down over
rock pitching (in places
below top water level)

unwashed
ballast
hardcore

rock pitching

concrete haunching
concrete slab

top water level

filter

lowest water level

SCALE 1:50

LEFT ABOVE This cross-section and elevation of the inner edge of Trimpley structural bund show the method of construction to achieve a soft edge for all normal water levels.

LEFT CENTRE The upper edge of the structural bund before filling with water, showing the top of the concrete lining softened with stone fill, the upper edge of which consists of grassed unwashed ballast.

LEFT BELOW The inner face with water, stones and an irregular grass upper edge.

the rim of the concrete reservoir base with large rocks and irregular soiling to give the effect of a 'shingly beach with vegetation invading from the top'.[5] The surrounding access road was formed from unwashed gravel over hardcore that was then sown with grass and grazed by sheep. This 'reinforced grass' was also used for the sailing club car park, leaving the impression of general pastureland. Finally, with typical attention to detail, Colvin made sure a meticulous maintenance schedule was drawn up. When sending this to the Water Department she suggested that it should be pinned up in a position where it could be seen by both ground staff and visitors.[6] Today Trimpley's setting is described as 'idyllic'.[7] a 'picturesque beauty spot' with a 'hidden world of wonderful wildlife',[8] and the reservoir and its surroundings are used for a wide variety of recreational purposes, a testimony to Colvin's resolute vision.

But reservoirs, dealing with water and light, were perhaps easier to handle sympathetically than the heavier, more challenging buildings of industry. In 1947, in *Land and Landscape*, Colvin had expressed her anxiety about the industrial landscape:

So many existing factories and industrial buildings have been erected without recognition of the potential beauty of such specialized structures that it will take more and better examples of modern industrial architecture than we yet possess to convince the general public of the great possibilities inherent in their design. So much depends too on the context, that good qualities of mass and proportion are often overlooked even when they exist.[9]

She anticipated that the 'siting of the more massive industrial buildings' would be a 'critical problem for the future'.[10] By the time she came to write a second edition of the book in 1970, many more examples of such large buildings were available. In her chapter 'Industry in the Landscape', she noted how, in the past, 'isolated human structures in remote places' had contributed to the

'grandeur' of the landscape and was able to express the hope that:

> Our power stations, oil refineries, factories and water-works must take their place, in time, with the pyramids, castles and temples of the past. Perhaps they may succeed, visually at least, if something more than sheer materialism enters into their making. Some care for their effect on their surroundings – at least some simple recognition of man's place in nature and of his responsibility to the land and to the future – is needed.[11]

BELOW A distant view of the setting of Trimpley reservoir in the Severn valley with the pumping station on its right.

In the post-war years many writers had expressed such optimism about the potential beauty of industrial landscapes, but Colvin recognised that not everyone would appreciate the good looks of these new buildings. However, as she noted in a 'criticism' of Sir Frederick Gibberd's Didcot power station (1964–8) in Berkshire,[12] 'the sculpture of new technology', like art 'inspired by battle scenes, by air raids and by Rome in flames',[13] might appeal to the eye even if not to the mind. Some might be fine features in themselves but planting was crucial to concealing the clutter that invariably surrounded them and to providing a balance to their size.

Colvin was sympathetic to the arguments against the siting of Didcot power station. In fact she had represented the objectors at the inquiry. As a result of the evidence given by her and by Sylvia Crowe as consultant for the Central Electricity Generating Board (CEGB), the power line eastwards was aligned to avoid the Goring Gap – the two of them agreed on the need for an underground length. Nevertheless, professionally she was impressed by the success of Gibberd's landscape design which followed the precepts she promoted and that she had already put into practice at an earlier date, as we shall see, for example, at Drakelow in 1959. But she was generous in her comments about Didcot: 'The closer we come to the giants the more we can admire Sir Frederick's admirable work of easing them into this inappropriate and resentful setting.'[14] The appearance of the huge cooling towers had provoked a wide range of reactions:

> To many it is a shock of horror…an unpardonable intrusion in the calm Thames valley. Others…are moved to enthusiasm by the strange beauty of the cooling towers, and at least one convincing poem has been inspired by the view of the group seen from different positions and in different lights.…[15]

Gibberd's landscape treatment had, she felt, 'the merit of great simplicity'. The towers were sited in two asymmetrical groups of three rather than the two rows of four originally planned, and earth mounding and planting screened the 'inevitable clutter' round the base of the buildings. She appreciated the way the trees balanced the scale of the towers and provided a foil to their mechanical shape without attempting to screen them from view, although she was a little critical of the 'staccato character' of the planting – 'a sinuous flow…might have related the concrete structures more decisively to each other'. Some of Didcot's towers are visible from the grounds of the Manor House in Sutton Courtenay, one of Colvin's major post-war garden commissions. When they were built, the owner wanted to screen them with trees but Colvin felt they were themselves a significant feature in the landscape – giant 'eyecatchers' – and that the view of them should be retained, as indeed it was.[16]

During the late 1950s and 1960s, the Central Electricity Generating Board, set up by the 1957 Electricity Act, presided over a massive expansion of the electricity supply industry, including the building of more than 55 new power stations. The Board was required by the Act to recognise the impact its proposals would have on the natural beauty of the countryside and on the flora, fauna, natural features, buildings and objects of special interest. The size of the power stations and the vast new network of transmission lines that was also constructed were to have a major impact on the environment in many parts of the country but, largely thanks to the appointment of architect and town planner Sir William, later Lord, Holford to the CEGB's board, landscape architects were called in to advise.

The ILA's increasing concern for good industrial landscape had been expressed immediately after the war in October 1949 in Thomas Sharp's presidential address, entitled 'Temples of Light and Power'. In this

RIGHT ABOVE The massive cooling towers of Didcot power station eased by Sir Frederick Gibberd's 'admirable work' into their 'inappropriate and resentful setting'.

RIGHT BELOW Behind the trees to the right, the cooling towers of Didcot power station can be seen from the grounds of the Manor House, Sutton Courtney. An urn in memory of Brenda Colvin is centre left.

he considered the problem of whether town or country landscape was more capable of 'absorbing the great edifices required by some of our modern utilities'. Cooling towers, he felt, could have 'great aesthetic and dramatic qualities as abstract shapes', but they were unsuited to towns because 'they outrage the human scale, to which all things in a town must be related'.[17] At this time, however, there was little opportunity for landscape architects to be involved in industrial landscape and it was not until 1957 that the institute proposed its first national annual conference on the subject of 'The Landscape of Industry'. In November that same year, speaking at a Royal Society of Arts conference on 'Perils and Prospects in Town and Country', Colvin agreed with the general feeling that 'little money would be forthcoming for the sake of beauty alone', but went on to suggest that 'we should make the most of our wonderful opportunity to create artificial mountains by getting current colliery waste tipped into good shapes and planting them with trees'.[18]

In the early 1960s the institute's journal addressed the subject of the industrial landscape in papers and discussions from its general meetings, looking for example at possible solutions for the problems of scale and of transmission lines in the landscape. There was discussion in it too of the advantages of using excavated earth from building works to produce a more interesting modelling of the ground and to improve the setting of factories and other industrial buildings. In October 1964 the institute mounted a touring exhibition entitled 'Industry in Landscape' which one reviewer said made it clear that 'our landscape architects' time is better spent creating lakes and hills in the best tradition of British landscape than in bedding lupins outside factories'.[19] Gradually, appreciation of the value of landscape architects was growing.

Earlier that year Colvin had opened the institute's 'Discussion for Members only' on 'Landscape Work for the CEGB' and summarised the common problems of dealing with coal-fired power stations.[20] As they were of necessity usually sited in 'flat, monotonous landscapes', on or near a coalfield and on rivers or estuaries, the 'enormous cooling towers, chimneys and main buildings seen from afar, above trees, buildings and other constructions may give interesting variety of form....It would be impossible, even if we wished, to screen the larger components of power stations, and the problem is rather to integrate and relate them to their surroundings.' The 'impression of huddle and clutter' given by coal stores, railway sidings, car parks, sheds, stores and operational space, could, she suggested, be screened by ground modelling and planting – a strategy Gibberd was to follow at Didcot. Such banks and trees would provide an 'extensive horizontal mass' that would 'balance the huge verticals of the installations, and...graduate the scale to that of the surrounding agricultural pattern'. In a landscape where there were no trees or vegetation, she felt that ground modelling alone would achieve those effects but her own experience was of working in places where trees and hedges were in keeping with the local landscape.

Colvin had, of course, already covered the topic of 'ground modelling' in 1947 in *Land and Landscape* in the context of adapting a countryside site to any new large industrial structures. She had also suggested that there was no reason why waste material, rather than just being used for 'levelling up to a flat surface', should not be used 'to create contours of positive beauty like natural hills and valleys, or totally new forms'. Touchingly, she regretted the loss of the 'dump of brick rubble' which had been piled up in Hyde Park during the bombing of London in 1940-41 and which she felt had given a glimpse of how things could be in the future:

For some reason...the ramp carrying lorry loads to the top was made with curved lines, which, with the sharp escarpment at the top, possessed real beauty. Grassed over and crowned with a group of stately sycamores – the tree which sprang up on all the bombed sites – it would have made a fine addition to the park landscape. Consisting as it did of London's crumbled homes, it would have become a war memorial having significance of a totally different order from any to be erected later.[21]

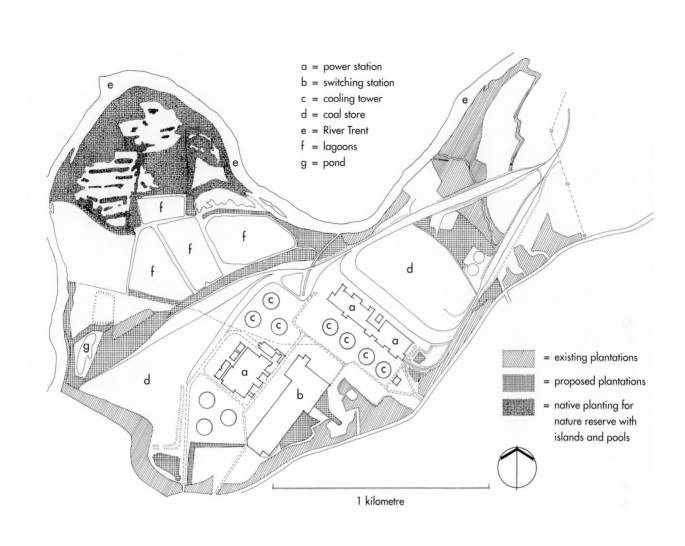

a = power station
b = switching station
c = cooling tower
d = coal store
e = River Trent
f = lagoons
g = pond

= existing plantations

= proposed plantations

= native planting for nature reserve with islands and pools

1 kilometre

Where a site 'devastated by abandoned industries' was to be used for new buildings, she believed that old spoil heaps, rather than just being flattened, had the potential to give interesting land forms, with new and better contours well related to the new building layout.

Colvin put her beliefs into practice in her own work on the landscape of a number of power stations.[22] In 1959 she was commissioned by the CEGB at Drakelow 'C' power station in Staffordshire, the third and largest power station to be built there.[23] Her initial, and in places poetic, landscape report typified her approach to the treatment of these giant structures. It considered the general problem of the whole Drakelow site in relation to the surrounding landscape and views from

ABOVE The landscape proposals plan for Drakelow power station (1962 and later), showing pre-existing and proposed woodland and the nature reserve in gravel workings.

various roads in a wide area of countryside. In spite of the 'impression of a doomed forgotten landscape lamenting lost glory', with derelict machinery, discarded vehicles and trees that had died as a result of building works decaying where they stood, 'their corpses creating a scene of desolation and despair', she was surprisingly optimistic and considered that the site could become 'a fine landscape of the future'.[24]

TOP The nature reserve beside Drakelow power station.
ABOVE Sunken access leads to the bird hide in the nature reserve.

In time her optimism was justified and Drakelow received an award under the 'Countryside in 1970' scheme. This was the reward for her innovative and ecologically sound proposals which included woodland belts around the edge of the site, detailed landscape treatment for the 'non-operational' space within it, and a wildfowl nature reserve on lakes created by gravel extraction for construction purposes (see also p.154). Nature conservation provision for children in the form of a duck pond and a 'nature walk' were planned in consultation with local schools and became popular features. Colvin felt that this encouragement of interest in wildlife was an insurance against vandalism and that it would widen the children's appreciation of landscape conservation.[25] The influence of their surroundings on children was a subject she felt strongly about – a picture of a Victorian village school in the second edition of *Land and Landscape* is captioned: 'This grim tarmac

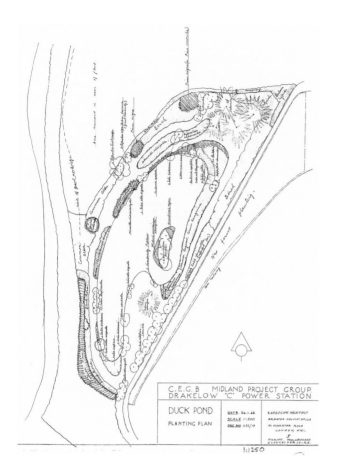

C.E.G.B MIDLAND PROJECT GROUP
DRAKELOW 'C' POWER STATION

DUCK POND

PLANTING PLAN

1:1250

she fought to avoid the planned siting of two cooling towers on an established wooded area known as the 'New Covert'. She proposed screen planting around the coal storage area and railway lines, car parking areas below road levels to facilitate screening, and additional tree belts to help distant views of the site.

However, trees could only appear as the base from which the cooling towers and chimney were to rise, so in her report Colvin suggested that the composition would be improved by 'some other form' contrasting with that of the towers to be seen above the trees. She queried whether this could be done by means of 'an artificial hill built of surplus ash'. If this was built up by lorries, 'a pleasing curved form' could be made. There would be 'no attempt to reproduce naturalistic contours' but rather to 'provide variety of outline to the group by means of an additional man made form'. Some trees could be established along its crests, but the main effect should depend on 'clean unplanted contours'.[28]

As always, at Drakelow and elsewhere, maintenance was an important issue for Colvin and she considered it vital to leave no 'undefined or nondescript areas liable

enclosed by prison-like railings can scarcely foster any appreciation of beauty at the impressionable stages of childhood.'[26] Today the Drakelow Nature Reserve is an important site for overwintering birds, a place visited by rare birds such as the great egret and the bittern, and home to a wide range of resident waterfowl.[27]

Believing that to achieve the 'fine landscape' she felt possible the landscape aspects of the new power station could not be considered in isolation, Colvin made a range of recommendations for the whole site as well as the area outside it. As the overhead cables presented the 'worst visual features', she suggested that some simplification of the transmission lines, using fewer pylons, should be considered. She was adamant that agriculture and forestry where possible were the best means of keeping the majority of the ground in presentable order and so areas from which gravel was extracted were therefore restored to agriculture as soon as possible. In particular

to weed infestation and unauthorised dumping of rubbish'. In addition to the land restored to agriculture, any odd areas left over were planted with trees rather than grass to reduce maintenance costs and improve the general appearance. Her involvement at Drakelow was to continue until 1974.

Colvin's use of ground modelling at Drakelow was to be one of the earliest uses in the post-war landscape of a man-made landform, but her approach contrasted with that of Geoffrey Jellicoe. In his naturalistic landscape plan for Guinness at Park Royal, London, in the same year, he used some 20,000 tons of subsoil excavated from a tunnel to form two attractively shaped hills to enhance the view of the brewery. It was a bonus that the money saved by not having to transport the subsoil to landfill was donated by the contractor to pay for one issue of the institute's journal. These Guinness hills and the low hills Jellicoe modelled from waste excavated during the building of Rutherford High Energy Laboratories in 1960 were intended to look natural and to hide the industrial buildings. And Jellicoe endowed his ground modelling with symbolic meaning – he described the hills at the Rutherford Laboratories as 'guardians of the underground monster'. Colvin's solution was more honest. In a caption to a picture of the Guinness hills in *Land and Landscape*, she drily commented that the 'contours please whether or not we seek for symbolism in their sculptural form'.[29] The contours she shaped at Drakelow – and, later, elsewhere – were unashamedly

artificial and yet, rather than disguising the large industrial elements, they enhanced the site, balancing the giant features and 'easing' them into the landscape.

In 1961 the CEGB commissioned her to work on a new coal-fired power station at Eggborough in Yorkshire. The commission was to lead to a long-term ground-breaking project. For the power station site itself, her design included extensive woodland belts and high banks around the outside edge of the site aimed at screening the low-level industrial activity. In time, providing for the wider lives of its employees, part of the site was restored to allotments, playing fields, a small golf course and a bowling green.

In her initial landscape proposals Colvin considered that although the main structures of the new power station would become 'a dominating feature of a wide landscape', if carefully treated they could be 'visually acceptable in this region otherwise rather featureless and lacking distinction'. Broad planting would balance the vertical height and mass of the buildings and considered treatment of ground levels and planting would screen the more unsightly lower elements of the group. She had a clear grasp of the need for a large-scale landscape concept when treating industrial-type landscapes, and the plantations at Eggborough successfully set off the giant structure, extending it horizontally about three or four times the width of the power station itself. The railway that came in gave her a welcome opportunity for planting along its length for about a mile, thereby achieving a really large-scale setting that hid the base of the power station. As at Drakelow, she also made suggestions in connection with the siting of main power lines to avoid 'unfortunate complication' to the 'existing unsightly wirescape of the area'.[30]

And it was in these proposals for Eggborough that Colvin raised the question of ash disposal. If a site for tipping ash was available, she considered that

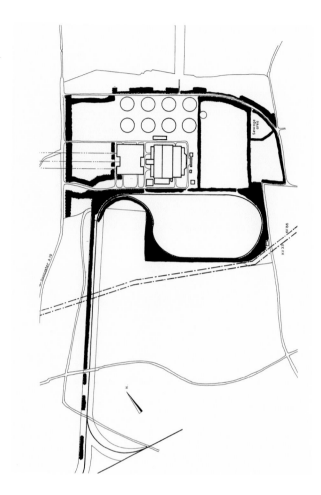

LEFT In the 1964 landscape plan for the new Eggborough power station in a flat open landscape, the black areas show new tree belts, often to be planted on artificial hills around the edge of the site. The length across the four cooling towers is 0.5 kilometres which indicates the sweeping scale of the project.

ABOVE The desolate state of the Eggborough site on completion of construction in 1969, before restoration, reveals the size of the task facing Colvin.

the 'tip' should be designed as a fine feature to contribute positively to the surrounding landscape…. I urge the necessity for positive form as against amorphous nonentity. Brayton Barff and Hambelton Hough provide good precedents for small hills in the region and I would urge in this case a frankly man-made hill, sculptural in outline like an early fortress or camp such as Maiden Castle.[31]

In 1962, pioneering the idea of preparing a restoration scheme before site work began, the CEGB appointed Colvin to prepare a design for the project that became known as Gale Common. Her proposal for the disposal of pulverised fuel ash (PFA or 'fly ash') waste from Eggborough and Ferrybridge coal-fired power stations was a most significant – and spectacular – project. Her approach to the problem was novel and 'poetic'.[32]

It was a 'neat virtuous circle of land restoration'[33] – land which had subsided as a result of the mining of coal would be raised with tipped ash and returned to productive agriculture. To this neat practical theory that, incidentally, would probably not be allowed nowadays because the low-lying wet land would be deemed too interesting and would be taken on as a nature reserve, she added an imaginative sculptural view. Her preliminary report, expanding on the idea first suggested in the Eggborough proposals, cited 'the objective of creating a completely new landscape feature, of distinguished and pleasing form, contributing to the interest of the landscape, as do existing hills' but also as 'an abstract sculptural group….No attempt at reproduction of other earthworks is proposed…. A frank artefact may be preferable to a naturalistic hill in this flat area where it can scarcely be seen as part of the

TOP LEFT In the early years after the opening of Eggborough power station, the north corner of the restored site, which had been the labour camp, was allotments for members of staff with a small kickabout pitch and the boundary screen mound beyond.

TOP RIGHT Immediately inside the northwest edge screening, the area used during construction as labour camp, car park and materials storage was made into a recreation landscape (photo 1985).

CENTRE LEFT The recreation landscape photographed in October 1992.

CENTRE RIGHT The northwest edge screening for Eggborough, with trees on mounding, was developed into a nature conservation area, as were all the extensive new woodlands planted around the site (photo October 1992).

BELOW The twenty-year-old tree belt, planted on a mounding along the A19 northwest of the power station, screens all the complexity of low-level equipment and moving vehicles (photo 1988).

surrounding geological structure.'[34] With the report she included photographs of some of the many early earthworks still existing in England, including one of Chaddenwick Down near Mere in Wiltshire.[35] These – and perhaps that wartime 'dump of brick rubble' – were to provide the inspiration for the detailed Gale Common plan.

Defying the convention of the time which was either to bury the ash or to make waste heaps as low-key as possible, Colvin planned an 'unabashed and obvious' artificial form with spiralling roads and contoured hilltops to be built out of the waste.[36] The PFA was to be pumped in water slurry from the power station and disposed of in lagoons inside the hill to dry out. Initially she presented her plan in the manner of Repton with 'before' and 'after' pictures of the landscape. She intended that the terraced formation of the hill would be retained as a permanent feature. The objective was

to create, on what was unproductive land, new contours that would be capable of 'sound economic use'.[37] It would become 'a farmland plateau, with sheep grazing on the banks, and cultivation on the upper levels with shelter belts and hedges.'[38] The number of terraces had to be reduced when the engineers had second thoughts on the construction and changed to a system of tracks and bunds on the artificially elongated northern end of the hill that was to emphasise its man-made character.

Work started on the nearly 200-hectare site in 1965 and continues today, a huge hill of ash being built beside the M62 motorway, rising high on the flat open landscape and visible from far and wide. In fact Gale Common has been constructed almost entirely after Colvin's death, thanks to her well thought-out system for continuity

ABOVE The lynchets on Chaddenwick Down, near Mere, Wiltshire, inspired Colvin's ideas for treating the sides of Gale Common Hill.

of design input. At one point in 1972, though, Colvin & Moggridge's landscape consultancy was terminated by the CEGB's North West Region. Typically, Colvin's reaction was prompt – and firm. Knowing that he had always 'urged the necessity for skilled landscape advice on major CEGB projects', she wrote direct to Lord Holford, still a member of the board, to protest, expressing her fear that 'a large area of dereliction may replace the hill form as intended'. She noted that the project had received considerable publicity, 'always giving credit to the CEGB for the conservation value of this work, and for their fulfilment of the amenity obligations'. Her

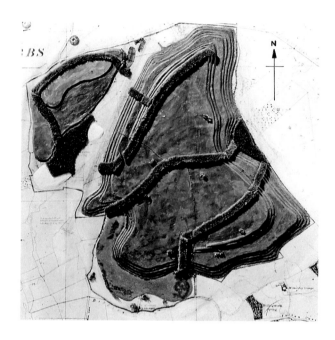

OPPOSITE This plan of Gale Common Hill was drawn in 1967 from the design prepared in early 1964. The hill is being built in three stages by filling raised lagoons with ash pumped in water from two coal-fired power stations (Eggborough and Ferrybridge), the sides of the lagoons being built mainly from waste shale from the nearby Kellingly colliery. Woods and fields are shown on the hill top; subsequent design development has put fields on the hillside and open grazing on the hill top. The hill is 1.5km wide by 2.2km long and over 50m high at the northern end.

RIGHT ABOVE The first model of Gale Common Hill was made in 1963 from plasticine, the correct quantity for the scale of the model having been supplied by the engineers, Rendel, Palmer and Tritton. This meant that each evening, the staff member who had been shaping the model had to scrupulously scrape all plasticine from their fingernails to avoid loss of volume.

RIGHT CENTRE This 1986 aerial photograph – with snow – of Gale Common Hill Stage 1 under construction shows Eggborough power station in the distance. The lower part of the left-hand side of the hill shows the final profile in place. The lagoons on the hilltop are clothed in marshland vegetation which floats upwards as the lagoons are filled, a clever device by the CEGB ecologist to avoid lightweight dust particles blowing off the top surface.

RIGHT BELOW Ash being pumped into the Stage 1 Gale Common lagoon in 1992, with its mat of floating vegetation, and birch trees in the background.

Above: The site as existing, looking east.
Below: The same view with the completed hill. The sections below look west.

threat to 'make some public disclaimer of the end result' now that the original scheme had been jettisoned was effective. The firm was reappointed.

The design has been gradually modified as circumstances change, but Colvin's original idea remains the inspiration for each development. At the start of the project, typically pessimistic about the durability of her created works but showing great foresight, she mused on what would happen to the ash within the hill. Would it remain soft or become in effect a stone and be quarried? Or might PFA as a raw material become valuable enough to be dug out again? This last thought showed great foresight – PFA is now indeed a valuable material for blockmaking and

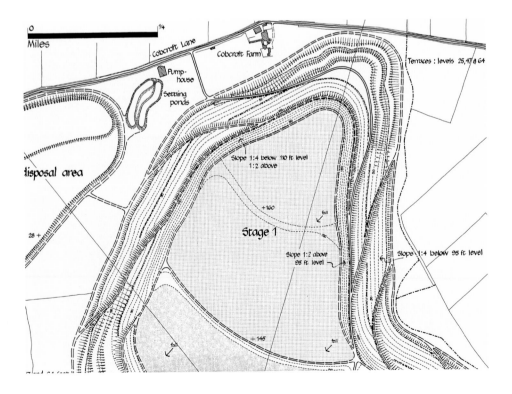

LEFT Colvin's 1967 contour design for Stage 1 of Gale Common Hill which has been substantially constructed to this design. Tracks spiral up the hill in a clockwise direction. The northern end of the steep-sided lagoon is terraced to enrich the silhouette. Contours are drawn 10 feet (3m) apart.

LEFT A photograph of the pre-existing site, looking east across the flat landscape, with Eggborough power station on the left, is compared with a drawing by Peter Swann of the proposed Gale Common Hill when completed, seen from the same place. **RIGHT** This photograph of the completed north end of Gale Common Hill taken in 1992 shows the terraced silhouette of Colvin's 'unabashed and obvious' artificial landform.

may yet be quarried on the hill.[39] In defiance of such concerns, however, in 2003 Stage 1 (the northern end) of the three phases she had proposed was substantially complete. The third phase has recently received detailed planning consent on the basis of plans prepared by Colvin & Moggridge in 1984 and which received outline planning permission in January 1986. Taking its inspiration from the patterns created by ancient lynchets on chalk downs and yet projected to be still under construction, managed by different owners, 50 and more years after its conception, this one project unites Colvin's ideas about the connections between past and future, and about time as an important dimension in the creation of landscapes.

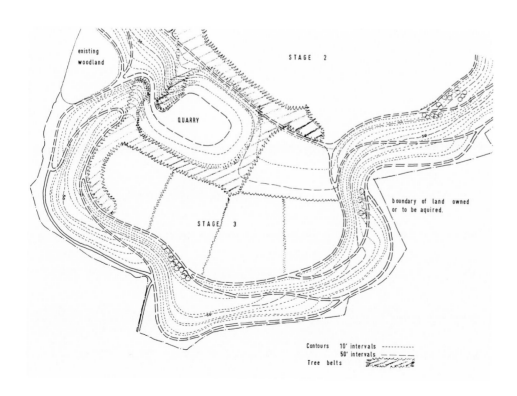

LEFT A prescient plan of the southern end of Gale Common Hill with a possible quarry, prepared in 1964. Pulverised fuel ash is now a valuable material for blockmaking and a quarry may indeed come to be needed on the hill.

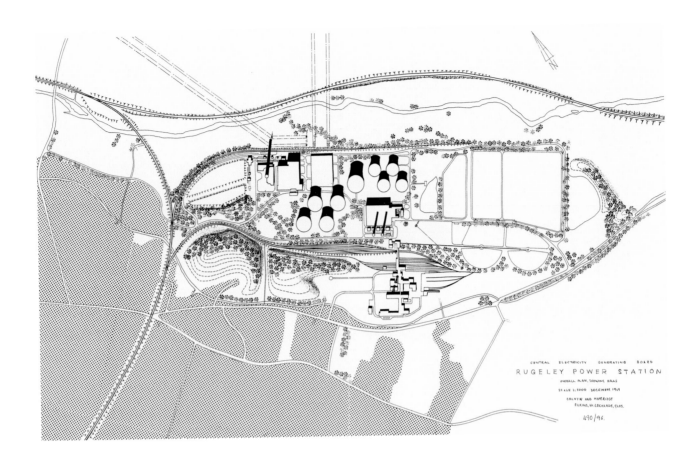

CENTRAL ELECTRICITY GENERATING BOARD
RUGELEY POWER STATION
OVERALL PLAN, SHOWING HILLS
SCALE 1:5000 DECEMBER 1964
COLVIN AND MOGGRIDGE
FILKINS, Nr. LECHLADE, GLOS.
490/96.

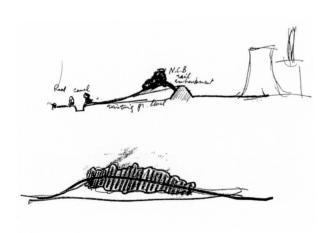

TOP The overall plan of Rugeley power station shows the proposed hills; the new B station is the four left-hand cooling towers.

ABOVE This design sketch of proposed hills to the south west of the power station to screen the town comes from Colvin's site notebook of May 1964.

On a far smaller scale at Rugeley, a CEGB commission in 1964 that continued to 1975, Colvin used waste ash and shale to create screening hills. The project doubled the size of the existing coal-fired power station on a site that was close to the town where Colvin felt 'any possible means of breaking up the large industrial extent should be tried.'[40] With new planting taking the place of former hedgerows, a spinney on raised shale contours in the colliery screening the railways and coal store from the south, and raised contours formed by extension of the new lagoon linking with the existing ground and spinney, she achieved a broad-based setting in scale with the vast concrete shapes. At Drakelow 'C', Frank Dark, the architect, had chosen a warm red colouring for two of the towers. Colvin felt this was effective on clear days at bringing them forward visually from the other four grey towers, but that the Burton climate 'too often clouds all in a grey dimness'.[41] Here at Rugeley, in consultation with the architects Watson and Coates, she proposed

LEFT ABOVE This sketch from the landscape report for Rugeley power station (January 1965) shows the view looking northeast from rising ground south of the A51, with the proposed spinney on raised shale contours in the colliery area.

LEFT BELOW This model of the landscape plan shows the proposal for two dark peaty-coloured cooling towers to reduce the otherwise too massive bulk of grey concrete; the belt of trees in the foreground is 1.2 kilometres long.

BELOW The four B station cooling towers are on the left with transmission lines running across to the right; existing trees combined with new planting in the foreground form a broad-based setting.

colouring two of the four cooling towers a dark peaty brown to define their shape against the otherwise too massive bulk of grey concrete. But there was little remedy at the time for the 'unfortunate landscape effect' of two sets of transmission lines, apart from tree planting that might ultimately improve the view.[42]

A small footnote to Colvin's association with the CEGB has recently come to light in the form of a set of three photographs of her work on the landscape setting at the CEGB South Project Group Offices at Squires Lane in Finchley, north London in 1960 and 1961.[43] The architects were Farmer & Dark, a firm who had introduced Colvin to several jobs in the 1950s and 1960s.[44] In this lakeside setting Colvin designed a simple landscape that must have been much enjoyed by the board's employees.

For all of the larger CEGB commissions the question of management was crucial. 'In strictly economic terms,' she wrote in some notes on landscape maintenance for the institute's journal, 'it is obvious that a landscaping scheme is going to prove a ceaseless waste of money, stock and manpower unless it is managed with the proper forethought and skills.'[45] In fact, with its ownership of these massive sites, the CEGB had become a very important landowner. Colvin felt it was fair to regard them – and the other industries that administered large amounts of land in Britain – as 'heirs of the former great landowners whose care for the beauty of their estates has left us so fine a heritage'. Frequently private estates had been taken over directly from the previous landowners with all their woods and farmland intact. In fact industry could 'make or mar the landscape of the future according to whether or not it accepts the responsibilities towards the land which were formerly assumed without question by the owners of fine estates.'[46] The whole of the land should be 'productive' of something, she felt, even if, as in the case of landscape quality, what it produced was an 'invaluable asset'.

With its profound effect on the landscape, she considered human activity had almost reached 'a geological scale. Our extractive industry changes the levels and ground forms over huge areas.' While she

recognised that change had to be accepted as a necessity, she considered that 'we have far greater powers of control over the changes than was formerly thought possible, and we are learning that the controls must be applied throughout the process of change and not as an afterthought.'[47] The intrusion of industry into the newly created National Parks was a particular problem.

ABOVE A small jetty runs out over the water beside the CEGB's Southern Project Group offices in Finchley.

OPPOSITE ABOVE The simple, clean lines leading to the striking willows at the water's edge match the clean architecture of the CEGB's offices.

OPPOSITE BELOW The simplicity of the mown grass and willows merges into more naturalistic planting including irises in the water.

It was during the 1930s that groups such as the Ramblers' Association, the Youth Hostel Association and the Council for the Preservation for Rural England had lobbied the government for measures to protect and allow access to the countryside for the benefit of the nation. The pressure culminated in the 1945 White Paper on National Parks, produced as part of the Labour Party's planned post-war reconstruction. The following year, Colvin, James Adams and Sylvia Crowe submitted their evidence to the National Parks Committee on behalf of the ILA. Finally, in 1949, the government passed an Act of Parliament to establish National Parks to preserve and enhance their natural beauty and provide recreational opportunities for the public. Lewis Silkin, Minister for Town and Country Planning, described it as 'the most exciting Act of the post-war Parliament'.

In its 1947 report the National Parks Committee had recognised that 'the most serious menace to the landscape' of the Peak District came from the exploitation of its minerals, in particular limestone. It described some of the damage: 'The heights round Buxton emit black smoke, Dove Holes is raw and heaped with tips, a recent quarry gashes the side of Eldon Hill' and went on to suggest that 'measures should be taken to check the defacement now in progress and to remedy what has already been inflicted'.[48] Nevertheless in 1952 there were 26 applications for permission to continue and extend existing quarry workings within the Peak District National Park. Surprisingly the Peak Park Planning Board only asked the minister to reject two applications – from Eldon Hill and the adjacent Sparrowpit quarries – on the ground that the 'distressing scars' constituted 'a disastrous incident' in an otherwise unspoilt stretch of countryside. When she was called to speak on behalf of the application at a public inquiry, Colvin conceded that the quarry was unsightly and that it would not be possible to screen the quarry face, which in her view was not objectionable per se. However, she

BELOW Planting of larger trees at the Bowater Paper offices provided an effective contrast to the reflecting walls of the new buildings.

felt that the quarry face and the upper parts of the associated buildings would be improved if seen above a belt of trees which would in itself be valuable in what was a rather bleak landscape. Restrictions on how far the quarry could be extended were accepted by the company. The quarry was finally closed in 1999 and is still undergoing landscape treatment with vegetation beginning to grow on the quarry face. Eldon Hill was one of a few quarries on which Colvin worked in the early 1950s.[49]

Elsewhere in the Peak District, in 1955 Colvin was commissioned to prepare a landscape scheme for the Peak Planning Board to improve the appearance of derelict tips at the Ecton copper mines in the Manifold Valley. Here trees were planted in soil pockets on the terraces of the old workings and on the hillside above them. In spite of the remedial work she undertook, Colvin remained convinced that the 'great lesson to be learned from the terrible legacies of the past is that it is far more difficult to put things right on land formerly ravished by industry than to restore land to sound use in the course of operations.'[50] This was a view that she argued consistently through the post-war years. In a criticism of Gibberd's Potash Mine at Boulby in Yorkshire written in 1974, she posed the question: 'Are we always to go by the known short-term considerations or should we try to assess the loss of landscape quality in the interests of unborn generations?'[51] Too often, it seemed, decisions were taken on economic grounds solely in the interests of the present generation.

On a smaller industrial scale, in 1956 Colvin designed the landscape for the Bowater Paper Corporation offices at Northfleet, Gravesend. According to the ILA journal's review of the institute's display at Chelsea in 1958, 'pride of place among the more complex buildings and their landscapes goes to the Bowater Paper Mill landscape designed by Miss Brenda Colvin, dramatically presented by photographs of a model'.[52] Young trees 'of more than normal nursery size' were used here to form a counterpoint to the glassy reflecting walls. The reviewer felt it could be argued that 'for a detached building, this was more effective than

the provision of a "setting" of English parkland to a building which dominates'. Colvin was to use a picture of the mill to illustrate the point that 'quick effects are usually called for in landscape planting' as clients and architectural colleagues tend to 'press for immediate results'. A compromise solution, she suggested, was to use a few specimen trees in a matrix of forest-type planting, or by using each type of planting in separate areas.[53] At the W.H.Smith warehouse at Swindon in 1964 (see p.104) she used a mix of long- and short-term planting schemes, but emphasised that if only fully grown trees and shrubs were used it would reduce planting 'almost to a three-dimensional problem' – as if a painter were 'to forgo the use of perspective'. She felt strongly that:

> The pleasure of watching things develop in time, and of noting and enjoying each different phase as it appears, is not to be relinquished lightly – to miss out these intermediate stages is to lose one of those contacts with the soil which our period can ill afford; and the artificial completion of the project at one stroke is one of those means by which 'civilization' (or that sophistication which we call civilization) impoverishes the realities of living in time.[54]

In 1970 Colvin published a second, considerably revised edition of her book *Land and Landscape* and dedicated it to Geoffrey and Susan Jellicoe. It was greeted enthusiastically by her friend, the landscape architect J.St Bodfan Gruffydd:

> How splendid that this marvellous book should come back to us, and in new form, to bring us all up to date!...We have here a standard work on landscape architecture to take us well into the 21st century. Miss Colvin has a poet's feeling for the evolution of the land.[55]

New techniques and problems had necessitated much updating. Preparing the revision was stressful work for Colvin, now in her seventies: 'she would shut herself into her office with drafts and potential illustrations and struggle fiercely to perfect each sentence or caption.'[56] Nevertheless, the emphasis was still on our ecological relationship to the landscape and Colvin's forceful opening to Chapter One remained unchanged. In her Foreword, with considerable foresight, she saw the dangers of mankind's disregard for nature: 'The tendency of our age is towards ever greater domination of nature by man, though we are dimly aware that the last word will be with nature unless we can adapt our new powers to the crescendo of evolution without overriding the natural laws ensuring healthy survival and duration.' She acknowledged that in the years since the first edition of the book:

> immense changes have taken place in our landscape, in our powers of altering it and in the rate at which changes occur....In 1947, the threat of over-population was scarcely felt, though the rate of general development was already a threat to landscape in these islands and the havoc that might be caused to our land by growing technical power was becoming evident. But now the pressure of increasing numbers of people greatly increases the risk of havoc and makes the remedies more difficult.

The new edition, she felt, was a 'very small contribution' towards the 'vast combined operation…needed to prevent the destruction of any small country's dwindling charm and to ensure for its people…a landscape worth living in.'[57] In addition, her public landscape work, together with her other writings and her involvement with the crucial decision-making forums influencing landscape strategies all meant that her contribution to making 'a landscape worth living in' was enormous. Writing Colvin's obituary for the Wye College magazine, Sylvia Crowe referred to the 'tranquil riverside gardens [Colvin] designed beside Salisbury Cathedral' as a 'fitting memorial to her work.'[58] In truth the same could be said of any of those of her larger landscapes that have survived.

Writing about her own beliefs and the profession of landscape architecture in Muriel Emanuel's *Contemporary Architects*, published in 1980, Colvin noted how landscape design differed from architectural design in the fundamental aspects of both time and space:

> Most landscape design projects take far longer to mature than those of architecture, and they are far more vulnerable to short-term destruction or inadvertent neglect....The basis of landscape design is biological rather than geometrical: the laws of nature remain dominant over human fashion and convention.[59]

Her approach to her large-scale and long-term projects reflected this belief. Frequently, working in this field, she had to fight battles and take a stand in favour of the landscape against the power of high finance, politics and planners, and against entrenched groups including professionals such as engineers as well as objectors. But out of it all she managed to create innovative, often soulful landscapes. And all were created on the basis of ideas she had developed through garden design. She believed that 'each garden went to the heart of the matter of landscape architecture, posing in miniature the problems to be solved in the largest project'.[60] Her later gardens were to be skilfully designed with a fluency and certainty that came from her long experience and reflection on the philosophy and practice of landscape architecture.

RIGHT At the Bowater Paper offices, Colvin used larger than usual young trees for a reasonably quick effect.

ABOVE An important post-war garden commission for Colvin was Sutton Courtenay where she replaced Norah Lindsay's Persian Garden with a much simpler 'jewel' garden with a sculpture group by Charoux at its centre.

Modern private gardens

'In a modern world, a garden must be easy to maintain; for this reason…
it might be assumed that modern gardens could not compete in interest with
the great gardens of history. This is not true, for the smaller the garden,
the greater the perception of detail.'

GEOFFREY AND SUSAN JELLICOE[1]

THROUGHOUT THE POST-WAR YEARS, alongside her large-scale public work, Colvin continued designing private gardens and there are some 180 garden commissions shown in her notebook. She gained great satisfaction from the smaller more intimate scale of this work because of her profound interest in plants and planting design. In the 1970s she even planned to write a book on planting – she had intended to include a section on the subject in her revision of *Land and Landscape* but had to 'drop' the plan as 'there was already more subject matter than could be packed into the space allowed me by the publishers'.[2] Draft titles for the book were 'The Garden for Four Seasons' or 'The Constant Garden v. the Instant'. Drawing on her twenty years of experience developing her own garden in the Cotswolds, the book would have emphasised how 'the care of pleasure gardens could be reduced and simplified without loss of quality in design' while still making it possible to keep them 'looking interesting and shapely at all seasons'. This was the overall philosophy she brought to her post-war gardens work.

As with her earlier gardens, much of this work has not survived but evidence from photographs, plans and a few surviving gardens reveals the extent of her considerable talent in this sphere. Additionally, recognising the quality of her work, several of her designs were featured in garden books of the period. One of the first was Peter Shepheard's *Modern Gardens*, published in 1953. In this Shepheard selected garden designs from around the world, designs that seemed to him 'to possess a common touch of the contemporary spirit'. He said he had let his choice be led by his belief that 'the modern garden should find its inspiration in the contemporary scene; that if it looks backward for a precedent, it should turn not to the Renaissance gardens of Europe…but to the gardens in which from time to time man has come to terms with nature and made her partner to his design.'[3] Among the 50 or so selected gardens, Shepheard included two of Colvin's designs – a small town garden in Hampstead and the Manor House at Sutton Courtenay in the Thames Valley.

In the years between the wars socialite and garden designer Norah Lindsay had created a magical garden for herself at the Manor House which was widely regarded as one of the most beautiful gardens in England. Her romantic laissez-faire style had led to a luxuriant garden, crammed with planting. Lindsay's niece Lady Diana Manners remembered it 'with flowers literally overflowing everything and drifting off into a wilderness'.[4] Writing about the garden herself in *Country Life* in 1931, Lindsay commented that 'In a garden where labour is scarce and the soil beneficent, all manner of tiny seedlings get overlooked till, lo and behold! a handsome clump has established itself in the most unlikely position'. She described the whole effect as being 'that of thoughtless abundance', attributing to it 'an air of spontaneity in the planting, as if the flowers and trees had chosen their own positions and, like the house, been overlooked by the rushing tide of men'.[5] But, in spite of this effusion, it was not a 'modern' garden in Shepheard's terms, it was a garden that looked back to Europe. Lindsay had

been greatly influenced by her travel abroad and, like the Italian Renaissance gardeners before her, included much topiary in her designs.

During the 1930s David Astor, the son of Lindsay's friend Nancy Astor, had been a frequent visitor to the Manor House. He was at Balliol and often went over from Oxford to help in the garden at weekends. Returning from the war in 1945 Astor found that for financial reasons Lindsay needed to sell the house and he decided to buy it. He knew the garden well and therefore realised immediately that without its creator it could not survive and that he would not have enough time to devote to it – it was already suffering badly from neglect. He had heard

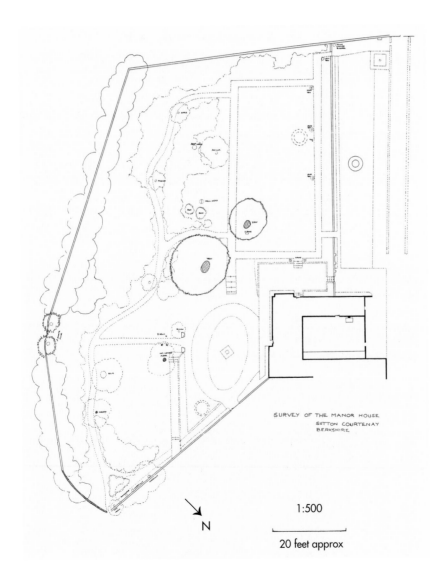

SURVEY OF THE MANOR HOUSE
SUTTON COURTENAY
BERKSHIRE

N

1:500

20 feet approx

LEFT Plan of the gardens around Sutton Courtenay Manor House which were completely remodelled in 1948–50. Thereafter minor changes continued to be made for the next twenty years. Wild gardens spread northwest from the house to a Thames riverside walk leading to a copse about 300 metres away. The entry drive and front door were relocated from the southeast to the northeast side of the house and the gardens remodelled to the southeast and south. A new 'jewel' garden was created to the southwest.

RIGHT ABOVE The curved terrace leads up steps to the lawn on the southwest of the house. The yew on the right was retained from the existing garden (photo c.1952).

RIGHT BELOW The former gate pillars were retained as part of the garden to the southeast of the house.

of Colvin through John Hill of the interior decorators, Green & Abbot,[6] and in 1948 he invited her 'to advise on alterations'.[7] As they worked together to redesign the garden, he was to appreciate her 'talent and her pioneering spirit'.[8] It was to be a long-term commission, involving work on both the garden around the house and the wider landscape towards the River Thames. Colvin wrote about her initial work there at some length in the Institute of Landscape Architects' journal in November 1953, illustrating the article with her own photographs.

By the time of her first visit Astor had instigated a number of changes. A new entrance and drive already in use meant that Colvin could replace the former gravel forecourt to the southeast of the house with a paved terrace with curved hedges of lavender. Its clean

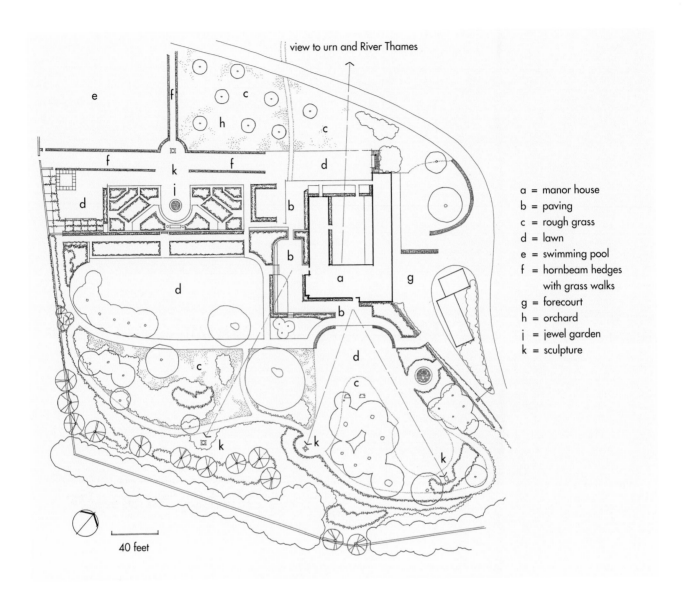

view to urn and River Thames

a = manor house
b = paving
c = rough grass
d = lawn
e = swimming pool
f = hornbeam hedges
    with grass walks
g = forecourt
h = orchard
i = jewel garden
k = sculpture

40 feet

sweeping lines ran out towards the informal garden beyond, where mown grass walks led between the trees. The old gate pillars that had marked the previous entrance were retained as 'objets trouvés', and 'a tangle of plants of various heights was placed between and around the piers...setting them apart from the present day coming and going, and leaving them to brood, undisturbed, over the forgotten past'. They are still there today.

Beyond the terrace the lawn that replaced the forecourt divided near the old gateway into two wide walks which were each given a focal point – a stone urn for one and a small group sculptured by Siegfried Charoux for the

ABOVE Colvin's layout plan for the gardens to the south of Sutton Courtenay when she was appointed in 1948, showing the sightlines to the objects in the garden. There were still many fine plants from Norah Lindsay's garden. **RIGHT** A sculpture group by Siegfried Charoux to the south, with the trees around trimmed to frame it in views from the house (photo c.1952).

ABOVE The long border, punctuated with existing yew trees, beside the lawn to the southwest of the house.
RIGHT Looking back towards the house, the long curving path with its echoing line of Jersey elms separates the lawn and the wild garden.

other. The planting of the walks and their 'terminal points' was 'designed to give a sense of depth and of undetermined distance'. In fact they are not far from an unseen road boundary which Colvin hoped would remain 'unheard' behind a dense background planting of trees and shrubs. Parallel to the boundary, at right angles to the two walks, a gently winding grass path led from a gate near the new drive, first revealing the urn and the small Charoux group and then, further on, a more important group by the same sculptor, each object appearing in turn as the path turned in its direction. Colvin's plan shows the careful siting of all three objects to serve as focal points for the grass walks and to provide a link between the house and garden. The second group was set in the southeast angle of the garden known as the 'wild garden'. It was framed by 'carefully trimmed branches of flowering trees' and behind the group, to highlight it, Colvin planted silver-leafed eleagnus.[9]

Norah Lindsay's elaborate formal Long Garden, immediately to the south of the house, which had been divided into many compartments marked by clipped hedges and punctuated by topiarised yew and box, had all been swept away before Colvin saw it. Of course not everyone approved of the changes and some blamed her for them: some years later Colvin's assistant Anthony du Gard Pasley happened to meet a woman who lived nearby. She complained that there had been a wonderful garden at Sutton Courtenay but 'then some dreadful woman came along and made it all look like a public

park'.[10] The truth was that it had been 'considered too elaborate for present day conditions'[11] and that, during the war years, it had in any case begun to go to ruin. What Colvin found in the Long Garden when she first visited was 'an empty expanse dominated by some very fine old yew trees and enclosed on the south and west by high brick walls'. Drily she wondered whether perhaps 'it was the emptiness of this expanse, after such a clean sweep, which led to my summons'.

She decided to keep the space very open, making a 'fine lawn'. The herbaceous planting against the wall to one side was balanced on the other by the wild garden. A path marked the boundary between lawn and wild garden and 'careful thought was given to [its] line and siting…its long curve has been stressed by a row of Jersey elms following the same curve on a line whose base is formed by an ancient yew near the house'. Around the house Colvin found a series of terraces or small courts that corresponded to the ground plan of the house. She emphasised the variety of their levels and underlined their different characters by the treatment of the planting and paving materials. To contrast with the pillared arcade on one side of a small courtyard enclosed on the west side of the house, she built a raised bed for 'foliage plants of sculptural form'.

A passage created by tall hornbeam hedges that linked the southwest terrace to the kitchen garden was retained except at a central point where Colvin opened it out to give more width to what had been Lindsay's rose-filled Persian Garden. This was redesigned as the 'jewel' garden, a simplified parterre, 'in the hope of reducing its long and narrow proportions'. A plan of additional planting from 1960 shows the box-edged beds filled with 'Hidcote Blue' lavender, *Senecio cineraria*, yellow and white roses, and regal lilies, with tulips, 'Silver Blue' petunias and wine-red winter-flowering violas planted to provide colour

LEFT Grass walks, planted with wild flowers and bulbs, led from Sutton Courtenay house to the river.
BELOW One of the channels in the wild garden towards the river.

through winter and spring. The vine pergola with tiled floor and a wall fountain at the north end of this garden were all kept, and Colvin added some ferns and foliage plants that were given 'a cool shady position on a ledge under the vines', watered by an unseen pipe linked to the fountain. Reluctantly she conceded that a lawn between the rose garden and the pergola 'may accommodate a swimming pool at a later date'.

Beyond the wall and the pergola lay the vegetable garden and orchard. To the west of the house grass walks led to the river bank. The Manor House lies on an ancient site, a dry piece of land in the middle of a complex watery maze of cuts, channels and pools, beside a stream called the Mill or Ginge Brook which joins the River Thames not far downstream from Abingdon. Close to the river were meadows that Lindsay had carefully preserved as 'cool green savannahs flowing serenely along the river's

ABOVE Looking back
to the house at Sutton
Courtenay across the
meadows beside one of
the river's backwaters,
planted with daffodils;
newly planted whips can
be seen in the foreground.
RIGHT Colvin's
photograph of the
riverside walk, newly
modelled in about 1952.

bank' – she found their 'solitude…refreshing after the crowded coloured gardens'.[12] Not surprisingly, Colvin was in sympathy with this more naturalistic approach and noted how 'in spring the livestock poses charmingly among the daffodils beneath weeping willows'. She planted a curving avenue of golden alder (*Alnus incana* 'Aurea') – a favourite tree of hers – whose bark would 'make one of these walks rosy throughout the winter'. A large quantity of the delicate fragrant *Narcissus* 'Tresamble' was to be planted beside it.[13] Another walk was shaded by silver poplars. But some stretches were left clear to maintain views from the house and terraces to the Thames. Along the main river bank she contrasted open views with 'lengths of dense and bosky shade where thickets of bamboo and *Cornus siberica alba* growing under willows and poplars emphasize the contrast of light and shadow'. Large numbers of trees were planted throughout all this wilder section and beyond the property 'for the benefit of the village in general'.[14]

Colvin had a very close relationship with Astor. The swimming pool question was perhaps a rare topic on which they seem to have sparred but her reluctance to spoil the jewel garden prevailed and the swimming pool was positioned on the far side of the hornbeam *allée*. Later Astor wanted to enlarge the pool. When Colvin's structural engineers said that it would not be possible, she wrote to let him know. Matching Colvin's ability for the dry riposte, Astor replied that he was sorry to hear it would not be possible to enlarge the swimming pool. How much would it cost?[15] Money may not have been too much of a concern for him but the question of maintenance was certainly important and in 1961 the size of the vegetable garden was reduced by half and returned to meadow to reduce labour.[16]

Colvin's involvement with Sutton Courtenay continued for many years. The spare clean lines of her design close to the house are now somewhat blurred with self-sown seedlings and other alterations, the plantings in the wilder parts of the garden have become overgrown, and the whole has suffered from a degree of neglect. The rising water table also means that some of the trees nearer the river have died.[17] Nevertheless

Colvin's stated intention of seeking 'to unite the old and the new' in her treatment of the whole garden was and remains successful.[18] The more formal areas close to the house retained a degree of their former exuberance in planting yet suited the new owner's need for lower maintenance, and the graduation from formal to informal is skilfully handled with the move from exotic to indigenous planting easing the move from the house out to the plantation beyond.

Shortly after Colvin started working for Astor at Sutton Courtenay he bought the Compton Beauchamp estate in Wiltshire, and when in the late 1960s he considered moving to the moated house and had it restored and improved, he naturally asked her, in addition to her work on the woodland there, to advise on the restoration and planting of the garden.[19] Colvin's design was planned to show off Astor's extensive outdoor sculpture collection, most of which was in the grounds at Sutton Courtenay. The sculptures were to be displayed in alcoves created by curvaceous shrubberies, arranged so that they were seen in succession. Henry Moore's *King and Queen* was at the far end of the garden, visible from a distance and providing a conclusion to the sequence of more hidden works. Planting of the garden was well advanced when, in the early 1970s, the Astor family decided that they did not wish to leave Sutton Courtenay and so the Compton Beauchamp house with its grounds was sold, although Astor retained the estate which included White Horse Hill.

The garden at Compton Beauchamp was terribly overgrown when Colvin first visited, as a rare brief note of hers detailing some of the work needing to be done reveals:

Centre Walk to Gate:
Trim back box blobs by degrees
    " hedges (box) drastically
Clean nettles & ground elder behind (dig?)
Keep all shrubs, only cutting out dead wood/suckers now[20]

On that first visit she was accompanied by one of her staff, and when they heard a little voice hidden in the undergrowth – a baby in a pram – Colvin exclaimed, 'Oh, there's Sleeping Beauty!'[21] She may not have had any children of her own but she had a great sympathy with children and a remarkable understanding of their needs. Her nieces always appreciated the fact that she never talked down to them but spoke to them as adults.[22] Hal Moggridge's daughter Harriet echoes this feeling. She used to visit Colvin at home and walk round the garden with her. On one occasion, aged about ten, she went on an outing with her to White Horse Hill.

BELOW A sculpture in the garden at Compton Beauchamp with the house beyond. Colvin's caption written on the back of this photograph was: 'Each enclave may become the setting for sculpture or other items to be viewed singly … the system provides for objects of widely differing period and character to agree with the overall plan and the house, itself the product of many centuries'.

She remembers feeling 'grown up in her company as she appeared to treat me like an adult. Looking back, I realise that this was true except that she also managed to tell me things that I would find interesting and in a clear and vivid way…. She conveyed the impression that she found me interesting to talk to and I enjoyed this and her conversation. She was reserved but at the same time open.'[23]

Her understanding of a child's needs led Colvin to design an enchanting children's garden for Astor at his north London home.[24] This 1953 garden was featured in Marjorie Allen and Susan Jellicoe's *The New Small Garden* which was published in 1956 and again in their *Town Gardens to Live In* of 1977.[25] It was 'almost wholly devoted to the basic pleasures of young children. The elements of contented play are all found…sand, water, grass and delicious rounded pebbles that make an engrossing pattern under the water and are so exciting for small feet.'[26] Its main feature was a pebble pool,

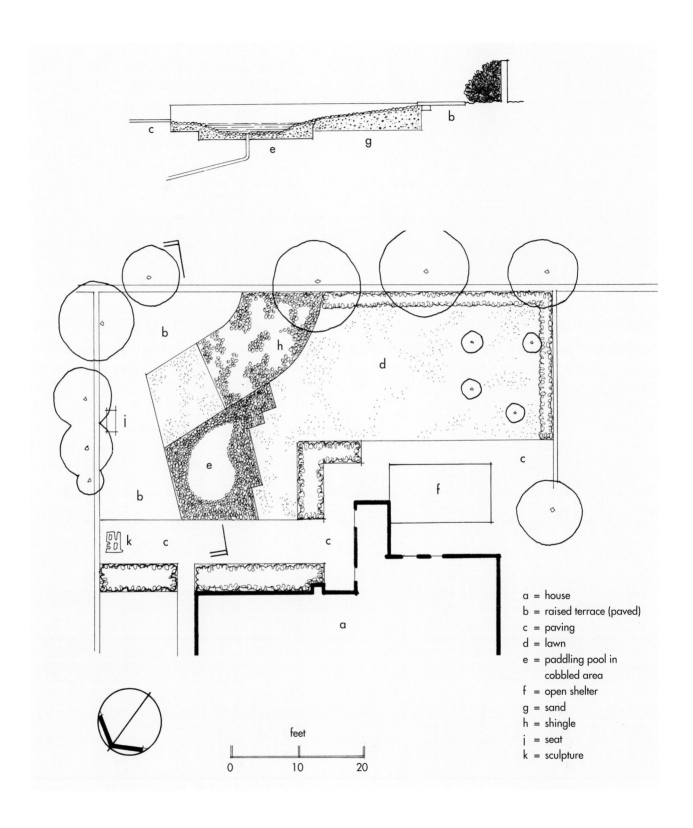

b

c ——— e g b

b

h

d

i

e

b

c

f

c

a

k c c

feet

0   10   20

a = house
b = raised terrace (paved)
c = paving
d = lawn
e = paddling pool in
      cobbled area
f = open shelter
g = sand
h = shingle
i = seat
k = sculpture

ABOVE The plan for the Astors' children's garden in London with a cross-section of the pebble paddling pool, showing the drain to empty the pool when it was not in use (top).

surrounded by sand and shingle, with boulders acting as steps up to a paved terrace where a seat is shaded by trees. The combination of sand and pebbles effectively re-created the pleasure of the seaside. As Allen and Jellicoe noted, too often 'Children…are in danger of being tidied out of existence' – but this was certainly not the case in this garden. The practical details are taken care of too: the pool is filled by a hose and has a plug-hole for easy emptying;[27] sand and shingle are contained in their separate compartments by a band of stone; half-standard flowering cherries shade the lawn which also provided a useful area for hanging out washing; climbers decorate the walls and create a screen. Colvin exhibited her plan for the other half of this London garden at the Chelsea Flower Show in 1956 – a large pear tree was preserved in a largely paved garden that flowed around its outline. Varied planting included many of Colvin's favourite sculptural shrubs and herbaceous perennials. For a while it was also home to Henry Moore's *King and Queen* sculpture, later moved to Compton Beauchamp, and Colvin had to try 'to make sense of fitting in this most unsuitable bit of sculpture'.[28] Over the years the Astors truly appreciated the contribution that Colvin made to their gardens – after her death, an urn was placed in her memory in the grounds of the Manor House, Sutton Courtenay (see p.163 bottom).

Children were catered for again in Colvin's design for another small London garden, also featured in Allen and Jellicoe's earlier book.[29] Presented with the small rectangular garden of a newly built terrace house, separated from its neighbours only by chain-link fencing, she met the challenge successfully. By using a series of curves in the layout, she broke up the rectangular shape and, by putting the main feature – a small pool – in the corner diagonally opposite the entrance from the house, leading the eye across the longest distance in the garden, she dramatically increased the feeling of space. The owners had asked for a children's plot to be included in an inconspicuous spot. To give an immediate sense of privacy, Colvin used bamboo screens near to the house and one of these also hid the view of the potentially untidy children's area from the house and

BELOW The seaside effect of the pebble paddling pool.
BOTTOM Colvin's own photograph of the garden she designed for the Astors at 12 Elm Tree Road, NW8.

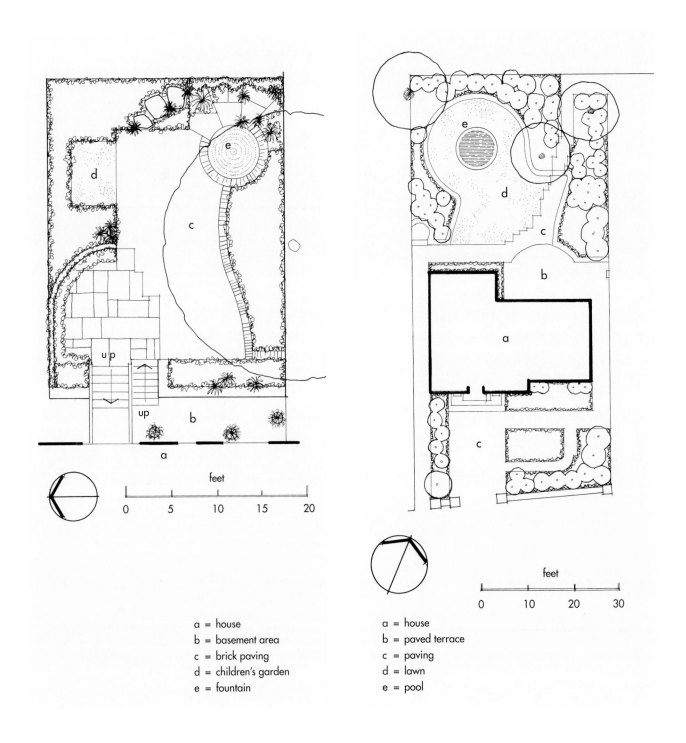

a = house
b = basement area
c = brick paving
d = children's garden
e = fountain

a = house
b = paved terrace
c = paving
d = lawn
e = pool

ABOVE LEFT AND OPPOSITE ABOVE Colvin's plan for the small rectangular garden of a newly built terrace house in London included bamboo screening and a change of paving to indicate the move from the seating area. Placing the pond at the farthest point from the entrance to the garden makes the most of the space.

ABOVE RIGHT AND OPPOSITE BELOW Colvin's use of curves increases the feeling of space in the small back garden of a house in Hampstead, London. Sculptural foliage in the border catches the light and contrasts with the simple lawn and pool, and trellis provides some privacy from neighbouring houses.

the stone-paved sitting area. A step down and a change of flooring to brick marked the transition from the sitting space to the rest of the garden where the pool and a raised platform behind it were the main features. The raised area acted as a stand for containers which could be brought in to provide seasonal colour to contrast with the rest of the planting which was subdued in tone, relying on contrast of foliage. The pool had a small fountain and small holes around its top edge created a bog area suitable for moisture-loving foliage plants. Most of the planting needed little attention apart from pruning and there were spaces for bulbs and small plants, and a small herb garden near to the kitchen window. Colvin planted climbers against the chain-link fencing which also meant she could 'borrow' the planting of the neighbouring gardens.

Colvin's skill at creating successful garden spaces out of even the tiniest plots was seen in another small town garden in Hampstead, London, the second of her designs featured in Peter Shepheard's *Modern Gardens*.[30] Once again she used curves 'to counteract the rectangles of the site and give a sense of space'. Changes of level also contributed to the interest with a step down to the lawn with its small circular pool and with raised curved beds around its edge. Again the planting was of tall plants of striking form such as acanthus, *Viburnum rhytidophyllum* and sumach. Colvin used photographs of this garden to illustrate the use of plants for their sculptural effect in her article on 'Gardens to Enjoy' in the 1952 *Studio Gardens and Gardening* annual. She considered the simplicity of the plain grass and pool on the lower level created a 'foil for plants of sculptural quality, catching the light on the raised border'. The planting of 'free or non-geometrical type' contrasted with the grass and stone paving on the horizontal planes and the brick for the vertical planes. She was pleased with the effective strong curved shadow of the low brick wall.[31] Trellis added to the top of the wall – just as she had used in her early London gardens in the 1920s – gave privacy and scope for climbers.

The apparent simplicity of these three small town gardens is deceptive. All feature many elements of Colvin's particular skilful and innovative style: the use of existing features such as trees, including those beyond the garden's boundary; simple, well constructed hard landscaping; attractive year-round planting; consideration given to practical concerns (washing line, herb garden, ease of emptying pool) and ease of maintenance.

On a larger scale was the garden Colvin's brother Hugh asked her to design for his new home in 1955, twenty years after she had first designed a garden in Essex as a wedding present for him. The new house near Salisbury, Nunton House, was a Queen Anne house of soft pink brick, set sideways to the road with its main façade facing south over an area that had always been garden. A gravel forecourt is surrounded by some magnificent mature trees, including three ancient yews and, beyond it, typical of Colvin, is a mown lawn surrounded by taller grass full of spring bulbs. The effect is one of restful simplicity with only climbers and a few shrubs chosen mainly for their shape and texture to complement the mood.

To the east, beyond the yews, lies the rest of the garden, including a formal box-edged rose garden with a central lawn. This is enclosed by a wall-backed herbaceous border on one side and a hornbeam hedge separating it from the kitchen garden on the other. Halfway along the semicircular path at the edge of the rose garden, Colvin decided to break through the Georgian brick wall to make a straight vista to an attractive orangery, contemporary with the house, with its own sunken lily pool. Here, she designed a formal 'Dutch' garden with stone paving surrounded by four drum-shaped clipped conifers and two pairs of Irish yews linking the steps through the wall from the rose garden. Through a brick gateway lay a more relaxed woodland garden where Colvin included many of her favourites, including periwinkles, butcher's broom and giant hogweed (*Heracleum mantegazzianum*) as well as shrubs such as variegated dogwood, *Rosa glauca* and *Viburnum rhytidophyllum*, all positioned to make the most of their foliage. At the end of the walk is a bench seat sheltered by a box hedge. The woodland

RIGHT The new entrance to the orangery and its formal garden at Nunton House.

garden then continued through glades of shrub roses, *Hydrangea aspera* Villosa Group and *Viburnum plicatum* f. *tomentosum* 'Mariesii' and past a paddock. When 'Bay', Colvin's brother, announced he wanted to put a tennis court in the middle of this section, she was disgusted. She at least ensured that it was positioned well away from the house and well screened.[32] It is a garden which in 1980 the National Trust's adviser John Sales considered was one 'of great charm, full of interest and with many plants. It is held together by a firm plan which makes the most of its buildings and features and provides the maximum of variety.'[33]

Many of those favourite plants reappear in Colvin's attractive and effective design for a riverside strip between an old walled garden and the River Thames at the Old Parsonage at Buscot which is also reminiscent of the riverside areas of Sutton Courtenay (see also p.79).[34] This was one of her designs selected by Geoffrey and Susan Jellicoe for

BELOW At the riverside walk at Buscot Old Parsonage in Berkshire *Gunnera manicata* and *Cornus alba* 'Variegata' contrast in colour and texture with the white poplars and pollarded scarlet willows around them.

their 1968 *Modern Private Gardens* book. Here Colvin chose plants to help 'effect the transition from garden to meadowland'.[35] She grouped giant *Gunnera manicata* and variegated dogwood among white poplars and pollarded scarlet willows to provide contrast of texture and colour. Other plants included the sculptural giant hogweed, oak-leafed hydrangeas and viburnums in contrasting areas of mown and rough grass with bulbs and day-lilies. The trunks of existing trees were trimmed to ensure clear views through to the river and the new planting.

But Colvin's skill did not just lie in her planting design. Her response to the mechanics, the very basics of any scheme, was always clearly and skilfully thought out. In 1956 she was commissioned by Sir Anthony Lindsay-Hogg who had recently purchased the Old Rectory at Acrise, near Folkestone.[36] He was undertaking major works on the house and invited Colvin to design the garden for him. In its existing layout the driveway had led straight up to the front of the house, ending in a circular forecourt enclosed by shrubs. As she had done at other houses, Colvin decided to re-route the drive to the side of the house. This meant she could make a dramatic change to the front, letting in light and

TOP The drive at the Old Rectory at Acrise ran straight up to the front of the house when Colvin first visited.

ABOVE After Colvin's re-design of the drive, the front of the house was opened out to a generous lawn with mature trees and rough grass around the edge.

LEFT The still water of the enlarged pond reflected the façade of the Old Rectory.

203

opening up the view to a generous expanse of lawn with surrounding mature trees and, slightly to one side, a simple pond that she enlarged and positioned in such a way that it reflected the house. She was very keen on organising water so that it would give a reflection where it had previously reflected nothing – 'Still water reflecting a scene, yet giving it a different aspect and a new quality, provides fascinating opportunities for the designer.'[37] Although this was a relatively simple piece of geometry to carry out, it was a skill that was not often appreciated or clearly understood. Colvin discussed it in both editions of *Land and Landscape*, noting how the level of the water and the shape of the bank or verge could be controlled to reflect the pictures required and demonstrating with a diagram how to achieve the desired reflection. In addition to its aesthetic effect, the pond at Acrise also served a very practical purpose in that all the drainage from the front of the house was organised to run into it. The planting in this garden was simple but effective – mostly shrubs, with many bulbs planted in rough grass, lawns, separate 'rooms' created with yew hedging, and a number of raised beds close to the house for more colourful, seasonal planting. And,

again, existing trees were preserved but with trunks cleaned to open up the views. Out of a plot that was overgrown and rather claustrophobic, Colvin created a stylish, open garden with a great sense of space and interesting outlooks, with planting interest close to the house, and simple upkeep.

Colvin's expertise in designing effective layouts and hard landscaping, her skill in planting design, and her ability to work at a very practical level, creating a workable, simple-to-maintain design all came together in her work at Okeover Hall in Staffordshire. Here, in the late 1950s, the architect Marshall Sisson was responsible for the extensive reconstruction of Sir Ian Walker-Okeover's home, an eighteenth-century house by Joseph Sanderson, and Colvin was commissioned to restore the grounds. These were largely overgrown when she arrived – 'a real shambles' according to one of the gardeners of the time.[38] She preserved the main elements of the original eighteenth-century scheme but at the same time developed the gardens in her own characteristic style.

It was she who instigated changes to the arrival area, designing an open elliptical lawn in the centre, with a

LEFT The arrival area at Okeover Hall as Colvin rearranged it.
OPPOSITE LEFT ABOVE Looking back down to the front of Okeover Hall through the gates of the walled garden.
OPPOSITE LEFT BELOW The greenhouse that Colvin designed for the walled garden.
OPPOSITE RIGHT Colvin's viewing pavilion beside the discreetly sunken tennis court.

'blackamoor' holding a sundial in its middle. Straight across the courtyard from the main entrance of the house were the gates to what was a totally neglected walled garden. At the far end of this main north–south axis, up a slope, lay Sanderson's small 'Temple of Pomona', built in 1747–8. Colvin altered the gradient of this slope and created a wide grass path to lead up to the temple. The path was flanked by two wide herbaceous borders backed by espalier pears and edged with wide York stone paving which allowed the plants to flop over, softening the look of the walk. Looking back down the path from part way up the slope, Sisson's new front of the house was revealed, perfectly framed. The rest of this garden was a practical one, a kitchen garden for vegetables and fruit, and a greenhouse personally designed by Colvin who specified exactly what brick should be used. In the experience of Jerry Shenton who worked as a gardener at

Okeover for 42 years, it was a very successful greenhouse, one that was good to work in.

The other main axis of the garden layout was the east–west one on the far side of the house. This began with a terrace that Colvin designed with yellow roses below the windows of the south front of the house. Beyond this the ground rose and, after a flight of steps, a walk led through a number of old Irish yews and lead figures on the drums of pillars, passing a sunk garden to the right and ending at another small building designed by Sanderson. Known as 'The Necessary House', this had originally been a water closet, fed by an underground stream. To the north of this Colvin created a wild garden where most of the grass was left a few inches high with short walks mown through it. In the longer grass there were many bulbs for spring and around this area Colvin planted a number of trees, including golden alder and

tulip trees. Beyond the wild garden, Colvin designed a discreetly sunken tennis court – surrounded by grass banks, which she specified were to be 'finished at a gradient suitable for grass mowing'[39] – as well as a small viewing pavilion, framed by recessed box hedging.

For a successful outcome and continued good maintenance in a garden this size Colvin realised that she needed the cooperation of the professional gardeners and she always listened to their opinions on what she was planning, possibly more than she did to her clients' views. They found her very much in control but not dogmatic about her plans and they appreciated her expert horticultural knowledge and her friendly, considerate approach. She was generous too, giving Mr Shenton a signed gardening book as a token of her appreciation of his help as her work at Okeover came to an end.[40]

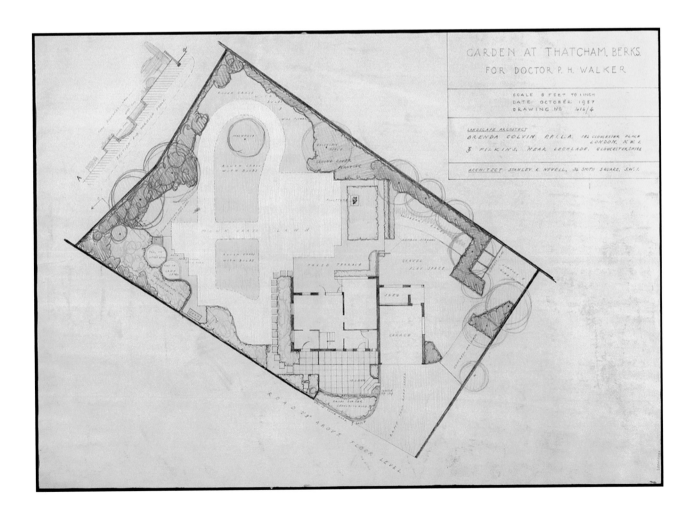

Colvin brought this very practical approach to the smaller gardens she worked on too. In October 1957, for example, she designed a garden for a new house owned by a Dr P.H. Walker at Thatcham in Berkshire.[41] This was on a much smaller domestic scale than Okeover and yet successfully managed to contain, on different levels, a great variety of elements, including rough grass with bulbs, a mown lawn, a gravel play space (backed with raspberry canes), a paved terrace, sculpture, pools and a paved platform for plants, as well as fitting in all the practical necessities – a compost heap, bonfire and rubbish heap – in a separate 'room' compartmented off from the rest of the garden. Jeremy Dodd's review of the design shown at the Chelsea Flower Show in 1958 and of a garden at Weybridge by Miss Marion Paynter commented that 'both showed a lack of unity between front and back "style" ', and yet it is a modern garden that sits well with the house and offers a good outdoor family space.[42] Additionally it would not have required high levels of maintenance and, increasingly throughout Colvin's career, that consideration had become a key factor. Writing about her own garden she said that her aim was 'eventually to make a labour-saving garden, its progress in that direction may be of interest to others who, like myself, have more enthusiasm than time at their disposal' – she was keenly aware of the requirements of her gardening clients. When, in 1962, she wrote her landscape report for the Church Commissioners on the newly built See House on the site of the former Bishop's Palace at Cuddesdon, Oxford, she acknowledged that the four-acre site was 'large for maintenance by one man'.[43] She therefore proposed a layout 'of the utmost simplicity, aiming at reduction of labour by logical grouping and convenient access to all parts, by avoidance of grass edges, clipped hedges and all elaboration, and by insisting on the need for levels suitably adjusted for mechanical mowing and other equipment.'[44]

In general, then, Colvin's style was simple, unfussy. She created uncomplicated broad effects and her gardens were uncluttered and elegant. This was certainly true of the tiny courtyard garden she designed for the office she shared with Sylvia Crowe at 182 Gloucester Place in London.[45] In their *New Small Garden*, Allen and Jellicoe described it as 'a garden to be looked at rather than sat in, but…just big enough to give its owners a feeling of contact with the soil and growing things'.[46] In this almost sunless spot, Colvin whitened the walls to get as much reflected light as possible and chose plants that would all grow well in shade. A set of three Italian oil jars were a chance find in a neighbourhood ironmongery shop and, to keep them off the floor which was in fact the roof of the basement below, a number of brackets at different heights were fixed to the wall.[47] The overall effect is very attractive and must have been a source of great pleasure for those working in the office.

In her own homes Colvin was freer to experiment and less bound by considerations of maintenance for her clients. After the war she moved to a house near Rickmansworth.[48] The house itself was not large but had a spinney and a dell behind it, a close contact with nature that she appreciated. Her nieces used to go and

LEFT ABOVE A simple modern layout complements this modern house at Thatcham in Berkshire.
LEFT BELOW The 1957 plan for the garden in Thatcham.
RIGHT The 'office yard' as Colvin termed it at 182 Gloucester Place.

plants and gardening. She was always a keen gardener – when her parents wanted to know what she would like for her twenty-first birthday she asked for a 'butt-load of manure'[50] – and in her later years would garden in the afternoons after a morning working in the office. Her garden was also a small personal haven at a time when professionally she was occupied with the design of such huge sites as the Gale Common ash disposal site. Against what might be expected of a landscape architect's garden, she confessed that the layout rather than having any 'special design interest' was 'determined almost wholly by existing buildings and walls in relation to the shape of the ground. My part in its evolution is concerned chiefly with the planting.' It is a small garden, no more than half an acre, but has an interesting shape because part of it had been a farmyard with separate divisions of space, enclosed by stone walls. Neighbouring buildings and walls add interesting variety of height and offered Colvin welcome 'odd corners and niches' for wall climbers and shrubs. By removing a footpath flanked by narrow borders and a hedge that had previously divided the garden in two, she opened up sightlines and increased the sense of space and movement within it. An existing tree – a large horse chestnut – is the centrepiece around which the rest of the main garden flows, the planted areas forming what she described as a 'sweeping S-curve' dividing them from the lawn and rough grass. The longest axis of the garden runs from northwest to southeast and Colvin enjoyed the way that between these points 'the open space widens out and is constricted alternately in accord with existing features'. Because of this effect of 'tension and release – a significant attribute of all design', she gave particularly careful thought to the shape and character of the curving line. As a result the different areas of the garden flow effortlessly into each other.

stay with her there and loved the house although their father – Colvin's brother – was rather scathing about it. Then in 1954 Colvin bought Little Peacocks, a classic Cotswold village house at Filkins near Lechlade, initially as a weekend retreat but with an eye to retirement – she was 57 at the time. A few years later, no doubt persuaded by her neighbour John Cripps, the magazine's editor, she wrote an article about her 'Small Cotswold Garden' for *The Countryman*.[49] She was hesitant about doing this because she did not really consider it 'ripe' enough and because she had not been able to 'spend time or money as lavishly as I would wish to make it as I want it to be'.

Here in her own garden she was free of constraints and concerns about maintenance – although she hoped that with time it could become a 'labour-saving garden' – and she could experiment and indulge her love of

LEFT The Spinney, named after the area of woodland behind it, Colvin's house in Rickmansworth.
RIGHT A plan of the garden at Little Peacocks with its central 'sweeping S-curve', showing (bottom right) the office that was built in 1965.

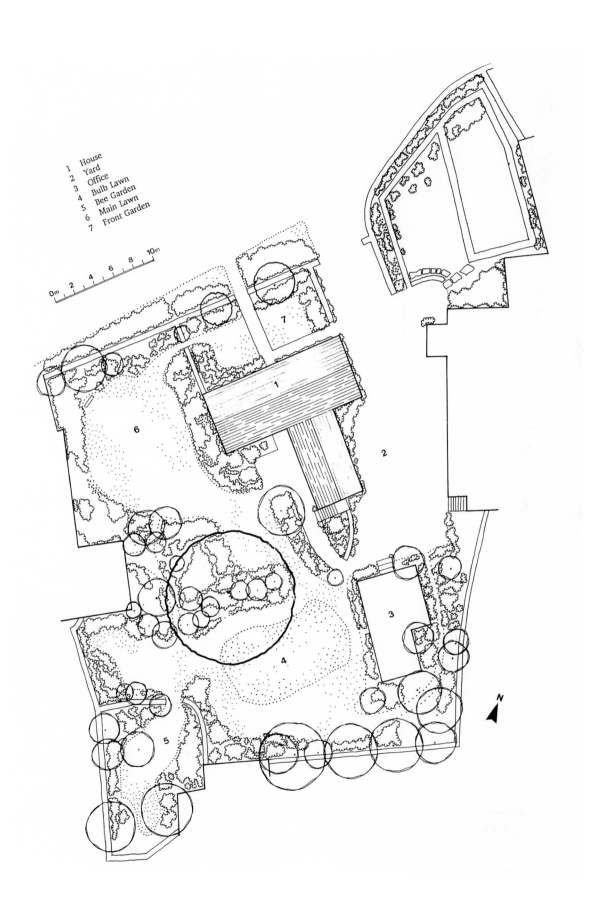

1 House
2 Yard
3 Office
4 Bulb Lawn
5 Bee Garden
6 Main Lawn
7 Front Garden

0m 2 4 6 8 10m

LEFT The west corner of Little Peacocks garden in June 1969, lit by morning sun, showing rich colour foliage (purple *Cotinus, Rosa glauca, Prunus spinosa purpurea, Pyrus eleagnifolia, Salvia officinalis pupurescens*) with mauve and white highlights of *Allium christophii, Iris 'White City', Rosa* 'Blanc Double de Coubert', *Verbascum bombyciferum* – and the daisies in the lawn enjoyed before mowing.

One of the most striking areas of planting was in the northwest corner, a colour scheme reminiscent of the shrub border she had designed at Boldre Hill in the late 1920s. Here a white painted Regency design seat was set back from the curve of the lawn against a range of dark-foliaged shrubs and climbers, including a purple vine, *Clematis montana rubens*, a purple form of blackthorn, purple sumach, *Cotinus coggygria* 'Royal Purple' and *Rosa glauca* (formerly known as *R. rubrifolia*), edged with purple sage and bergenia. In between the roses and sage, the season of flower colour was extended by irises, bulbs – black parrot tulips, 'deep crimson to blush-pink and white lilies'. But, best of all, *Lilium regale* was 'generously planted where its pink buds are seen with the rose at that wonderful moment when the expanding foliage gives a haze of bluish grey-green so inadequately described as *rubrifolia*'. As a vital counterpoint to the smokey purples, Colvin used a number of grey plants. They included the unusual silver-leafed *Pyrus elaeagnifolia* which was to become quite a feature, as well as *Elaeagnus commutata*, and the foliage of the iris. Seasonal white highlights –

sweet rocket, *Iris* 'White City' and the lilies – were also an important part of the mix. In his chapter on 'Colour, Its Values and Uses in the Garden' in his *Art of Planting*, Colvin's 'careful blending of all sorts of purplish and grey tones' was praised by Graham Stuart Thomas.[51] It was an extremely elegant combination.

The garden had some very practical elements too. One of two smaller walled 'rooms' in the southwest corner was devoted to bees. Colvin had two hives but was not especially expert at handling them and called on an old Swanley friend and former assistant – Miss Bindley, a clergyman's daughter who lived in Somerset – for help. Bindle, as she was known, used to visit once or twice a

RIGHT Colvin (left) and landscape architect Mary Mitchell seated on the southwest terrace by the kitchen door in 1964; partners' lunch was held here on summer days.

year to look after the bees. Next to the Bee Garden was a compartment devoted to rubbish and compost. Colvin removed an old 'leggy and unsightly' macrocarpa hedge that had screened this area and planted new evergreens as specimens in strategic positions. On the compost heap she used to grow marrows and ornamental gourds. She deemed two apple trees in the southeast corner 'too good to sacrifice' even though they were too flimsy for an area that she felt needed a fairly large evergreen group. As a compromise, she planted box and other evergreens under them to provide the dark background she wanted. There were more apple trees on the east boundary and these too were retained. Across the entrance drive from the house was another walled area that became dedicated to fruit and vegetables – a garden that provided asparagus for the partners' lunches she shared with Hal Moggridge. Close to the L-shaped house, a paved area in an angle facing southwest, partly shaded by an old Blenheim apple tree, was planned for 'rare lazy intervals and for outdoor meals'. The kitchen door opened on to this sitting area and nearby was a border of 'pot herbs'. A keen cook, Colvin found it 'essential to have these close at hand when cooking' and this terrace became a favourite spot.

One area that has flourished in the intervening years is the bulb lawn that was created over the hardcore of the old farmyard where there was very little topsoil. Over the years all the plants in this have seeded themselves and spread enormously. Starting almost on New Year's Day the first snowdrops start to flower with *Cyclamen coum*, and the display continues with *Anemone blanda*, *A. apennina* and wild daffodils, *Narcissus pseudonarcissus*, a small handful of which Colvin pocketed when they were stripping topsoil from the Gale Common scheme in Yorkshire. She had a hearty dislike of what she used to refer to as 'yellow telephones' – the large-flowered hybrid daffodils such as 'King Alfred'. The bulb lawn's first season ends with cowslips, fritillaries and meadow saxifrage and then it becomes a miniature hayfield where everything is allowed to seed for about a month before being cut down. Later in summer, the colchicums and cyclamen begin to appear and the lawn has a final trim in late autumn.[52]

TOP The bulb lawn, here in 1993, goes from strength to strength.
ABOVE Colchicums come into flower under the horse chestnut in autumn.

The garden in spring seen from the office in 1989.
Characteristic planting in spring with tulips and daffodils in flower but contrasting foliage to provide interest through the year.

Little Peacocks was the second of Colvin's designs to appear in Geoffrey and Susan Jellicoe's book of *Modern Private Gardens,* in which they selected a number of gardens that they felt met the changed 'spiritual need for gardens' of the modern world.[53] Her own description from this of her aims and to what extent she felt she had succeeded is so clear and succinct that it is worth repeating here:

> The planting is intended to give continuous calm enjoyment at all seasons, rather than dazzle the eye in the height of summer. The ground is well covered with low plants chosen for beauty of foliage: many are evergreen and there are masses of spring bulbs. In and over the ground-cover plants are many flowering shrubs, roses, viburnums, hydrangeas, tree paeonies, etc., to provide flower all through the year....
>
> I have tried to get a feeling of quiet space in this small area, enclosed as it is by grey stone walls and farm buildings. I try, too, to engender a sense of anticipation and interest by the progression from one interesting plant group to the next in a rhythm, giving definite contrasts without loss of unity. But it is difficult to reconcile simplicity with one's enthusiasm for plants in so small a garden, and I probably let the plants jostle one another too much.[54]

Although she emphasised the importance of foliage contrasts in colour, form and texture, she still felt that if this 'permanent sculptural basis' was satisfactory, then the flowers, when they appeared, would be that much more effective. It was the combinations that were important. She liked her garden to be orderly rather than manicured and enjoyed the daisies when they appeared on the main lawn (see also pp.92 and 95). Hers was a style of planting well suited to most owner-gardeners.

Following an illness, Colvin spent long weekends at Little Peacocks, working from there for part of the week. Finally, in 1965, she decided to close up in London and bring her practice down to Filkins. Against the east boundary wall she built a new 'temporary' building to house her two or three staff and finish off the jobs she

had on her books. It was beside this building that a few years later she discovered a rose seedling that Graham Stuart Thomas considered was probably a hybrid of a 'Kiftsgate' rose in the garden and an 'American Pillar' rambler next door. A vigorous rambler with wonderful semi-double blush pink flowers, it was named after its discoverer, *Rosa* 'Brenda Colvin'.[55] As it turned out, however, rather than reducing, Colvin's practice expanded and she took on Hal Moggridge as her partner in 1969. That temporary building is still in the garden, the firm is still based at Little Peacocks and the garden is still lovingly maintained very much in her spirit by people who knew and worked with her – Stephanie and Chris Carter. It is an atmospheric place in which Colvin's powerful character still seems present. Hal Moggridge has described the garden and her determined way of achieving the look she wanted:

> [It is] a subtle blend of many different plants held together by a strong overall composition; at every time of year the rich textures of foliage are lightened by many flowers always in perfect colour relationship to one another. To obtain this balance of form and colour individual plants have always been treated with determination; a flower of slightly the wrong shade would be dug up with ferocity, a shrub which showed signs of growing too large cut back as if it were behaving with deliberate offensiveness.[56]

The garden at Little Peacocks was very much Colvin's own personal garden – her laboratory for trialling plants that she might use in other contexts and a place where she could grow her own favourite plants in her own particular way. In a sense it was her work at Sutton Courtenay that epitomised her garden design philosophy more clearly. Expanding on her pre-war work, it featured 'outdoor rooms' close to the house and, in progression, further from the house, an increasingly

naturalistic approach to planting and design with, throughout, an emphasis on ease of maintenance. As she argued in her 1952 article on 'Gardens to Enjoy', a garden can be thought of as 'an extension of the house...[it] is a place to live in and should be designed primarily for that purpose, and be given all the shelter and seclusion and resting places needed. But it is also a place which provides endless variety and change as the year goes round, with rich contentment for the eye at every stage.'[57] Colvin's innovative and clear-sighted ideas have since been expressed by all of the celebrated garden designers of today.

The legacy

'And so Brenda Colvin's own time ran out and her formidable creative energy is stilled. But not her ideas for they have become the commonplaces of tomorrow.'

HAL MOGGRIDGE, 1981[1]

THE CENTRAL CONTRADICTION in Colvin's character – a retiring nature masked by and compensated for by apparent abruptness and occasional outbursts – is perhaps key to understanding the discrepancy in the way her influence has been underestimated by many compared with that credited to Sylvia Crowe and Geoffrey Jellicoe. For some thirty years the three of them formed what Hal Moggridge has termed 'a kind of landscape triumvirate'.[2] Their composite influence on the field of landscape architecture in twentieth-century Britain was widespread and certainly the contribution of all three was generously acknowledged by more careful commentators. Together they 'raised the consciousness of the profession by moving out from the garden and country estates to engage in social and political issues....They operated within crucial decision-making forums influencing landscape structures and strategies.'[3] Yet the majority of critical assessments of the development of twentieth-century landscape design do Colvin a great disservice by giving Crowe and Jellicoe considerably greater credit, perhaps in part because, unlike them, Colvin was no self-publicist. Her two contemporaries are, however, more generous in their estimates of her contribution. For Jellicoe, 'Perhaps, above all, her place in history is assured for her unstinted efforts to help create an independent landscape profession in a country previously dominated by gifted laymen'.[4] In 1956 Crowe wrote: 'I gratefully acknowledge my debt to all who have contributed to the present school of thought on landscape, and in particular to Brenda Colvin...and to G.A.Jellicoe';[5] she recognised that Colvin was 'a marvellous leader...her influence can't be overestimated. She had both vision and steadfastness of purpose.'[6]

When one takes stock of Colvin's legacy the word 'steadfast' is most apposite. Steadfast she certainly was in her long-term dedication to the cause of the wider landscape. In addition to her committed work in setting up and successfully establishing the Institute of Landscape Architects and the International Federation of Landscape Architects, she supported many individuals working in the field. Before landscape schools were established she took in students; later she employed newly qualified graduates and gave them practical experience. And she personified that move forward for women to become fully accepted professionals. Her election as the first woman president of a design or planning profession in particular led the way to women's greater involvement in those professions.

Despite her apparently formidable appearance, and a meticulous, almost perfectionist approach to her work, at heart she was an immensely likeable, enthusiastic and generous person with a wonderfully dry sense of humour. Consequently she had a profound influence on all those who worked with or for her. Peter Youngman called her 'a person of great integrity and selflessness, devoted to the cause of fine landscape that she believed in so strongly.'[7] She put her principles into practice in her work; she was an activist, according to Michael Laurie, 'at a time when the profession needed more than orators and gurus'.[8]

And she had vision. She led the new thinking about the involvement of landscape architects in the early stages of planning. Through her books, articles and lectures, her ideas impressed new generations of architects and planners. Many, Crowe included, were 'indebted to Brenda's ideas and writings (which helped us all to understand better our role as landscape architects rather than garden designers).'[9] She was an early conservationist, drawing attention to the fact that until we understood more about the ultimate effect of technological advances on soil fertility or on human health we should err on the side of conservation: 'The landscape humanity creates will reflect the condition of human ecology: only in landscapes reflecting healthy balance can human life remain worth living.'[10] She had great sensitivity to the way people lived and an acute awareness of their needs, whether it was shelter from wind or pleasant walkways and safer roads. She never stopped considering the issues, 'sparking away, throwing off ideas'.[11] Not long before she died she was speculating on where the first real crunch as a result of world population growth would fall and suggested it could be over water. She may not have forecast global warming but – given current predictions that climate change will lead to a wave of millions of 'environmental migrants', the destabilisation of areas vital to global security, the radicalisation of politics, north–south conflict, famines, and wars over water, energy, and other natural resources – her suggestion seems remarkably prescient.

Colvin's influence on garden design is perhaps more subtle – although she wrote many articles, she never wrote a book on the subject. It is undeniable, however, that her style of planting was always at the leading edge of current developments and became – and, more impressively perhaps, remains – both popular and practical. She herself, of course, would have said that she did not have a style but, with her clean uncomplicated designs, what she created were stylish gardens of great energy, easy to keep and revealing great sensitivity and profound knowledge in the handling of the plants used. The sculptural plants and contrasting foliage that she emphasised have indeed become the 'commonplaces' of today.

Her belief in continuity and long timescales led her to perpetuate her practice. It was on this basis that she invited Hal Moggridge into partnership in 1969 and then retained Chris Carter as a staff member in 1972, a partner-in-waiting. As a consequence they were able to continue working on several long-term projects and to go on promoting her ideas. Neither Sylvia Crowe nor Geoffrey Jellicoe succeeded in perpetuating their practices. She was generous with her staff too. One year, when the firm did not make much money, she handed the whole amount to Moggridge; when the Carters were unable to find a house to live in, she offered them – at a very preferential price – a barn in a nearby village that she had been converting to use as staff digs; she shared her home with the students who came to work for her, cooking them meals in the evening. Her staff were very much a part of her life – on a Friday afternoon, they would be invited in for a sherry.

The weekend was ahead and she was going to miss their company. Given her tempers, it could be an explosive place to work but it was nevertheless a good place to be, frequently with interesting discussions on much wider issues than just the job in hand.

Throughout her career, right from her determined and defiant stand against authority as a young student at Swanley, Brenda Colvin revealed herself to be a compelling, powerful and decisive woman, and her character was to define and indeed limit recognition of her legacy. In the course of her life she witnessed enormous changes in the nature of her work, in society as a whole and in the world around her. When she embarked on her profession in 1922 it was a rare thing for a woman to go out and start her own business. Most women at that time were expected to stay at home and pursue domestic interests rather than seek paid employment. Women were not even granted the right to vote on the same terms as men until 1928. On the surface garden design might have seemed a relatively gentle occupation but, given that she was not a naturally outgoing person, Colvin needed to develop an assertive, feisty attitude if she was to be successful with her own practice, getting gardens built and dealing with gardeners and contractors. She certainly achieved that. Candid and courageous, she was never afraid to express her views, to take a stand against authority and to speak out for what she believed in, however unpopular that might be. On occasions she could be fierce. And yet at the same time, all her life, there was a shyness there, and a talent for self-effacement that belied her impressive achievements and her abilities.

Even with her family she was never easy and compliant, but always utterly and completely honest. On her first visit to her niece Hilary who had just moved into a fairly grand house in Belfast, she went straight to look at the garden. Her comment? 'What a dull layout.' This was typical – as was her family's reaction to this sort of behaviour: they did not take offence and she was always held in great affection by them. It was rumoured in the family that she had had a romantic attachment that was brought to an end by the First World War but, as one of the generation of young women for whom there was a lack of 'marriageable' young men, she was destined to remain single.[12] That was a cause of deep regret to her. On one occasion one of her staff had nervously announced that she would have to resign because she was expecting her first child. Colvin ticked her off, calling her a 'naughty' girl, and her assistant James Riley who had overheard the conversation felt obliged to raise what he considered her inappropriate reaction with her. Colvin's response was the heartfelt confession that there had been a time when she would have done almost anything to have a child.[13] And Cass Moggridge recalls her saying how her thirties had been the hardest time in her life because it was so difficult being single and knowing that she would never have children.[14]

She was a strikingly good-looking woman – tall, willowy and elegant. On occasion she would show her height to advantage by dressing up in sweeping Indian clothes and John Brookes remembers in the Gloucester Place office sneaking looks at 'saucy' photographs of her on holiday in Europe in the 1930s diving into water with nothing on. Having travelled alone to the United States and fairly extensively in Europe, she was a worldly woman and adventurous, and her travels alone and with the International Federation of Landscape Architects contributed to her awareness and appreciation of landscape. In her personal life she was a rather solitary person, happy with her own company. Although she had a number of good friends, mostly people involved with the profession, she was never deeply social. Even with Sylvia Crowe who shared an office with her for so many years and who had accompanied her on caravan trips, there was always a sense of reserve. But this reserved manner concealed a generous, kind person who was much liked and respected by all who knew her.

Colvin never really recovered from the shingles she had in 1975. As her condition deteriorated and her sight faded, she expressed a wish to stay at Little Peacocks and all those around her worked hard to make that possible. Her secretary Mac took charge and Cass Moggridge organised a rota of locals and friends who willingly came to read and talk to her. Colvin had enjoyed being involved in village life in Filkins. She had attended church there and did the church flowers occasionally, more to be sociable and join in with the community than out of any deeply held beliefs. She was an open-minded woman and so was very interested in James Lovelock's *Gaia* when it was published in 1979. His theory of earth functioning as if it were a living organism was very much in tune with her own thinking. But all in all, she was not a particularly religious person.

On the day she died, 27 January 1981, Cass remembers going in to see Colvin who sat up in bed, saying 'I want porridge and brown sugar for breakfast'. She passed away while the porridge was being prepared. She was buried in the cemetery at Filkins and a memorial service was held at St James's Piccadilly on 17 March with the church being decorated with flowers brought up from her garden at Little Peacocks.[15]

A few years before, Colvin had found herself 'driven' to express her own beliefs about the purpose of life in a privately published collection of poems and prose under the title *Wonder in a World* (1977). It is a very personal work, an 'Agnostic's Progress', that reveals her joy in life: 'Well may we count our blessings and be grateful for the conditions on this planet so amazingly adapted to the evolution of the creative spirit of man.'[16] If the landscape profession may be considered to have had a positive effect on our surroundings in the past 60 years, we should perhaps count our blessings and be grateful for the pioneering contribution of Brenda Colvin. The time is long overdue for her influence and inspiration to be given the recognition they deserve. I hope in some small way to have achieved a little of that in this book.

Notes

PROLOGUE, pp.8-11

1. Letter to 'Junior Staff' from Dr John Groundes-Pearce, 7 March 1973. I am grateful to Pat Grover for this letter from her archive and for information about the office party that she was largely responsible for organising. She, Chris Carter, James Riley and Jennie Heming were the 'junior staff' who sent out the invitations. Replies went to Pat Grover at the cottage she rented in nearby Shilton.
2. Text by Brenda Colvin, dated 9 February 1973, displayed at the office party held at Little Peacocks, Filkins, on 2 March 1973, saved in a folder by Pat Grover.

BEGINNINGS, pp.12-21

1. Brenda Colvin quoted in Sheila Harvey (ed.), *Reflections on Landscape: the Lives and Work of Six British Landscape Architects* (Aldershot, 1987), p.139.
2. Ibid.
3. Interview with Julia Joynt, daughter of Colvin's brother Hugh, 23 September 2003.
4. Brenda Colvin quoted in Tony Aldous with Brian Clouston, *Landscape by Design* (London, 1979), p.121.
5. Colvin's father Elliot Graham Colvin (1861–1940) married Ethel Augusta Colvin (1867–1944), a cousin and eldest daughter of Sir Steuart Colvin Bayley, K.C.S.I., at St Paul's Calcutta, on 6 December 1888.
6. This is the year that Elliot Colvin gives for his appointment in his draft memoir, British Library Mss Eur E359/13, but 1902 is the date given in *Who's Who*.
7. The Indian Civil Service (ICS) originated as the elite civil service of the Indian Government under British colonial rule in India. It had succeeded the Honourable East India Company's service when the Crown took over India in 1858 and was responsible, under the Viceroy, for the civil administration of India from that year until August 1947 when India and Pakistan became independent. Elliot Colvin entered the service in 1882 and, in a fairly typical career path, rose through the ranks: Assistant Magistrate, Bengal, 1883; Assistant Political Department, 1884; Political Assistant, Rajputana, 1885; Private Secretary to Lieutenant-Governor of Bengal, 1887; First Assistant Agent to the Governor-General in Baluchistan, 1889; Settlement Officer, Saran and Champaran, 1891; Magistrate and Collector, Champaran, 1895; Settlement Commissioner, Alwar and Bharatpur, 1896; Political Agent, Eastern Rajputana States, 1897; Revenue and Judicial Commissioner, Baluchistan, 1897; General Superintendent, Thagi and Dakaiti, 1901; Resident in Kashmir, 1903 [or 1902 – see Note 6]; Agent to the Governor-General in Rajputana, and Chief Commissioner, Ajmer-Merwara, 1905–17. He retired from the service in 1918.
8. Interview with Peter Youngman, 26 June 2003.
9. Harvey (ed.), *Reflections*, p.139.
10. Brenda Colvin, 'Planting Design', *Journal of the Institute of Landscape Architects* (March 1951), p.3.
11. As described in J.B. Colvin's 'Green Book' (Withypool, 1970) containing Colvin family trees and biographical notes, compiled by James Bazett Colvin, British Library Mss Eur Photo Eur 145.
12. Much of the information about Sir Elliot Colvin's career and movements comes from his own draft memoir, British Library Mss Eur E359/13.
13. I am very grateful to Esmé Hodge of the Hextable Heritage Centre for sharing her extensive knowledge of Swanley Horticultural College's history, and to Liz Davies of Swanley Town Council for allowing me to use the archive photographs.
14. In April 1889 Arthur Harper Bond bought Hextable House and 43 acres of land for £5,500. He was a founder member of The Horticultural College and Produce Co. By the end of the year he had 13 male students paying fees of £80 per annum, but this was not enough to keep the company afloat so Bond applied for help to Kent County Council. He was granted an award for 20 scholarships of £60, but there was some disquiet at public money being given to a college run for profit so the Horticultural College was licensed by the Board of Trade as a non-profit making company in 1891.
15. In 1898 Daisy Greville, Countess of Warwick, founded Warwick Hostel in Reading to offer training to 'surplus women in the lighter branches of agriculture'. This expanded and moved to Studley Castle in Warwickshire in 1903, becoming Studley Horticultural & Agricultural College for Women. Frances Wolseley founded her College for Lady Gardeners at Glynde c.1902. There were also horticultural courses for women at Reading University, at the Royal Botanic Society in Regent's Park, and at the Botanic Gardens in Edinburgh and Glasnevin. Beatrix Havergal, who had studied at the Thatcham Fruit and Flower Farm School near Newbury, established her school of horticulture for young ladies at Waterperry House near Oxford in 1932.
16. Letter of 1900 quoted in Kay N. Sanecki, 'The Ladies and the Gentlemen', *Hortus* No. 32 (Winter 1994), p.64.
17. I am grateful to Joyce Bellamy for background information on the Metropolitan Public Gardens Association. Fanny Wilkinson, who had been principal at Swanley from 1902 until her resignation in June 1916, had also worked for the Association as landscape gardener and no doubt Agar was taken on as her successor on Miss Wilkinson's recommendation.
18. Handwritten note in Agar's membership file at the Landscape Institute.
19. *The Horticultural College Magazine*, May 1919.
20. Brenda Colvin, 'Beginnings', *Landscape Design*, February 1979, p.8.
21. Dr Kate Barratt became principal of the college in 1922, exactly 20 years after she had become a student there. She remained until 1939.
22. *The Horticultural College Magazine*, May 1920.
23. Ibid.
24. Colvin, 'Beginnings'. As Colvin left Swanley mid-course she does not seem to have been eligible for any diploma or qualification.

25. Interviews with Anthony du Gard Pasley, 13 November 2002, and John Brookes, 18 April 2002.

26. Brenda Colvin, *Land and Landscape* (London, 1970), p.93.

27. Colvin, 'Beginnings'.

28. Colvin, quoted in Aldous with Clouston, *Landscape by Design*, p.121.

29. Damage had been caused by military activity during the period from 1915 until 1920. The military camp situated at the southern end of Wimbledon Common was a transit camp, with a substantial battle course to prepare the soldiers for the trench warfare on the western front. The camp was finally dismantled in 1922.

30. The Treaty of Neuilly-sur-Seine was signed on 27 November 1919. The treaty established borders over contested territory between Bulgaria, Turkey, Greece and Yugoslavia. As one of the Central Powers in the First World War, belligerent Bulgaria received the least land, and was required to reduce its army to 20,000 men, pay reparations exceeding $400 million, and recognise the existence of Yugoslavia.

A GOOD CONNECTION, pp.22-31

1. Brenda Colvin, letter dated 1 July 1930 to the Institute of Landscape Architects re a proposed scale of professional charges.

2. William Buckley Gladstone was the son of Murray Gladstone and Alicia Sidney Bayley who was Colvin's mother's younger sister. He was born in Calcutta in 1890.

3. I am very grateful to Lady Redman and her daughter Felicity and son Jeremy for showing me round the garden at Stair House and for permission to use their collection of old postcards of the house and garden.

4. Brenda Colvin, 'Beginnings', *Landscape Design*, February 1979, p.8.

5. 19 Evelyn Gardens, 258 King's Road and 25 Cheyne Row.

6. Interview with James Riley, 19 May 2003. Lady Heseltine is not aware of Colvin's connection with the garden at Thenford House.

7. William MacGowan, known as 'Mac', was Colvin's secretary after she had moved her office to her home in the Cotswolds.

8. Together with a few prints that were used in displays at the Chelsea Flower Show and some folders of negatives, two small albums of selected contact prints covering the years 1934–54 survived, along with most of the rolls of 35mm negatives from which they were taken, at the offices of Colvin & Moggridge in Filkins.

9. Seven guineas is approximately equivalent to £330 today.

10. Colvin, letter dated 1 July 1930 to the Institute of Landscape Architects.

11. According to the Chelsea catalogues, she was there in 1926, 1927, 1928, 1930 and each year from 1935 to 1939.

12. I am grateful to Ian Todd and the Surrey Vintage Vehicle Society for helping me identify this car and the one that appears on p.123.

13. MS of Colvin's draft for a book she was writing on garden design in 1974, titled either 'The Garden for 4 Seasons' or 'The Constant Garden v. the Instant'

14. Ibid.

15. Although there is no record of the commission in the school's archives, I am grateful to Michael Bevington of Stowe School for this information. My thanks also to Barry Smith of the National Trust at Stowe and Mick Thompson of Buckinghamshire Gardens Trust who kindly responded to my enquiries but were unable to find any reference to Colvin's involvement at Stowe.

16. Wycombe Abbey School has no record of this commission in its archives.

A SELF-SOWN SEEDLING, pp.32-9

1. Brenda Colvin, 'Beginnings', *Landscape Design*, February 1979, p.8.

2. *The Gardeners' Chronicle*, 9 February 1929, p.91. Fifty years later, in an article written for the Landscape Institute's Golden Jubilee in 1979 ('Beginnings', *Landscape Design*, February 1979, p.8), Colvin wrote that an advertisement for the Chelsea meeting had appeared in the Royal Horticultural Society's journal, but it seems that her recollection of events was not quite accurate. The only advertisement or notice I have been able to find is the one that appeared in the *Gardeners' Chronicle*. I am grateful to Christopher Ashill at the RHS Lindley Library for helping me to research this.

3. Postcard and letter in Brenda Colvin's membership file at the Landscape Institute.

4. Brenda Colvin quoted in Tony Aldous with Brian Clouston, *Landscape by Design* (London, 1979), p.120.

5. Ibid.

6. Ibid.

7. In July 1929 Colvin wrote with apologies that she could not attend the meeting of 'B.A.G.A'; by October she referred in a letter to the 'British Institute of Landscape Gardeners' (Landscape Institute, Brenda Colvin's membership file). The final decision to use the name 'Institute of Landscape Architects' was taken at a meeting on 28 January 1930 but backdated to 11 December 1929 when Thomas Mawson was elected president.

8. Colvin quoted in Aldous with Clouston, *Landscape by Design*, p.120.

9. Edward Milner's son Henry joined his father's practice in the 1870s. The firm was taken over by Henry's son-in-law Edward White and, known as Milner White, survived until the retirement of Frank Marshall in 1995, at which time it was the oldest garden design and landscape architecture practice in the British Isles, an honour now held by Colvin & Moggridge.

10. Colvin, 'Beginnings'.

11. Sheila Harvey (ed.), *Reflections on Landscape: the Lives and Work of Six British Landscape Architects* (Aldershot, 1987), p.6.

12. Colvin, 'Beginnings'.

13. A letter in Colvin's membership file at the Landscape Institute shows that she asked for membership details to be sent to Agar in 1929.

14. Colvin, 'Beginnings'.

15. Colvin quoted in Aldous with Clouston, *Landscape by Design*, p.122.

16. Ibid.

17. Colvin, 'Beginnings'.

18. Brenda Colvin, *Land and Landscape* (London, 1970), p.96.

19. Colvin's paper, given at the Old Students' Guild's conference on 28 November 1931, is reproduced in *The Horticultural College Magazine*, No 69, May 1932, pp.4-8. In the spring 1935 issue of *Landscape and Garden*, Colvin reported on a lecture given by R.H. Mattocks at the ILA on the place of the park in the town plan. In it he also referred to the Westchester example and how it proved that generous provision

of open space properly planned was of economic value: the rateable value of the land increased and concessions granted to restaurants, amusement parks, etc. more than paid for the upkeep of the open spaces.

20. Aldous with Clouston, *Landscape by Design*, p.122.

21. Brenda Colvin, letter of 15 June 1931 to Mr Hart (Landscape Institute membership file).

22. Aldous with Clouston, *Landscape by Design*, p.122.

23. Ibid.

24. Colvin, 'Beginnings'.

25. Trevor Rowley, *The English Landscape in the Twentieth Century* (London, 2006), p.1.

26. H.V. Morton, *In Search of England* (London, 1927; 17th edn 1932), pp.5-6.

27. Clough Williams-Ellis, *England and the Octopus* (London, 1932), p.15.

28. In 1969 the name of the council was changed to The Council for the Protection of Rural England to reflect a change in approach to its activities. The council's name was changed again in 2003 to the Campaign to Protect Rural England, aiming to promote the beauty, tranquillity and diversity of rural England by encouraging the sustainable use of land and other natural resources in town and county.

29. Brenda Colvin, 'Quarterly Notes', *Landscape and Garden* (Spring 1934), p.60.

30. Brenda Colvin, 'Quarterly Notes, *Landscape and Garden* (Autumn 1934), p.45. Adams's speech was read by his son as Adams himself was unwell.

31. Hal Moggridge, 'Gardens and Landscapes 1930-2000', Conference Paper, Garden History Society and Twentieth Century Society, September 1998, quoted by David Lambert, 'Postwar Gardens and Landscapes in the UK: A provisional history for the post-war period', Draft 1 (22 March 2002).

32. Sheila Harvey and Stephen Rettig (eds), *Fifty Years of Landscape Design* (London, 1985), p.154.

A SMALL BUT SATISFYING LIVELIHOOD, pp.40-77

1. Brenda Colvin, 'Beginnings', *Landscape Design*, February 1979, p.8.

2. Ibid.

3. Brenda Colvin, 'Low Walls and Steps Give Variety – and Enchantment', *Good Gardening* (July 1936), pp.24-5.

4. Brenda Colvin, 'Pot Gardening', *Landscape and Garden* (Winter 1938), pp.214-15.

5. Ministry of Health, Misc. Reports 1941-9, 'Our Gardens' (Published for the Ministry of Health by HMSO, 1948). This 28-page booklet was published as a supplement to the Central Housing Advisory Committee Report on 'The Appearance of Housing Estates', issued in April 1948 by a sub-committee of the Central Housing Committee under the chairmanship of Lord Faringdon. It cost 1*s*.

6. Lady Allen of Hurtwood and Susan Jellicoe, *The Things We See 7: Gardens* (London, 1953); Susan Jellicoe and Marjory Allen, *Town Gardens to Live In* (London, 1977).

7. The house in Varengeville was called La Palette.

8. The Bonds are an old Dorset family and this commission was probably for Creech House or a house they owned in Corfe Castle.

9. In the notebook, the commission is noted for Mrs Swann although the name is spelt with one 'n' on the mount of photographs that were shown at the Chelsea Flower Show.

10. Percy Richard Morley Horder (1870–1944) was one of a group of early twentieth-century architects who were highly influential in re-introducing the romantic vernacular styles of the Elizabethan period. Many of his homes were in the style of Edwin Lutyens, having gables, stone dressings, mullioned windows and inglenooks.

11. Colvin also re-routed the drives at Acrise in Kent, her parents' house Gangbridge, her brother's house Oakley Hall in Essex, Okeover Hall in Derbyshire and almost certainly other gardens.

12. Brenda Colvin, 'Gardens to Enjoy' in *Gardens and Gardening Vol. 3: Hardy Plants, The Studio Gardens and Gardening* annual, eds F.A. Mercer and Roy Hay (London, 1952), p.9 and caption p.13.

13. I am very grateful to Julian and Harriet Cotterell, the owners of Steeple Manor, for inviting me to visit their garden, and for letting me see and publish these photographs.

14. Colvin, 'Gardens to Enjoy', p.10.

15. Brenda Colvin, 'In the New Forest', *Landscape and Garden* (Winter 1938), pp.202-4. The current owner of Boldre Hill, Mrs Anne Montague-Jones, who has been there since 1986, reports that the fields have been sold and the path is no longer there.

16. Brenda Colvin, 'Maze at West Stowell House', *Landscape and Garden* (Spring 1939), p.42.

17. Merlin Waterson, *Lady Berwick, Attingham and Italy* (n.d.), p.59.

18. Ibid.

19. Letter, Brenda Colvin to Lady Berwick, 19 June 1929. I am grateful to Sarah Kay of the National Trust for letting me see the correspondence between Colvin and Lady Berwick and the relevant extract from Merlin Waterson's book.

20. Graham Stuart Thomas, *Gardens of the National Trust* (London, 1976), p.99.

21. Colvin, 'Gardens to Enjoy', p.11 and caption p.14.

22. Brenda Colvin, 'Herbaceous Borders', *Landscape and Garden* (Autumn 1936), p.145.

23. I am grateful to Sacha Maxwell, Nora Kennedy's great-granddaughter, for the photographs of Sarn Hill.

24. I am grateful to Tim Mowl for alerting me to the existence of these plans and introducing me to Jane Carr who kindly allowed me to see and reproduce the plans for Conderton.

25. I am grateful to the owner, Deborah Richards, for replying to my enquiry about the current state of the garden. As the garden had been redesigned in 1996, there was little left of Colvin's design when I visited.

26. Brenda Colvin, 'A Hampshire Garden of about One Acre', *Landscape and Garden* (Winter 1935), p.142.

27. Elliot Colvin's draft memoir British Library Mss Eur E359/13.

28. Colvin, 'A Hampshire Garden', p.142.

29. Her mother died in May 1944.

30. I am very grateful to Jane and Jonathan Ruffer of what is now known as Ugley Hall (the village and house names have alternated between

Ugley and Oakley) who allowed me to visit their garden and study their copy of the planting plan. The clematis shown are: *C.* 'Comtesse de Bouchaud', *C. alpina*, *C.* 'Beauty of Worcester', *C. montana rubra* and *C.* 'Ascotiensis'. The roses on the planting plan, some of which are no longer available, were 'Madame Butterfly', 'Julien Pot[?]', 'Etoile de Hollande', 'Rose Marie', 'McGredy's Ivory', 'Lamia', 'Charles P. Kilham' down one side and 'Akol' [?], 'Shot Silk' with a note to change for yellow rose next year, 'Existing roses (excepting Shot Silk)', 'Mrs Henry Bowles', 'William F. Dreer', 'Lady Pirrie' and 'Angèle Pernet'.

31. Peter Beales, *Classic Roses* (London, 1997), p.420 and p.430

32. The house itself is now divided into two – the older, southern section is now called The Manor House, owned by Alan and Debbie Griffiths, and the other section to the north is now Savage's House, owned by Andrew Day, all of whom kindly replied to my enquiries.

33. Ron Sidwell, *West Midland Gardens* (Gloucester, 1981), p.226

34. I am very grateful to the Griffiths for allowing me to use their photograph of Colvin's original plan for Savage's House.

35. Nos. 41 (1923) and 187 (September 1931) in the gardens book, for Lady Margaret Shaw, daughter of Lord Inchcape. Colvin displayed her photograph of this woodland walk at the Chelsea Flower Show in 1953.

36. First published in March 1935, *Good Gardening* was edited by H.H. Thomas who had previously edited *Popular Gardening*.

37. Colvin's car's registration CYH is from a series of registrations issued by London County Council in June/July 1936. The car is a 1936 Series II Wolseley – a 12/48 Sliding Head Saloon. I am grateful to Ian Todd and the Surrey Vintage Vehicle Society for identifying the car model.

38. Colvin's MSS and photographs at Colvin & Moggridge.

39. Interview with Anthony du Gard Pasley, 13 November 2002. He commented, 'I've always thought there's something very symbolic about the idea of these two in 1939, as it were standing on the edge of a precipice, solemnly drawing things in the sand. I've always been very touched by that story.'

40. Interview with Anthony du Gard Pasley.

41. Interview with Robert and Molly Wheatley, 3 September 2003.

42. Colvin, 'Beginnings'.

43. Ibid.

44. In addition to the gardens mentioned in this chapter, there are photographs of Bramble Rough (No. 127), Upper House, Great Bowden (No. 157), Woolley Grange (No. 211), Mount Hall (No. 214), Conigre House (No. 223), Manor of Groves (No. 226), Drybrook (No. 230), Clovelly, Merrow (No. 239), Little Cliff, Rye (No. 240), Aston Somerville (No. 247), Burford House near Tenbury (No. 286) and a couple of other unidentified gardens.

45. Sidwell, *West Midland Gardens*, p.109.

46. Today there are three houses with this name in the Haywards Heath area.

47. Interview with John Brookes, 18 April 2002.

AN ENTHUSIASM FOR PLANTS, pp.78-95

1. Brenda Colvin quoted in Susan and Geoffrey Jellicoe, *Modern Private Gardens* (London, 1968), p.47.

2. Interview with Barbara Moth, 1 July 2003.

3. Brenda Colvin, 'Some Differences in French and English Garden Design', *Landscape and Garden* (Autumn 1937), pp.142-4.

4. Quoted by Peter Shepheard in Sheila Harvey (ed.), *Reflections on Landscape: the Lives and Work of Six British Landscape Architects* (Aldershot, 1987), p.69.

5. Brenda Colvin, *Land and Landscape* (London, 1970), p.89.

6. Harvey (ed.), *Reflections*, p.32.

7. Colvin, *Land and Landscape* (1970), pp.89-90.

8. Ibid., p.93.

9. Madeline Agar, *Garden Design in Theory and Practice* (London, 1913), pp.206-39

10. Brenda Colvin, 'Planting Design', *Journal of the Institute of Landscape Architects* (March 1951), p.3.

11. Brenda Colvin, 'Planting as a Medium of Design', *Journal of the Institute of Landscape Architects* (August 1961), p.8.

12. Ibid., p.3.

13. Colvin, 'Planting Design', p.3.

14. Ibid., p. 8.

15. Ibid., p. 4.

16. Cecil Stewart provided the drawing used on p.128 of the first edition, Richard Westmacott that on p.200 of the second edition.

17. Colvin, *Land and Landscape* (1970), p.201.

18. Brenda Colvin, 'Plant Form in Relation to Architecture', *Landscape and Garden* (Autumn, 1934), p.21.

19. Colvin, 'Planting Design', p.4.

20. Colvin, *Land and Landscape* (1970), p.88.

21. Colvin, 'Planting Design', p.4.

22. Ibid., p.7.

23. Harvey (ed.), *Reflections*, p.141.

24. John Brookes, 'Review of *The Modern Garden* by Jane Brown', *Gardens Illustrated* (March 2001), p.108.

25. Colvin, 'Planting as a Medium of Design', p.8. Impressive though it is, in the years since its introduction in 1893, giant hogweed has proved itself to be a dangerous plant (chemicals in its sap can cause 'photosensitivity') and invasive throughout the UK and it is now an offence to 'plant or otherwise cause [it] to grow' in the wild.

26. Colvin, 'Planting Design', p.8.

27. Harvey (ed.), *Reflections*, p.142.

28. Brenda Colvin, notes for 'Swanley Lectures on Garden Appreciation', dated 1940, among private papers at Colvin & Moggridge.

29. Brenda Colvin, 'How Really Delightful the Average Garden Can Be', *Good Gardening* (March 1936), p.9.

30. Brenda Colvin, 'Grey-Leaved Plants', *Landscape and Garden* (Summer 1934), p.44.

31. Colvin, notes for 'Swanley Lectures', dated 1940. A handwritten curriculum vitae, dated 20 June 1941, in Colvin's membership file at the Landscape Institute includes lecturing in Planting Design at Swanley and the Regent Street Polytechnic.

32. Colvin, 'Herbaceous Borders', *Landscape and Garden* (Autumn 1936), p.145.

33. Colvin, 'Plant Form', p.22.

34. Interview with Anthony du Gard Pasley, 13 November 2002.

35. Interview with Anthony du Gard Pasley.

36. Now *Brachyglottis greyi*.

37. Colvin, 'Planting Design', p.7.

38. Colvin, 'Planting as a Medium of Design', p.8.

39. Colvin, 'Plant Form', p.22.

40. Harvey (ed.), *Reflections*, p.141.

41. Brenda Colvin, 'New Ways of Filling a Garden', *Good Gardening* (April 1936), pp.9-10.

42. Brenda Colvin, 'Daydreams with a Purpose', *Good Gardening* (June 1936), p.14.

43. Quotes from Christopher Lloyd in BBC Two's tribute 'Gardener Provocateur', 8 pm, 22 December 2006.

44. Colvin, 'Herbaceous Borders', p.147.

45. Colvin, 'Pot Gardening', p.215.

46. Elizabeth B. Kassler, *Modern Gardens and the Landscape* (New York, 1964), p.13.

47. Brenda Colvin, 'Gardens to Enjoy' in *Gardens and Gardening Vol. 3, The Studio Gardens and Gardening* annual (London, 1952), pp.9-12.

48. Colvin, 'Planting as a Medium of Design', p.10.

49. Brenda Colvin, *Land and Landscape* (London, 1947), p.68. She reiterated the point in the second edition of the book (1970), p.119.

50. S. and G. Jellicoe, *Modern Private Gardens* (London, 1968), p.47.

51. Colvin, 'Grey-Leaved Plants', p.44.

52. Ibid., p.45.

53. Colvin, 'Planting as a Medium of Design', p.8.

54. *Observer*, 25 February 1962, p.33. As a member of the *Observer* gardening panel, Colvin contributed articles in 1962-4.

55. Geoffrey Jellicoe, 'Brenda Colvin', *Contemporary Architects*, ed. Muriel Emanuel (London, 1980), p.163.

TREES IN TOWN AND COUNTRY, pp.96-111

1. Brenda Colvin, 'Tree Planting' in A.E. Weddle (ed.), *Techniques of Landscape Architecture* (London, 1967), p.176.

2. No. 358 in Colvin's notebook.

3. Brenda Colvin, 'Tree Planting on Compton Beauchamp Estate, Wilts', *Journal of the Institute of Landscape Architects* (February 1959), pp.2-4.

4. *Independent*, 14 December 2001.

5. Brenda Colvin, *Trees for Town and Country: A Selection of Sixty Trees Suitable for General Cultivation in England* (London, 1947). The book was prepared for the Association for Planning and Regional Reconstruction during the war.

6. Interview with Chris Carter, 2 September 2003. He regrets that he was not there in person to see the architect's reaction. As a student Chris Carter worked at Colvin & Moggridge in his summer holidays for three years from 1965. He returned to the firm in 1972 becoming an associate fairly quickly and, following Colvin's death in 1981, he became a partner.

7. Richard Sudell, 'Trees and Men', *Journal of the Institute of Landscape Architects* (October 1947), p.3.

8. Chris Beetles, *S.R. Badmin and the English Landscape* (London 1985), p.27. In fact, Badmin was a little optimistic as, unfortunately, architects did not always see how trees would end up and, according to Chris Carter (letter 3 June 2008), the Letraset trees much used in the 1970s and 1980s (without proper acknowledgement to Badmin) would often appear in completely the wrong scale – a mature Lebanon cedar only 3 metres high, for example.

9. Mary Keen, 'Tree Time Treats', *Independent on Sunday*, 15 May 1992.

10. Colvin, *Trees*, p.5.

11. Brenda Colvin, 'Trees and Landscape Architecture', *Journal of the Institute of Landscape Architects* (October 1947), p.13.

12. Colvin, *Trees*, p.5.

13. Colvin, 'Trees and Landscape Architecture', p.13.

14. Brenda Colvin, 'Landscape Architecture in the New Towns. A Symposium: Part III', *Journal of the Institute of Landscape Architects* (July 1950), pp.6-10.

15. Ibid., p.7.

16. I am grateful to Sylvia Grace Borda, Research Associate, Emily Carr Institute, and lecturer at Queen's University Belfast, for sharing her knowledge of East Kilbride with me for this chapter and Chapter 8. In her photographic project, *EK Modernism*, with over 8,000 images, she chronicles the new town's original modernist layout and examines key architectural buildings within each of its district areas. She also produced a website, www.eknewtown.com. The work was completed as part of a public art commission through the East Kilbride Arts Centre, South Lanarkshire Council and the Millennium Commission, Urban Culture Programme, and the Lighthouse, Scotland's Centre for Architecture, Design and the City.

17. Colvin, *Trees*, p.5.

18. Brenda Colvin, 'Planting Design', *Journal of the Institute of Landscape Architects* (March 1951), p.4.

19. Brenda Colvin, *Land and Landscape* (London, 1970), p.217.

20. Colvin, 'Planting Design', p.6.

21. Brenda Colvin, 'Plant Form in Relation to Architecture', *Landscape and Garden* (Autumn, 1934), p.20.

22. Ibid., p.21.

23. Brenda Colvin, 'Landscape Use of Lawns', *Landscape and Garden* (Winter 1937), p.220.

24. Brenda Colvin, 'Some Differences in French and English Garden Design', *Landscape and Garden* (Autumn, 1937), p.143.

25. Colvin, 'Trees and Landscape Architecture', p.13.

26. Colvin, 'Planting Design', p.4.

27. Colvin, *Land and Landscape* (1970), pp.320-1.

28. Ibid., p.127. The W.H. Smith warehouse was No. 501 in Colvin's notebook for 1964.

29. Colvin, 'Trees and Landscape Architecture', p.14.

30. Brenda Colvin, 'Design with Plants 1: Of Time and Trees: What the Eye Will See, the Imagination Foresees', *Landscape Design* (February 1974), p.9.

31. 'Aldershot New Military Town: Landscape Report', May 1964 (Colvin & Moggridge), p.1.

32. Interview with James Riley, who worked extensively with Colvin at Aldershot, 19 May 2003.

33. 'Aldershot New Military Town: Landscape Report', p.3.

34. Colvin, 'Design with Plants', pp.8-11.

35. Colvin, 'Planting Design', p.6.

36. Colvin, 'Design with Plants', p.11.

37. Colvin, *Land and Landscape* (1970), p.224.

38. The other members of the committee were Geoffrey Jellicoe, geographer L. Dudley Stamp, town planner Gordon Stephenson, forester Fraser Story and Clough Williams-Ellis.

39. *Wartime Journal of the Institute of Landscape Architects* No 6 (October 1944).

40. Brenda Colvin, *Land and Landscape* (London, 1947), p.157.

41. *Wartime Journal* (October 1944).

42. Brenda Colvin, 'Trees in Towns and Their Treatment for Landscape Effect', *Journal of the Royal Horticultural Society* (Vol. 85, September 1960), pp.447-51.

43. Colvin, *Land and Landscape* (1947), plate 89.

WORKING FOR SPLENDOUR, pp.112-27

1. Quoted in 'Extracts from a meeting at the Royal Society, Burlington House, W1 on 18 November 1942', *The Wartime Journal of the Institute of Landscape Architects* No. 3 (April 1943), p.8.

2. Sheila Harvey (ed.), *Reflections on Landscape: The Lives and Work of Six British Landscape Architects* (Aldershot, 1987), p.35.

3. *Landscape and Garden* (Autumn 1937), p.190, listed 70 members - 19 Fellows, 35 Associates, 3 Members, 4 Probationary Associates, 5 Students and 4 Honorary Trade Associates. After this issue, the journal did not include a list of members but invited readers to apply for a full list from the Hon. Secretary.

4. Brenda Colvin, 'Beginnings', *Landscape Design* (February 1979), p.8.

5. Ibid.

6. Geoffrey Jellicoe, 'Brenda Colvin', *Contemporary Architects*, ed. Muriel Emanuel (London, 1980), p.2.

7. Correspondence in Colvin's membership file at the Landscape Institute.

8. 'The New President', *Journal of the Institute of Landscape Architects* (November 1951), p.2.

9. No. 236 in Colvin's notebook.

10. Letter in Brenda Colvin's membership file at the Landscape Institute.

11. Letter quoted in Harvey (ed.), *Reflections on Landscape*, p.144.

12. Letter from Brenda Colvin to Mr Burton, 3 January 1961.

13. Interviews with Julia Joynt, 23 September 2003, and Barbara Oakeley, 26 June 2003.

14. Interview with Julia Joynt, 23 September 2003.

15. Letter from Mrs Mary Kaye, 12 July 2003.

16. In October 1945 the journal re-emerged as *Journal of the Institute of Landscape Architects*. The title was changed again in February 1971, to *Landscape Design*.

17. 'Ruined City Churches', letter from Marjory Allen of Hurtwood, David Cecil, Kenneth Clark, F.A. Cockin, T.S. Eliot, H.S. Goodhard-Rendel, Julian Huxley, Keynes and E.J. Salisbury to *The Times*, 12 August 1944, reproduced on p.4 of *Bombed Churches as War Memorials* (Cheam, Surrey, 1945).

18. *Bombed Churches as War Memorials* (1945), pp.23-30.

19. Geoffrey Jellicoe, 'The Wartime Journal of the Institute of Landscape Architects' in Sheila Harvey and Stephen Rettig (eds), *Fifty Years of Landscape Design* (London, 1985), p.9.

20. Ibid.

21. Ibid.

22. Harvey (ed.), *Reflections on Landscape*, p.115.

23. Evidence in papers in Brenda Colvin's membership file at the Landscape Institute.

24. Brenda Colvin, 'Landscape as an Expression of Social Evolution', *Wartime Journal of the Institute of Landscape Architects* No. 2 (June 1942), p.8.

25. Quoted in 'Conference on the Landscape Architecture in the County of London Plan Held at the Royal Academy of Arts, Wednesday 24th November 1943', *Wartime Journal of the Institute of Landscape Architects* No. 5 (April 1944), pp.10-11.

26. 'An Appeal to Professional Members', *The War-time Journal* No 1 (August 1941), quoted in Harvey and Rettig (eds), *Fifty Years*, p.10.

27. Harvey and Rettig (eds), *Fifty Years*, p.46.

28. Interview with Peter Youngman, 26 June 2003.

29. 'The New Towns Committee of the Ministry of Town and Country Planning: Evidence Submitted by the I.L.A.', *Journal of the Institute of Landscape Architects* (April 1946), p.16.

30. 'The National Parks Committee of the Ministry of Town and Country Planning: Evidence Submitted by the I.L.A.', *Journal of the Institute of Landscape Architects* (April 1946), p.21.

31. Harvey and Rettig (eds), *Fifty Years*, p.47.

32. Places visited include Amersham, Aynho (Oxfordshire), Bournville, Eltham, Farnham, Gerard's Cross, Hammersmith, Hampstead Garden Suburb, High Wycombe, New Cross, Northolt, Northwood, Oxford, Rickmansworth, Roehampton, Ruislip, Southampton, Sutton at Hone (Kent), Watford and Western Avenue

33. Notes in Brenda Colvin's membership file at the Landscape Institute.

34. Harvey and Rettig (eds), *Fifty Years*, p.57.

35. Letter from Anthony du Gard Pasley, 20 April 2003.

36. 'Presidential Address delivered by Miss Brenda Colvin at a General Meeting on October 18th, 1951', *Journal of the Institute of Landscape Architects* (November 1951), pp.3-7.

37. Peter Youngman, 'The Legacy' in *Sylvia Crowe*, eds Geoffrey Collens and Wendy Powell (LDT monograph No. 2, Reigate, 1999), p.171. Interview with Peter Youngman, 26 June 2003.

38. Colvin, 'Beginnings'.

39. The Town Planning Institute received its royal charter in 1959.

40. Brenda Colvin (ed.), 'Quarterly Notes', *Landscape and Garden* (Winter 1934), pp.51-2.

41. Geoffrey Jellicoe, 'War and Peace', *Landscape Design* (February 1979), p.10.

42. Ibid.

43. Sylvia Crowe, 'International Scene', *Landscape Design* (February 1979), p.14.

44. Harvey (ed.), *Reflections on Landscape*, p.38.

45. Crowe, 'International Scene'.

46. Brenda Colvin, 'Garden Architecture', *Country Life* (12 September

1952), pp.764-5; 'A Landscape Architect's Impressions of Israel 1962', *Journal of the Institute of Landscape Architects* (November 1962), pp.16-17; 'Curtain Raiser on Landscape', *Journal of the Institute of Landscape Architects* (November 1963), pp.14-16.

47. Brenda Colvin, Sylvia Crowe, Geoffrey Jellicoe, 'Letter to the Editor', *Landscape Design* (February 1976), p.6.

48. Harvey (ed.), *Reflections on Landscape*, p.36.

49. Wanda Zaluska, née Stachniewska, had lived with Colvin for a time before her marriage to Count Zaluski. She died of cancer in the late 1960s. Anthony du Gard Pasley kindly supplied this information in his letter of 4 May 2003.

50. Interview with Anthony du Gard Pasley, 13 November 2002.

51. Jellicoe, 'Brenda Colvin', *Contemporary Architects*, ed. Emanuel, p.163.

52. Letter from Barry Newland, 30 January 2005.

53. Interview with Hal Moggridge, 24 May 2008.

54. Hal Moggridge and Chris Carter, 'Profile: Colvin and Moggridge', *Landscape Design* (December 1986), p.22.

55. Hal Moggridge, 'The Work of Brenda Colvin', *The Garden*, Vol. 106 Part 11 (November 1981), p.453.

A LANDSCAPE WORTH LIVING IN, pp.128-53

1. Brenda Colvin, *Land and Landscape* (London, 1970), p.xxiii.

2. Sheila Harvey (ed.), *Reflections on Landscape: the Lives and Work of Six British Landscape Architects* (London, 1987), p.125.

3. Interview with Peter Youngman, 26 June 2003. The square in question was Gordon Square in Bloomsbury.

4. Harvey (ed.), *Reflections*, pp.125-6.

5. Peter Youngman, 'The Theory of Planning', *Architectural Review*, October 1948.

6. Brenda Colvin, *Land and Landscape* (London, 1947), p.1.

7. Sylvia Crowe, 'Book Review', *Journal of the Institute of Landscape Architects* (April 1948), p.16.

8. Brian Hackett in Harvey (ed.), *Reflections*, p.100; Peter Youngman, ibid., pp.125-6; George Plumptre, *The Garden Makers: The Great Traditions of Garden Design from 1600 to the Present Day* (London, 1983), p.200.

9. Geoffrey Jellicoe, 'Brenda Colvin', *Contemporary Architects*, ed. Muriel Emanuel (London, 1980), p.164.

10. Brenda Colvin, 'Presidential Address', *Journal of the Institute of Landscape Architects* (November 1951), p.4.

11. David Cowling, *An Essay for Today: The Scottish New Towns 1947 to 1997* (Edinburgh, 1997), p.104.

12. In order of designation: Stevenage, Crawley, Hemel Hempstead, Harlow, Hatfield, Welwyn, Basildon and Bracknell.

13. Colvin's work at East Kilbride is not listed in her notebook, but she was certainly working there in 1950. East Kilbride was the first new town to be designated under the Clyde Valley Regional Plan of 1946 and set the standard for Scotland's later new towns at Glenrothes, Cumbernauld, Livingston and Irvine.

14. Brenda Colvin, Sylvia Crowe and H.F. Clark, 'Landscape Architecture in the New Towns. A Symposium: Part III', *Journal of the Institute of Landscape Architects* (July 1950), pp.6-10.

15. Cowling, *Essay for Today*, p.22.

16. See p.222, n.16.

17. Interview with Peter Youngman, 26 June 2003.

18. Colvin, *Land and Landscape* (1970), p.106.

19. Colvin, 'Landscape Architecture in the New Towns', p.7.

20. Colvin, *Land and Landscape* (1947), pp.193-4.

21. Cowling, *Essay for Today*, p.12.

22. Peter Youngman, 'Landscape Planning' in Sheila Harvey and Stephen Rettig (eds), *Fifty Years of Landscape Design*, pp.47-8.

23. Letter from D.A. Woods to Brenda Colvin, 5 November 1962.

24. 'Aldershot New Military Town: Landscape Report', May 1964 (Colvin & Moggridge papers), p.2.

25. Hal Moggridge, 'Brenda Colvin', *Oxford Dictionary of National Biography*, eds H.C.G. Matthew and Brian Harrison (Oxford, 2004), p.834.

26. 'Aldershot New Military Town: Landscape Report', p.1.

27. Hal Moggridge, 'Aldershot New Military Town – Landscaping: A Note of First Impressions – February 1970' (Colvin & Moggridge).

28. Draft 'Notes for consideration at ad hoc meeting September 30th', 29 August 1968.

29. Interview with Chris Carter, 2 September 2003.

30. Moggridge, 'Brenda Colvin'.

31. 'Aldershot Military Town', Minutes of meeting held on 16 December 1968, at Union Building, Hospital Hill, Aldershot, to consider the administrative and technical arrangement for the formation of the refuse tip at Camp Farm.

32. 'The Landscape System', *c.*1963 (Colvin & Moggridge papers).

33. Ibid.

34. Colvin, *Land and Landscape* (1947), p.244.

35. *Landscape and Garden* (Autumn 1936), pp.158-9.

36. Colvin, *Land and Landscape* (1947), p.245.

37. Christopher Tunnard, *Gardens in the Modern Landscape* (London, 1938), p.161.

38. S. Daniels, 'On the Road with Humphry Repton', *Journal of Garden History* 16 (1996), p.179.

39. Brenda Colvin, 'Roadside Planting in Country Districts', *Landscape and Garden* (Summer 1939), pp.86-8.

40. Colvin, *Land and Landscape* (1970), p.354.

41. Colvin, 'Roadside Planting', p.86. The quotation is from Shakespeare's *Hamlet* (II, ii, ll.110-11).

42. J.W.R. Adams (Fellow of the ILA), Professor G. Blackman, Brenda Colvin (Fellow of the ILA), Dr W. Fox, F. Newcomer (Ministry of Transport), E. Prentice Mawson (Fellow of the ILA) and A.G. Wise (Associate of the ILA) made up the committee. Their report, 'prepared on behalf of the Council', was published in the October 1946 edition of the *Journal of the Institute of Landscape Architects*.

43. 'Roads in the Landscape', *Journal of the Institute of Landscape Architects* (October 1946), p.4.

44. Ibid., pp.4-8.

45. Colvin, *Land and Landscape* (1947), p.245.

46. Ibid., p.249.

47. Brenda Colvin, 'The London-Birmingham Motorway: a new look at the English landscape', *Geographical Magazine* 32 (1959), p.243.

48. Ibid., p.246.

49. Interview with Peter Youngman, 26 June 2003.

50. Christopher Hall, 'Motorways the Mulley Way', *Guardian*, 19 March 1970, p.13. Christopher Hall was secretary of the Ramblers' Association and formerly chief information officer at the Ministry of Transport.

51. Harvey and Rettig (eds), *Fifty Years*, pp.136-8.

52. In 1965/66 Colvin also undertook work with the architects Maguire & Murray in the North Quad.

53. I am grateful to Ursula Mitchel, Archivist at Queen's University, Belfast, for this information from the university's archives, including Minutes of Building Committee meeting on 19 May 1961; Minutes of Halls of Residence Sub-Committee meeting on 15 December 1961.

54. Colvin, *Land and Landscape* (1970), p.106.

55. Queen's University Estates Department website http://www.qub.ac.uk/directorates/EstatesDepartment/EstatesPlanningDivision/CapitalDevelopmentProgramme/

56. Cadw: Welsh Historic Monuments, *Register of Landscapes, Parks and Gardens of Special Historic Interest in Wales – Carmarthenshire, Ceredigion and Pembrokeshire*, pp.86-92. I am grateful to Gwynne Griffiths and Kaye Moxon of Cadw for letting me see the Register entry and Colvin's proposals and to Robert McCleary of Aberystwyth University for sending me the aerial photographs of the site at the time when Colvin first started work there.

57. Arthur Hellyer, 'Lessons of a Maritime Garden', *Country Life*, 13 October 1977, p.1026.

58. *Ligustrum* in Var, *Prunus lusitanica, Arbutus unedo*, escallonias (tall evergreen forms), *Garrya elliptica, Berberis darwinii, Cotoneaster salicifolia, C. frigida, C. henryi, C. franchetii, Eleagnus* (tall evergreen forms), *Eucalyptus dalrympleana*, griselinia and pittosporum.

59. Michael Sanderson, *The History of the University of East Anglia Norwich* (London, 2002), p.139.

60. Letter from Lasdun to Thistlethwaite, 31 January 1968, quoted in Sanderson, *History*, p.168.

61. Letter from Joan, Lady Evershed to Thistlethwaite, 17 December 1966, quoted in Sanderson, *History*, pp.168-9.

62. Brenda Colvin, 'University of East Anglia Interim Landscape Report and Approximate Estimate of Cost', December 1967, p.1.

63. Letter and notes from Hal Moggridge, 11 July 2003.

64. Interview with Hal Moggridge, 11 April 2002.

65. Sanderson, *History*, p.169.

66. Ibid.

67. Letter, Brenda Colvin to Frank Thistlethwaite, 4 November 1968.

68. Hal Moggridge, 'The University of East Anglia: Commentary' (no date).

69. No. 407 in her notebook, marked down as Trinity Square.

70. Pepys is buried at St Olave's Church nearby. To mark his association with the garden it contains a sculptured head of him that was presented in 1983 by F.E. Cleary.

71. F.E. Cleary, *The Flowering City* (The City Press, 1969), p.40.

72. J.H. Whitlock, *The City Gardens* (The Corporation of London, 1951), p.7.

73. Jeremy Dodd, 'Chelsea Flower Show', *Journal of the Institute of Landscape Architects*, August 1958, pp.5-7.

74. Colvin, *Land and Landscape* (1970), p.307.

75. Ibid., p.344.

INDUSTRY IN THE LANDSCAPE, pp.154-83

1. Brenda Colvin, *Land and Landscape* (London, 1970), p.344.

2. Brenda Colvin, *Land and Landscape* (London, 1947), p.155.

3. Interview with Hal Moggridge, 11 April 2002.

4. Colvin, *Land and Landscape* (1970), p.343.

5. Brenda Colvin, 'The Landscape of Reservoirs', *Landscape Design* (August 1971), p.24.

6. Letter from Colvin & Moggridge to R.C. Whitehead, City of Birmingham Water Department, 22 April 1969.

7. According to the Trimpley Sailing Club website. The reservoir is used for sailing, rowing and fishing, and the surrounding area is used by walkers and ramblers.

8. Severn Trent Water website www.stwater.co.uk/server.php?show=ConWebDoc.1821.

9. Colvin, *Land and Landscape* (1947), p.223.

10. Ibid.

11. Colvin, *Land and Landscape* (1970), p.344.

12. Didcot has been in Oxfordshire since the 1974 boundary changes.

13. Brenda Colvin, 'Power Station, Didcot, Berkshire: Criticism', *Architectural Review* (August 1974), p.92.

14. Ibid.

15. Simon Young, Colvin's editor at John Murray, wrote a poem about the power station.

16. Interview with head gardener Inara Gipsle, 9 October 2002.

17. 'Presidential Address', *Journal of the Institute of Landscape Architects* (October 1949), pp.6-9.

18. 'Beauty and the Cost Problem', *Guardian*, 22 November 1957, p.7.

19. Diana Rowntree, 'Industry in the Landscape Exhibition at the RSA', *Guardian*, 28 October 1964, p.9.

20. Published in the *Journal of the Institute of Landscape Architects* (May 1964), pp.12-14. Also on the platform were Sylvia Crowe and Derek Lovejoy (1925-2000), landscape architect, who founded what is now one of the largest landscape practices in Europe, Derek Lovejoy and Partners.

21. Colvin, *Land and Landscape* (1947), pp. 225 and 228-9.

22. Power station schemes listed in her notebook are Keadby 1951 (Nos 336 and 337), Stourport 1951 (No. 338), Drakelow 1959 (No. 432), Eggborough 1961 (No. 454), Rugeley 1962 (No. 490), Meaford 1966 (No. 506).

23. Drakelow 'C' was decommissioned on 31 March 2003 and the cooling towers were finally demolished in September 2006.

24. 'Central Electricity Generating Board – Drakelow C Power Station: Landscape Report' (October 1959).

25. Colvin, *Land and Landscape* (1970), p.144.

26. Ibid., p.288.

27. The reserve is now owned by Derbyshire Wildlife Trust.

28. 'Central Electricity Generating Board – Drakelow C Power Station: Landscape Report'.

29. Colvin, *Land and Landscape* (1970), p.163.

30. 'Central Electricity Generating Board – Eggborough Power Station: Preliminary landscape proposals', April 1962.

31. Ibid.

32. Hal Moggridge, 'A Frank Artefact', *Landscape Design* (April 1993), p.22.

33. Letter from Chris Carter, 3 June 2008.

34. Brenda Colvin, 'Gale Common, Preliminary Landscape Report, November 1962' (Colvin & Moggridge). The site for the waste was named after Gale Common, one area within it.

35. This picture was also used on the back of the jacket of the second edition of *Land and Landscape*.

36. Brenda Colvin, 'Current Work: III Gale Common, Eggborough, Yorkshire', *Landscape Design* (November 1968), p.24.

37. 'Central Electricity Generating Board – Eggborough Power Station: Preliminary landscape proposals'.

38. 'Landscape Work for the C.E.G.B.', p.12.

39. Letter from Chris Carter, 3 June 2008.

40. 'Central Electricity Generating Board – Rugeley Power Station: Landscape Report' (January 1965), p.1.

41. Colvin, *Land and Landscape* (1970), p.212.

42. 'Central Electricity Generating Board – Rugeley Power Station: Landscape Report', p.7.

43. Nos 442 and 452 in the notebook.

44. Nos 336-8, 356, 377, 402, 403, 442, 443, 449 and 452 in the notebook.

45. Brenda Colvin, 'Landscape Maintenance of Large Industrial Sites', *Journal of the Landscape Institute* (November 1968), p.25.

46. Colvin, *Land and Landscape* (1970), p.332.

47. Ibid.

48. Reported in the *Guardian*, 19 July 1947, p.3.

49. Other quarries listed in her notebook are Crofthead Quarry at Bishopsbriggs, and Warton Crag in Lancashire in 1951, and Torr Works (also known as Merehead Quarry) in Somerset in 1974, although Colvin did not work on the last.

50. Colvin quoted in a report on the Council for the Preservation of Rural England's national conference in Cromer held on 6 October, *Guardian*, 7 October 1967, p.3.

51. Brenda Colvin, 'Potash Mine, Boulby, Yorkshire', *Architectural Review* (August 1974), p.100.

52. Jeremy Dodd, 'Chelsea Flower Show 1958', *Journal of the Institute of Landscape Architects*, August 1958, pp.5-7.

53. Brenda Colvin, 'Tree Planting', *Techniques of Landscape Architecture*, ed. A.E. Weddle (London, 1967), p.176.

54. Colvin, *Land and Landscape* (1970), pp.126-7.

55. 'Book Reviews', *Journal of the Institute of Landscape Architects* (November 1970), p.42.

56. Sheila Harvey (ed.), *Reflections on Landscape: the Lives and Work of Six British Architects* (Aldershot, 1987), p.144.

57. Colvin, *Land and Landscape* (1970), pp.xxi-xxiii.

58. Sylvia Crowe, 'Brenda Colvin C.B.E., P.P.L.I.', *Agricola* (1980), pp.53-4. Swanley Horticultural College was amalgamated with Wye College in 1948.

59. Muriel Emanuel (ed.), *Contemporary Architects* (London, 1980), p.163.

60. Harvey (ed.), *Reflections*, p.150.

MODERN PRIVATE GARDENS, pp.184-213

1. G. and S. Jellicoe, *Modern Private Gardens* (London, 1968), p.10.

2. Brenda Colvin, 'The Garden for 4 Seasons or The Constant Garden v. the Instant' (unpublished typescript).

3. Peter Shepheard, *Modern Gardens* (Ipswich, 1953), p.24.

4. Jane Brown, *Eminent Gardeners: Some People of Influence and Their Gardens 1880-1980* (London, 1990), p.60.

5. Norah Lindsay, 'The Manor House – I. Sutton Courtenay, Berks', *Country Life*, 16 May 1931, pp.610-16.

6. Letter from Bridget Astor, 15 April 2003.

7. Brenda Colvin, 'Sutton Courtenay Manor Berkshire', *Journal of the Institute of Landscape Architects* (November 1953), pp.5-8.

8. Letter from Bridget Astor, 15 April 2003.

9. In time, Colvin's carefully sited sculptures had to be removed from the garden for security reasons. The Manor House, Sutton Courtenay is no longer owned by the Astors. The Charoux figures are currently on loan to the Siegfried Charoux museum in Austria.

10. Interview with Anthony du Gard Pasley, 13 November 2002.

11. Colvin, 'Sutton Courtenay', p.7.

12. Lindsay, 'The Manor House', p.312.

13. Letter from Brenda Colvin to Mr Burton, 3 Ginge Brook, Sutton Courtenay, 3 January 1961.

14. Colvin, 'Sutton Courtenay', p.8.

15. Interview with Anthony du Gard Pasley, 13 November 2002.

16. Letter, Brenda Colvin to Mr Burton, 3 January 1961.

17. Interview with head gardener Inara Gipsle, 8 October 2002.

18. Colvin, 'Sutton Courtenay', p.6.

19. See p.96.

20. MS notebook, Colvin & Moggridge.

21. Interview with Diana Ford, 15 May 2003.

22. Interview with Julia Joynt, 23 September 2003.

23. Email from Harriet Moggridge to Cass Moggridge, 24 May 2008.

24. 12 and 14 Elm Tree Road, St John's Wood, London – No. 355 in Colvin's notebook.

25. Lady Allen of Hurtwood and Susan Jellicoe, *The New Small Garden* (London, 1956) and Susan Jellicoe and Marjory Allen, *Town Gardens to Live In* (London, 1977.)

26. Allen and Jellicoe, *New Small Garden*, p.109.

27. The paddling pool was used as an example in Geoffrey Jellicoe's chapter on 'Water' in A.E. Weddle (ed.), *Techniques of Landscape Architecture*, pp. 132-4.

28. Interview with Anthony du Gard Pasley, 13 November 2002.

29. Probably No. 341 in Colvin's notebook from 1952 at Pembroke Gardens in Kensington.

30. Shepheard, *Modern Gardens*, p.68. This is probably No. 299 (1944-5), 1 Prince Arthur Road, Hampstead.

31. Brenda Colvin, 'Gardens to Enjoy' in *Gardens and Gardening Vol. 3: Hardy Plants, The Studio Gardens and Gardening* annual, eds F.A. Mercer and Roy Hay (London, 1952), captions p.16.

32. Interview with Julia Joynt, 23 September 2003.

33. John Sales, *West Country Gardens* (Gloucester, 1980), p.237.

34. No. 433 in 1959 in Colvin's notebook.

35. G. and S. Jellicoe, *Modern Private Gardens*, p.72.

36. No. 388 in 1956 in Colvin's notebook, then known as Acryse Manor.

37. Brenda Colvin, *Land and Landscape* (London, 1947), p.90, (London, 1970), p.157. Interview, Chris Carter, 2 September 2003.

38. Interview with Jerry Shenton, 3 September 2003.

39. Plans at Okeover Hall, Okeover, Ashbourne. I am grateful to Sir Peter Walker-Okeover Bt for inviting me to see these.

40. Interview with Jerry Shenton, 3 September 2003.

41. No. 414 in Colvin's notebook, 'through Arch. press books'. The architect was Stanley Nevell, 34 Smith Square, London SW1. Drawing No. 414/4, dated October 1957 and signed JAB [John Brookes], in the Landscape Institute archives.

42. Jeremy Dodd, 'Chelsea Flower Show 1958', *Journal of the Landscape Institute* (August 1958), p.5.

43. No. 472 in Colvin's notebook.

44. Brenda Colvin, 'See House, Cuddesdon, Oxford: Landscape Report', October 1962. I am grateful to Barbara Oakeley for the loan of a copy of this report.

45. Interview with Anthony du Gard Pasley, 13 November 2002.

46. Allen and Jellicoe, *New Small Garden*, pp.46-8. The garden also featured in the chapter on 'Pots and Containers' in Jellicoe and Allen, *Town Gardens to Live In*, p.144.

47. Interview with Anthony du Gard Pasley, 13 November 2002.

48. The house was in Sarrett Lane, Rickmansworth.

49. Sir John Stafford Cripps (1912-93), journalist, lived almost all his life in Filkins. He was editor of *The Countryman* from 1947 to 1971, making it an authoritative and influential voice for the countryside, as much concerned for employment, schools, shops, and transport as for conservation. He went on to become chairman of the Countryside Commission. Colvin's article appeared in the Winter 1959 edition of the magazine, pp.664-72.

50. Letter from Laurie Fricker, 23 November 2007.

51. Graham Stuart Thomas, *The Art of Planting* (London, 1984), p.34.

52. I am very grateful to Chris and Stephanie Carter for sharing their in-depth knowledge of the garden at Little Peacocks with me.

53. G. and S. Jellicoe, *Modern Private Gardens*, p.7.

54. G. and S. Jellicoe, *Modern Private Gardens*, p.47.

55. Peter Beales dates the rose to 1970 in his *Classic Roses* (London, 1985).

56. Hal Moggridge, 'The Work of Brenda Colvin', *The Garden* (Vol. 106 Part II), November 1981, p.447.

57. Colvin, 'Gardens to Enjoy', p.10.

THE LEGACY, pp.214-17

1. Hal Moggridge, 'The Work of Brenda Colvin', *The Garden* (Vol. 106 Part II) November 1981, p.453.

2. Hal Moggridge, '12 Gower Street', *Geoffrey Jellicoe*, ed. Sheila Harvey (LDT monograph No. 1, Reigate, 1998), p.16.

3. Ken Fieldhouse, 'Statements by Twentieth-Century Landscape Designers', *Garden History: Reviewing the Twentieth-Century Landscape*, 28: 1 (2000), eds Jan Woudstra and Cristiano Ratti, p.11.

4. Geoffrey Jellicoe, 'Brenda Colvin', *Contemporary Architects*, ed. Muriel Emanuel (London, 1980), p.163.

5. Sylvia Crowe, *Tomorrow's Landscape* (London 1956), p.9.

6. Sheila Harvey (ed.), *Reflections on Landscape* (London 1987), p.35.

7. Peter Youngman in Harvey (ed.), *Reflections*, p.126.

8. Michael Laurie, 'Women of Substance', *Landscape Design* (March 1999), p.56.

9. Peter Youngman, 'The Legacy' in *Sylvia Crowe*, eds Geoffrey Collens and Wendy Powell (LDT monograph No. 2, Reigate, 1999), p.172.

10. Brenda Colvin, *Land and Landscape* (London, 1970), p.379.

11. Interview with Chris Carter, 2 September 2003.

12. Interview with Julia Joynt, 23 September 2003.

13. Interview with James Riley, 19 May 2003.

14. Interview with Cass Moggridge, 24 May 2008.

15. I am grateful to Hal and Cass Moggridge and Stephanie and Chris Carter for sharing their memories of Colvin's last years with me, 24 May 2008.

16. Brenda Colvin, *Wonder in a World* (privately published, 1977), p.19.

Biographies

THOMAS ADAMS (1871–1940)

A leading British planning pioneer. Born on a farm outside Edinburgh, Adams moved to London as a journalist. He became acquainted with Patrick Geddes and the Garden City movement headed by Ebenezer Howard and was secretary to the Garden City Association and the first manager of Letchworth Garden City (1903–6). In 1914 he became a founder member and was first president of the Town Planning Institute. He subsequently became one of the founders of the Canadian planning movement. From 1923 to 1930 he was the director of the regional plan for New York City and its surrounding area. His two eldest sons became prominent planners – James W.R. Adams was planning officer for Kent, and Frederick J. Adams led the planning programme at Massachusetts Institute of Technology.

MADELINE AGAR (c.1874–1967)

Garden designer and landscape architect. Arrived to study at Swanley College in 1893, aged nineteen, and was there for two years. On leaving the college, Agar joined the Guild of Old Students and most of the information about her employment comes from news she supplied to the Guild's magazine and from her membership file at the Landscape Institute. In addition to the two books mentioned on p.18, she also published in 1921, jointly with Mary Stout, *A Book of Gardening for the Sub-Tropics with a Calendar for Cairo, including a vocabulary of Arabic gardening terms*. Among a handwritten list of her 'larger gardens' in her membership file, she included a garden in Cairo as well as ones at Place in Fowey, Cornwall, and Newton Stacey, Hampshire. In 1913 Agar was also responsible for the planting of architect Charles Voysey's 'Pleasance' garden in North Kensington, designed for the Horniman heiress, and local councillor, Emslie J. Horniman. Agar's father was Edward Agar, solicitor turned businessman. As co-founder of Wimbledon Hockey Club, he did much to revive the game of hockey which he was determined to establish on Wimbledon Common. I am grateful to Marie FitzGerald and Alan Elliot of the Wimbledon Museum and Freda Parker of The Wimbledon Club for their help in researching Madeline Agar's history.

MARJORY ALLEN, LADY ALLEN OF HURTWOOD (1897–1976)

Landscape architect. Studied at Reading University. During her time as vice-president of the Institute of Landscape Architects (1939–46) she became a close friend of Susan and Geoffrey Jellicoe. With Susan Jellicoe she published several books, including *Things We See: Gardens* (1953), *The New Small Garden* (1956) and *Town Gardens to Live In* (1977), but possibly her greatest interest was in child welfare. She campaigned for pre-school education and wrote several books on play, including an influential book on adventure playgrounds in 1954.

DAVID ASTOR (1912–2001)

Newspaper editor and philanthropist. Son of Waldorf and Nancy Astor, he grew up in the extraordinary atmosphere of Cliveden in Buckinghamshire, a hotbed of political debate. The Astor family owned the *Observer* from 1911, and David Astor was its editor from 1948 to 1975. Under his editorship it was a paper of ideas, liberal in the broadest sense, directed towards the interpretation of events, steady in its opposition to injustice and oppression, and prepared to take risks for the sake of its principles.

STANLEY ROY BADMIN (1906–89)

Watercolour artist, born in Sydenham, London. Badmin studied at Camberwell School of Art on a scholarship and at the Royal College of Art. Increasingly, he worked as an etcher and watercolourist, making his mark as an important educational illustrator, particularly admired for his accurate depiction of trees.

SIR REGINALD BLOMFIELD (1856–1942)

English architect, garden designer and author. Born in Devon, the son of a country rector, in 1881 Blomfield started training as an architect in the office of his uncle Sir Arthur Blomfield. A year later he was admitted as a student of architecture at the Royal Academy. In 1883 he set up on his own as an architect and became one of the early members of the Art Workers Guild. His book *The Formal Garden in England* (1892), written with F. Inigo Thomas, came out strongly in support of the style of architectural garden that he himself designed and attacked William Robinson's 'natural' gardening. Gardens, or parts of gardens, designed by him survive at Brocklesby Park (Lincolnshire), Caythorpe Court (Lincolnshire), Chequers (Buckinghamshire), Godinton House (Kent), Heathfield Park (East Sussex), Moundsmere Manor (Hampshire), Sulgrave Manor (Northamptonshire) and Waldershare Park (Kent).

PERCY CANE (1881–1976)

Born and educated in Essex, taking studies in both horticulture and architecture. A horticultural writer, he owned and published the magazines *My Garden Illustrated* and *Garden Design*. As a garden designer, his style is probably best classified as Arts and Crafts. Arthur Hellyer summed up the two characteristic features of his work as 'a mainly classical use of stonework . . . the other, for want of a better term, I call the slightly formalised woodland glade.' Cane was a very successful designer and won many medals at the Chelsea Flower Show where he exhibited most years from 1921 through to the early 1970s. His work can be seen at Dartington Hall, Devon, and Falkland Palace, Fife.

FRANK CLARK (1902–71)

Born in Manila. After a decade spent travelling the world and doing odd jobs, Clark realised he had most enjoyed making a garden in the Alaskan tundra, after a day spent counting salmon. This led him to an apprenticeship with Percy Cane and to collaboration with Christopher Tunnard. He was the first president of the Garden History Society and his pioneering book *The English Landscape Garden* was published in 1948. He then taught at the Universities of Reading and Edinburgh, inspiring the first generation of professionally qualified British landscape architects.

DAME SYLVIA CROWE (1901–97)

Garden designer, landscape architect and writer. Like Colvin, she studied at Swanley, arriving in 1920, the year Colvin left. After the Second World War, she shared an office with Colvin. She was president of the Institute of Landscape Architects from 1957 to 1959 and helped to found the International Federation of Landscape Architects. She worked on the landscaping of new towns at Basildon (Berkshire), Harlow (Essex, with Sir Frederick Gibberd), Warrington (Cheshire), and Washington (Tyne and Wear), and was employed by the Central Electricity Generating Board to landscape the setting of the nuclear power station at Trawsfynydd in Snowdonia. She was appointed Landscape Consultant to the Forestry Commission in 1964. Her book *Garden Design* (1958; 2nd edn, 1981; 3rd edn, 1994) is still of great value.

JOHN ST BODFAN GRUFFYDD (1910–2004)

Welsh landscape architect and one of the post-war leaders of the Institute of Landscape Architects. President of the ILA from 1969–71, he was landscape architect for Robinson College, Cambridge and helped found the landscape architecture school in Cheltenham (now the University of Gloucestershire).

STANLEY HART (?–1970)

Landscape designer. Started his career working with Percy Cane (1919–22), continued his studies after this and then worked as a designer and draughtsman at various nurseries before setting up his own practice in 1926–7. He was consultant architect to the National Playing Fields Association for two years and also to a number of the smaller contracting firms of landscape gardeners. In 1952 Hart moved to New Zealand where he lived for the rest of his life.

SHEILA HAYWOOD (1911–93)

Trained as an architect at the Architectural Association in London, 1929–34, and said that she received her landscape training 'from experience in the office of Geoffrey Jellicoe' whose assistant she was from 1939 to 1949. She became an Associate of the Institute of Landscape Architects in 1945 and a Fellow in 1956. She considered her most useful work was dealing with the restoration of worked-out gravel pits and in helping to establish a standard approach to this problem. She set up her own consultancy in 1949 and was consultant landscape architect to Bracknell new town.

OLIVER HILL (1887–1968)

English architect, landscape architect and garden designer. He was apprenticed to Edwin Lutyens, a family friend. Having gained a reputation as a country house architect, he began to design gardens. His early designs were in the Arts and Crafts style but he turned towards modernism in the 1930s. His work ranged from the formal garden at Moor Close, Berkshire (1924) to the modernist Joldwynds at Holmbury St Mary, Surrey (1934) and the Frinton Park Estate at Frinton-on-Sea (1937).

WILLIAM GRAHAM HOLFORD, BARON HOLFORD (1907–75)

Architect and town planner. Born and brought up in South Africa, Holford came to England in 1925 to study architecture at Liverpool University, where he won the Rome Scholarship in Architecture to the British School at Rome in 1930. He succeeded Patrick Abercrombie as Professor of Civic Design at Liverpool University in 1937. Holford was heavily involved with the development of post-war British town planning and was largely responsible for drafting the Town and Country Planning Act 1947. In 1948, he again succeeded Abercrombie as Professor of Town Planning at University College of London where he stayed until he retired in 1970.

GERTRUDE JEKYLL (1843–1932)

English author, artist, plantsman and garden designer. Jekyll designed over 400 gardens in the UK, Europe and America. Born in London, she spent most of her life in Surrey, latterly in a house designed for her by Edwin Lutyens at Munstead Wood, Godalming. She wrote many books about gardening that are still widely read and she contributed over 1,000 articles to *Country Life*, William Robinson's *The Garden* and other magazines. She was also a talented painter, photographer, designer and craftswoman. Her style of gardening was generally labour intensive and none of her gardens have survived although a few have been resurrected (Hestercombe, Somerset; The Manor House, Upton Grey). She was the first woman to receive the Victoria Medal of Honour from the Royal Horticultural Society.

SIR GEOFFREY JELLICOE (1900–96)

Architect, town planner, landscape architect, garden designer and author. He studied at the Architectural Association in London and, following a trip to Italy in 1923, wrote the classic book *Italian Gardens of the Renaissance* (1925) with Jock Shepherd. A founder member of the Institute of Landscape Architects, he was its president from 1939 to 1949, and was also one of the founders and first president of the International Federation of Landscape Architects.

In a career of almost 70 years, his work was varied and included the Cheddar Gorge Caveman Restaurant (1934), and several landscapes for private clients, often co-operating with Russell Page as planting designer. Among the latter were the Royal Lodge, Windsor, for the Duke and Duchess of York, and extensive new formal gardens at Ditchley Park (1935–9) for Ronald and Nancy Tree. Public works include the John F. Kennedy Memorial at Runnymede (1964) and the Water Garden in Hemel Hempstead. Probably his most ambitious garden design was for Sutton Place in Surrey (from 1980). Friendship with a number of leading modern artists led to his interest in Carl Jung and the role of the subconscious in landscape design.

SUSAN JELLICOE (1907–86)

Plantsman, photographer and author. In 1936 Geoffrey Jellicoe married Ursula [Susan] Pares who had joined his office as secretary. For 50 years they enjoyed a productive and happy marriage and co-operated professionally. Together they wrote the seminal book *The Landscape of Man*, starting in 1957, with Susan taking many of its photographs. By the time it was published in 1975, Susan had become an important figure in her own right in the world of landscape architecture. She was a fine plantsman and prepared planting schemes for many of Geoffrey's landscapes. An excellent landscape photographer, many of her photographs appeared in several books on which she collaborated, including *Modern Private Gardens* (1968) with her husband, and three books with Lady Marjory Allen, including *Town Gardens to Live In* (1977). She was an active member of the Garden History Society and edited the magazine *Landscape Design* for twenty years.

GILBERT H. JENKINS (1875–1957)
Architect and landscape architect. Became chief assistant to W.H. Romaine-Walker in 1901 and a partner in 1911. They worked together on the Tate's Duveen Gallery, the British Museum's Elgin Marbles Gallery, Rhinefield House and Great Fosters. Jenkins was born at Torquay, the son of a marble mason. His elder brother, Frank Lynn-Jenkins, was a sculptor. Gilbert Jenkins was the fourth president of the Institute of Landscape Architects, 1935–37.

NORAH LINDSAY (1873–1948)
Gardener and garden designer. Born to an upper class family, Lindsay lived her entire life among England's country house elite. She was beautiful, talented, high spirited, and a consummate hostess, mingling with the political and social luminaries of the age, all of whom were captivated by her. In 1924, at the age of fifty-one, facing financial ruin after the collapse of her marriage, she embarked on a garden design career that continued for the next two decades. She was largely responsible for the style of design and planting championed by Hidcote and Sissinghurst. Her commissions ranged from manor houses on the country lanes of England and grand aristocratic estates to royal gardens on the Continent. Her client base consisted of royalty, English nobility, and American expatriates.

SIR EDWIN LUTYENS (1869–1944)
English architect and garden designer. At the age of twenty, Lutyens met the forty-six-year-old Gertrude Jekyll. She became a formative influence on his work and they collaborated on many projects, producing some of the best country houses and gardens in England. As Jekyll's eyesight deteriorated, Lutyens produced the designs and Jekyll did the planting plans. Although often thought of as an Arts and Crafts architect, Lutyens's style is much more varied. Most of his gardens were designed for English country houses, but from 1912 for the Viceroy's Palace in New Delhi he designed a remarkable Mughal-style parterre. His unpaid work for the Imperial War Graves Commission after the First World War laying out battlefield cemeteries was impressive; he also designed the Cenotaph in London in 1919.

THOMAS MAWSON (1861–1933)
A prolific and influential garden designer and landscape architect whose work was largely in an Arts and Crafts style. He was born near Lancaster and initially worked with his uncle, a builder. In 1884 with his brothers he founded Lakeland Nurseries, Windermere, but he left in 1900 as his garden design business expanded. Initially he worked mostly in the north-west of England but increasingly in the south. In 1900 Mawson published one of the first books to be profusely illustrated, *The Art and Craft of Garden Making*. The book went through five editions by 1926 and was influential on garden taste of the time. In 1929 Mawson became

the first president of the Institute of Landscape Architects. One bit of practical advice he gave was that if you help a client to save money they will soon forget the saving and always remember the poor quality. His gardens incorporated both formal and informal elements and public parks were a speciality. Probably the best surviving example of his work is Dyffryn, Cardiff, Glamorgan.

EDWARD MILNER (1819–94)
Landscape gardener. Apprenticed to Joseph Paxton to work in the garden at Chatsworth, Milner then became Paxton's foreman at the Prince's Park, Liverpool and at Crystal Palace Park in Sydenham, and finally became an independent garden and park designer, working at Buxton, Lincoln, Bodnant and Gisselfeld in Denmark. His son Henry joined his practice in the 1870s.

HENRY MILNER (1845–1906)
Landscape gardener. Milner joined his father Edward's practice in the 1870s. In 1890 he published *The Art and Practice of Landscape Gardening*, which took most of its examples from his father's work. In 1897 Milner was one of the first to receive the Royal Horticultural Society's Victoria Medal of Honour. The family firm was taken over by Henry's son-in-law Edward White and, as Milner White, survived until the retirement of Frank Marshall in 1995, at which time it was the oldest garden design and landscape architecture practice in the British Isles, an honour now held by Colvin & Moggridge.

BARRY PARKER (1867–1947)
Architect and town planner. Parker went to the South Kensington School of Art in London in 1886, and studied interior design with T.C. Simmonds of Derby, 1887–9. He was later articled to the Manchester architect Faulkner Armitage from 1889 to 1893. In 1896 he went into partnership with Raymond Unwin (1873–1940), his second cousin and brother-in-law. They collaborated on architectural writing, including *The Art of Building a Home* (1901). In 1902 they were asked to design a model village at New Earswick near York for the Rowntrees, and the following year they were given the opportunity to take part in the creation of Letchworth Garden City. They became the planners and chief architects for the extensive cottage estates at Letchworth and Hampstead Garden Suburb. After the dissolution of the Parker & Unwin partnership in May 1914, Parker continued his town planning practice, advising on Porto, Portugal in 1915 and São Paulo, Brazil in 1917–19. From 1927 he advised Manchester City Council on the development of Wythenshawe, where he had a continuing role until 1941. His innovative master plan for this garden satellite of Manchester incorporated American-style parkways which he had admired since seeing them in New York in 1925.

WILLIAM ROBINSON (1838–1935)
Horticulturist and publisher. Born in Ireland and a student at Glasnevin. Robinson left Ireland in 1861 to take up a job at the Botanical Gardens of Regent's Park, London, and then worked for the leading horticultural firm of Veitch. He became a fellow of the Linnaean Society at the age of 29 and gardening correspondent of *The Times*. He wrote many books, including *The Wild Garden* (1870) and *The English Flower Garden* (1883)

to which Gertrude Jekyll contributed some sections. Having made his reputation with *The Wild Garden*, he started his magazine *The Garden* in 1871. Jekyll edited this for a couple of years as well as contributing many articles to it and to his *Gardening Illustrated* (from 1879).

JOHN DANDO SEDDING (1831–91)

Architect and writer. Trained in the office of G.E. Street, alongside fellow pupils William Morris and Philip Webb. After leaving Street's office, initially he inclined towards decorative work, concentrating on the study and design of embroidery, wallpapers, and metalwork, but after his marriage his architectural practice grew. He carried out church restoration work as well as designing new churches in the Gothic Revival style, with Arts and Crafts details.

PETER SHEPHEARD (1913–2002)

Architect and landscape architect, born and educated in Birkenhead. His consuming interest was natural history and he had a profound understanding of the relationship between the natural and the built environments. The Festival of Britain in 1951 gave him two major opportunities – one for housing design in the model development of Lansbury in Poplar, and the other in landscaping the downstream section of the South Bank exhibition site. In 1953 he published his *Modern Gardens*. In all his building projects, landscape played its part and throughout his career he designed gardens and outdoor spaces (Bunhill Fields, 1949 and 1963; Cheyne Walk Gardens, 1960; work at London Zoo, 1959–67). He was knighted in 1980.

RICHARD SUDELL (*c*.1900–68)

Landscape architect and author. The son of a Lancashire farmer, Sudell decided to become a landscape gardener at an early age. In 1915 he was a student gardener at Kew and left to join a firm of landscape contractors. From his office in Gower Street, he began publication of the Institute of Landscape Architect's journal and he was to be elected president of the Institute in 1955. His work was highly regarded abroad and he received many commissions for work in America. He was a prolific writer and his books, mostly for the general reader, include *Landscape Gardening* (1933), *The Town and Suburban Garden* (1950) and *Garden Planning* (1952).

F. INIGO THOMAS (1866–1950)

Artist and garden designer. Worked with Reginald Blomfield on the drawings for *The Formal Garden in England* and subsequently worked as a garden designer. His work can be seen at Athelhampton and Chantmarle, both in Dorset. Colvin herself visited and photographed Chantmarle in 1936.

INIGO TRIGGS (1876–1923)

Architect and garden designer. Through his books *Formal Gardens in England and Scotland* (1901), *The Art of Garden Design in Italy* (1906) and *Garden Craft in Europe* (1913) he influenced the Italian element of the Arts and Crafts style in England.

CHRISTOPHER TUNNARD (1910–79)

Landscape architect. Born in Canada, Tunnard came to England in 1929. After a European tour in the 1930s, he spearheaded a 'Modern' approach to landscape design and set down his ideas in his book, *Gardens in the Modern Landscape* (1938). After emigrating to America in 1939, he taught at Harvard and Yale.

ANDRÉ VERA (1881–1971)

French garden designer who worked closely with his brother Paul (1882–1951). His modernist principles were strongly influenced by the classical French garden style and his modernised version of the formal garden, with geometric shapes and much use of topiary, allowed for the use of bright colours and modern materials such as concrete.

EDWARD WHITE (1872–1952)

A highly respected landscape architect of the 1930s, partner in Milner White (see Henry Milner) and elected president of the Institute of Landscape Architects in 1932. He completed commissions in Ottawa, Calcutta and Europe, as well as many in the UK. The memorial gardens at Stoke Poges, completed in 1937, are probably his most important work. He saw them as the first of their kind in the country, 'intended for the repose of cremated ashes...designed and maintained in a fashion for which there is no existing precedent. An imperative condition is, of course, that the general appearance of the garden shall offer satisfactory unity'. He also designed the rock garden at Wisley in 1911 and a handsome Garden of Remembrance by the Crematorium at Kensal Green in 1938.

CLOUGH WILLIAMS-ELLIS (1883–1978)

Welsh architect, author and garden designer. His best surviving work is seen in the two gardens he created in Wales, for his family house at Plas Brondanw from 1908 and his fantasy Mediterranean village at Portmeirion from 1925. He also served on several government committees concerned with design and conservation and was instrumental in setting up the British National Parks after 1945. He wrote and broadcast extensively on architecture, design and the preservation of the rural landscape. He was knighted in 1971 for 'services to architecture and the environment'.

PETER YOUNGMAN (1911–2005)

Landscape architect and garden designer. Youngman studied history at Cambridge but became interested in garden design. He was apprenticed to a firm of nursery contractors in Chislehurst and then in 1935 was articled to George Dillistone, then vice-president of the Institute of Landscape Architects. His next job was with Thomas Adams, the planner, through whom he met the leaders of the planning profession. After the War, from 1948, he ran a landscape architecture course at University College London and was closely involved in the planning of Cumbernauld new town and Milton Keynes, and the 1960s expansions of Basingstoke and Andover. He was president of the Institute of Landscape Architects from 1961 to 1963.

Bibliography

WORKS BY BRENDA COLVIN

BOOKS

Land and Landscape (London, 1947; 2nd edn London, 1970)

Trees for Town and Country (London, 1947)

'Gardens to Enjoy' in *Gardens and Gardening Vol 3: Hardy Plants, The Studio Gardens and Gardening* annual, eds F.A. Mercer and Roy Hay (London, 1952), pp.12-23

'A Planting Plan' in *Bombed Churches as War Memorials* (The Architectural Press, 1945), pp.23-30

'Tree Planting' in *Techniques of Landscape Architecture,* ed. A.E. Weddle (London, 1967), pp.176-93

'Trees in the Countryside', in *Landscape Design with Plants*, ed. Brian Clouston (London, 1977), pp.7-13

Wonder in a World (privately printed, 1977)

ARTICLES

'Quarterly Notes', *Landscape and Garden* (Spring 1934), p.60

'Grey-Leaved Plants', *Landscape and Garden* (Summer 1934), pp.44-5

'Plant Form in Relation to Architecture', *Landscape and Garden* (Autumn 1934), pp.20-22

'Quarterly Notes', *Landscape and Garden* (Autumn 1934), p.45

'For Town Gardens', *Landscape and Garden* (Winter 1934), pp.21-3

'Quarterly Notes', *Landscape and Garden* (Spring 1935), p.39

'A Hampshire Garden of about One Acre', *Landscape and Garden* (Winter 1935), pp.142-3

'Winter's Bright Flowers and Cheerful Leaves', *Good Gardening* (January 1936), pp.4-6

'How Really Delightful the Average Garden Can Be', *Good Gardening* (March 1936), pp.8-11 and 46

'New Ways of Filling a Garden', *Good Gardening* (April 1936), pp.9-10

'New Ideas in Summer Bedding', *Good Gardening* (May 1936), pp.7-8

'Daydreams with a Purpose', *Good Gardening* (June 1936), pp.12-14

'Low Walls and Steps Give Variety – and Enchantment', *Good Gardening* (July 1936), pp.24-5

'How to Plan an Herbaceous Border', *Good Gardening* (September 1936), pp.12-13 and 50

'Herbaceous Borders', *Landscape and Garden* (Autumn 1936), pp.145-7

'Some Differences in French and English Garden Design', *Landscape and Garden* (Autumn 1937), pp.142-4

'Landscape Use of Lawns', *Landscape and Garden* (Winter 1937), pp.220-1

'The Herbaceous Border in Shade', *Landscape and Garden* (Summer 1938), pp.87-8

'In the New Forest', *Landscape and Garden* (Winter 1938), pp.202-4

'Pot Gardening', *Landscape and Garden* (Winter 1938), pp.214-15

'The Maze at West Stowell House', *Landscape and Garden* (Spring 1939), p.42

'Roadside Planting in Country Districts', *Landscape and Garden* (Summer 1939), pp.86-8

'Landscape as an Expression of Social Evolution', *Wartime Journal No 2 of the Institute of Landscape Architects* (June 1942), pp.8-9

'Trees and Landscape Architecture', *Journal of the Institute of Landscape Architects* (October 1947), pp.13-14

'Our Gardens', supplement to the Report on 'The Appearance of Housing Estates' issued in April 1948 by a Sub-Committee of the Central Housing Committee

'Landscape Architecture in the New Towns. A Symposium: Part III', *Journal of the Institute of Landscape Architects* (July 1950), pp.6-10

'Planting Design', *Journal of the Institute of Landscape Architects* (March 1951), pp.3-8

'Presidential Address', *Journal of the Institute of Landscape Architects* (November 1951), pp.3-7

'Garden Architecture', *Country Life* (12 September 1952), pp.764-5

'Sutton Courtenay Manor Berkshire', *Journal of the Institute of Landscape Architects* (November 1953), pp.5-8

'International Federation of Landscape Architects', *Journal of the Institute of Landscape Architects* (July 1955), pp.12-15

'The New President', *Journal of the Institute of Landscape Architects* (November 1957), p.2

'The London–Birmingham Motorway: A New Look at the English Landscape', *Geographical Magazine* 32 (1959), p.243

'Tree Planting on Compton Beauchamp Estate, Wilts', *Journal of the Institute of Landscape Architects* (February 1959), pp.2-4

'Trees in Towns and Their Treatment for Landscape Effect', *Journal of the Royal Horticultural Society* (September 1960), vol 85, pp.447-51

'Planting as a Medium of Design', *Journal of the Institute of Landscape Architects* (August 1961), pp.8-10

'Early-Spring Brilliance', *Observer*, 4 March 1962, p.39

'Feasting the Eyes and Nose', *Observer*, 15 July 1962, p.25

'Quick Screening', *Observer*, 28 October 1962, p.33

'A Landscape Architect's Impressions of Israel 1962', *Journal of the Institute of Landscape Architects* (November 1962), pp.16-17

'Counting up the Casualties', *Observer*, 24 February 1963, p.33

'Beauties of the Chelsea Fringe', *Observer*, 26 May 1963, p.35

'Wanton Touch', *Observer*, 15 September 1963, p.37

'Curtain Raiser on Landscape', *Journal of the Institute of Landscape Architects* (November 1963), pp.14-16

'Winter Colour', *Observer*, 9 February 1964, p.34

'Grass that Gives Colour Splash', *Observer*, 27 September 1964, p.33

'When All Is Gold …', *Observer*, 25 October 1964, p.32

'Current Work: III – Gale Common, Eggborough, Yorkshire', *Journal of the Institute of Landscape Architects* (November 1968), pp.20-24

'Landscape Maintenance of Large Industrial Sites', *Journal of the Institute of Landscape Architects* (November 1968), p.25

'Conservation of Landscape', *Journal of the Institute of Landscape Architects* (February 1970), pp.7-9

'The Landscape of Reservoirs', *Landscape Design* (August 1971), pp.23-6

'Design with Plants 1: Of Time and Trees: What the Eye Will See, the

Imagination Foresees', *Landscape Design* (February 1974), pp.8-11

'Power Station, Didcot, Berkshire: Criticism' and 'Potash Mine, Boulby, Yorkshire: Criticism', *Architectural Review* (August 1974), pp.92 and 100

with Sylvia Crowe and Geoffrey Jellicoe, 'Letter to the Editor', *Landscape Design* (February 1979), p.6

'Beginnings', *Landscape Design* (February 1979), p.8

SELECT BIBLIOGRAPHY

BOOKS

Madeline Agar, *Garden Design in Theory and Practice* (London, 1911; 2nd edn, 1913)

Tony Aldous with Brian Clouston, *Landscape by Design* (London, 1979)

Lady Allen of Hurtwood and Susan Jellicoe, *The Things We See 7: Gardens* (London, 1953)

Lady Allen of Hurtwood and Susan Jellicoe, *The New Small Garden* (London, 1956)

Jane Brown, *Eminent Gardeners: Some People of Influence and Their Gardens 1880-1980* (London, 1990)

Jane Brown, *The Modern Garden* (London, 2000)

Jane Brown, *The Pursuit of Paradise: A Social History of Gardens and Gardening* (London, 1999)

Katie Campbell, *Icons of Twentieth-Century Landscape Design* (London, 2006)

Geoffrey Collens and Wendy Powell (eds), *Sylvia Crowe* (LDT monograph No 2, Reigate, 1999)

Sylvia Crowe, *Garden Design* (London, 1958)

Sylvia Crowe, *Tomorrow's Landscape* (London, 1956)

Sheila Harvey (ed.), *Geoffrey Jellicoe* (LDT monograph No 1, Reigate, 1998)

Sheila Harvey (ed.), *Reflections on Landscape: the Lives and Work of Six British Landscape Architects* (Aldershot, 1987)

Sheila Harvey and Stephen Rettig (eds.), *Fifty Years of Landscape Design* (London, 1985)

Susan and Geoffrey Jellicoe, *Modern Private Gardens* (London, 1968)

Susan Jellicoe and Marjory Allen, *Town Gardens to Live In* (London, 1977)

Elizabeth B. Kassler, *Modern Gardens and the Landscape* (New York, 1964)

Peter King, *Women Rule the Plot: the Story of the 100 Year Fight to Establish Women's Place in Farm and Garden* (Duckworth, 1999)

David Matless, *Landscape and Englishness* (London, 1998)

Hal Moggridge, 'Brenda Colvin', *Oxford Dictionary of National Biography*, eds. H.C.G. Matthew and Brian Harrison (Oxford, 2004)

George Plumptre, *The Garden Makers: The Great Traditions of Garden Design from 1600 to the Present Day* (London, 1983)

George Plumptre, *The Latest Country Gardens* (London, 1988)

John Sales, *West Country Gardens* (Gloucester, 1980)

Peter Shepheard, *Modern Gardens* (London, 1953)

Ron Sidwell, *West Midland Gardens* (Gloucester, 1981)

Christopher Tunnard, *Gardens in the Modern Landscape* (London, 1938)

Clough Williams-Ellis, *England and the Octopus* (London, 1928)

ARTICLES

'Conference on the Landscape Architecture in the County of London Plan Held at the Royal Academy of Arts, Wednesday 24th November 1943', *Wartime Journal of the Institute of Landscape Architects* No 5 (April 1944), pp.7-12

Institute of Landscape Architects, 'Roads in the Landscape', *Journal of the Institute of Landscape Architects* (October 1946), pp.4-8

'The New President', *Journal of the Institute of Landscape Architects* (November 1951), p.2

'Landscape Work for the C.E.G.B.', Discussion for Members with Brenda Colvin, Derek Lovejoy and Sylvia Crowe, *Journal of the Landscape Institute* (May 1964), pp.12-14

L.J. Fricker, 'Forty Years A-Growing', *Journal of the Institute of Landscape Design* (May 1969), pp.8-15

J. St Bodfan Gruffydd, 'Review of *Land and Landscape* by Brenda Colvin', *Journal of the Institute of Landscape Architects* (November 1970), p.42

David Streatfield, 'Ideas into Landscape: Leaders Do Not Wait to Be Called', *Landscape Architecture* (January 1972), pp.32-5

Brenda Colvin, Sylvia Crowe and Geoffrey Jellicoe, 'Letter to the Editor', *Landscape Design* (February 1976), p.6

Arthur Hellyer, Lessons of a Maritime Garden', *Country Life*, 13 October 1977, pp.1026-7 (reprinted in Arthur Hellyer, *Gardens of Genius* (London, 1980))

Geoffrey Jellicoe, 'War and Peace', *Landscape Design* (February 1979), p.10

Sylvia Crowe, 'International Scene', *Landscape Design* (February 1979), p.14

'Brenda Colvin CBE, PPILA – Obituary', *Landscape Design* (May 1981), p.4

Hal Moggridge, 'The Work of Brenda Colvin', *The Garden*, Vol 106 Part 11 (November 1981), pp.447-53

Hal Moggridge and Chris Carter, 'Profile: Colvin and Moggridge', *Landscape Design* (December 1986), pp.20-22

Hal Moggridge, 'A Frank Artefact', *Landscape Design* (April 1993), pp.22-3

Michael Laurie, 'Women of Substance', *Landscape Design* (March 1999), pp.53-6

Garden History, 'Reviewing the Landscape: Statements by Twentieth-Century Landscape Designers', Vol 28 No 1 (Summer 2000), pp.2-16

Elaine Harwood, 'Post-War Landscape and Public Housing', *Garden History*, Vol 28 No 1 (Summer 2000), pp.102-16

Hazel Conway, 'Everyday Landscapes: Public Parks from 1930 to 2000', *Garden History*, Vol 28 No 1 (Summer 2000), pp.117-34

Brenda Colvin's Notebook

The handwritten content of the notebook is not always legible. Where the spelling of a word is not clear, this is indicated with a question mark in square brackets. Question marks not in square brackets appear in the original. The punctuation throughout the notebook is erratic but reproduced here as it was written (including some crossings-out). Although the notebook starts off in Colvin's hand, increasingly after 1937 other people make entries. The years noted in the margin and some other annotations, such as who had recommended her, were added to the earlier pages by Colvin at a later date (see p.23 for some examples) – these additions are shown in italics.

Entries from 1969 onwards, the year when Colvin & Moggridge was formed, are marked in brackets after the entry number with different categories indicating the degree of Colvin's involvement. The categories are: 1 = full involvement; 2 = some involvement; X = no significant involvement.

Hal Moggridge points out, however, that, 'The category "no significant involvement" by her needs the cautionary comment that, at least until the late 1970s, she was always there to give advice and guidance on the progress of jobs. We met for lunch every day when we were both in the office so that she had an indirect input all the time. She was also frequently in her own office in the wooden building to help all the staff, with each of whom she kept personally in touch.'

[Page 1]

1922?

1   Lulworth – W.B. Gladstone
2   Acton Round – *Wolryche Whitmore?*
3   Rodwell – *through Penrose-Thackwell*
4   Frognal (Planting plan)
5   Wishaw, Scotland – Lord Belhaven and Stenton
6   Weysprings
7   Mr Roxburgh's garden – Stowe School (*through Joy Coupley*)
8   St Margaret's Bay – *through Penrose Thackwell*
9   Lady Blenkinsop –   "   "
10 Mrs Morrison
11 Mrs Penrose-Thackwell
12 Mrs Fowler – Trull, Somerset (*through Newtons*)
13 Mrs Buckland
14 Mrs Verney (planting plans only)
15 Catchbulls [should be Catchbells] – Colvin, Stanway Essex
16 Mrs Tucker
17 Pamphlett [?] – The Farrells [?]
18 Hartcup – 9 Elm Tree Road

19 Goodenough – Filkins, Lechlade, Glos
20 Mrs Cleghorn
21 Mrs Blackett-Swiney – *Taunton through Newtons?*
22 Mrs Radcliffe
23 Sesame Club – *through Penrose Thackwell*

[Page 2]

1923?

24 Mrs Hickly
25 Mrs Fairleaver [?] – Bricketts Wood, Herts (*Gladstone*)
26 Mrs Fox – Robin's Close, Wellington
27 Mond *London – through Waddingtons*
28 Mrs Pollen –   "   *Gladstone*
29 E.W. Cooper
30 Chance – 5 Turner's Wood
31 Tallents
32 Cooper – Renton Furse [?], Crowcombe
33 Newton – Corfe Cottage
34 Mrs Scott, *Varengeville – France – through Swanley?*
35 Lady Pinney – Racedown, Crewkerne
36 Mrs Bond – *Dorset through Gladstone*

37 Pemberton – Trumpington Hall

38 Universaty [sic] Coll: School

39 Kidston – Hazelton Manor, Chippenham

40 Mrs Osborne

?41 *Lady Margaret Shaw – Woldingham?*

42 Mr Candlish – Fox Lydgate, Redditch, Worcs

43 Kirby

44 Russell – Silverwood, Camberly *RHS*

45 Baily – Lynells, Totteridge Green

46 Bannatyne – Wellington Avenue

[**Page 3**]

1924?

47 Macaulay – *Argyll* (*E.G.C.*)

48 Wolryche Witmore – *Dudmaston Bridgnorth Shrop.*

49 Mainwaring

50 Swann – Steeple, Dorset (*Gladstone*)

51 Henderson – Berkley, Frome, Som (*Blackley*)

52 Swainson

53 Fraser

54 T.G. Johnson

55 Roxburgh – Stowe (New House)

56 Fox – Rumwell Hall (Newton)

57} Mrs David Farquharson

58}   "   Nesham   "

59 Macnamara – *24 Carlyle Square*

60 Agnew – Woodhill, Hatfield

61 Governesses' Ben: Ass: – plans [?] at Beckenham

62 Mrs Peploe – Fawke House, Sevenoaks

63 Mrs Spencer Smith

64 Mrs Williamson – Edward Road, Bromley

65 Lady Clinton Baker – *Basford Hall Herts* (*formerly Rosa Henderson*)

66 Mrs Waddington – *Brampton Mill, Huntingdon*

67 Mrs Tennant – Little Holland Hall, Clacton

68 Mrs Thesiger Daniel – Pencraig, Llangefni, Anglesey

69 Mrs Byrne – Templewood Lane, Farnham Com

[**Page 4**]

70 Mrs McGrath – The Postern, Tonbridge

71 Mrs Hill – Spursholt, Romsey

72 Mrs Ingles – Cheddon Fitzpaine, Taunton

73 Mrs Johnson – Trull

74 Major J.B. Paget – Ibstock Place, Roehampton

75 Mrs Dewhurst – Tilstone Lodge, Tarporley

76 Mrs Pirie – 24 Tregunter Rd S.W.10

77 Lady Millais – Spreakfield, Frensham

1925

78 Mrs Peabody – Osborne House, Bolton Gdns

79 K. Gladstone – Greenways, Crow, Ringwood

80 Lady Agnew – 23 Upper Grosvenor St.

81 Mrs Lane – Arches Manor, Framfield, Sussex

82 Mrs Drage – 22 Mansfield Gdns Hampstead

83 Byrne – The Chesters, Farnham Com.

84 Mrs Cobden Sanderson – Cannes

85 J.R. Holland – The Pantiles, Englefield Green

86 Miss Grasett – 25 Hollylodge Garden

87 Mrs Hobson – 1 Bedford Square

88 Lady Boyne – Burwarton House, Bridgnorth

89 Mrs Blaauw – Mariners Charity, Lewes

1926

90 Mrs Lloyd – Harewood, Bletchingley, Surrey

91 Mrs Cunliffe – Thurston Pl and, Bury St Edmunds

92 Mrs Moncreiffe – 21 Sussex Place

[**Page 5**]

93 Mrs Gates – 2 Norfolk Road

1926-27

94 Mrs Crookshank [?] – Johnstounburn, Humbie, Midlothian

95 Mrs Donaldson Hudson – Chiswardine [sic], Market Drayton

96 Lady Crossely – Combermere Abbey, Whitchurch Cheshire

97 Mrs Waddy – West Hayes, Taunton

98 Miss Le Marchant – Green Dragons Chipping Campden

99 Mrs Gillum – Quarry Hill, Reigate

100 Mrs Howett [?] – Heathwood, W. Heath Road, Hampstead

101 Mrs Stewart – Woodend, Banstead, Surrey

102 Mrs Graham-Clarke – Glanrhos, Radnor

103 Mrs D'Arcy Baker – Hedsor Park *Herts?*

104 Mrs Harrison Hughes – 34 Queen Anne's Gate [and] Eddington House, Hungerford

105 Mrs Fairfax – Whitwell Hall, York

106 Mrs Knight – Chawton Dower House, Alton, Hants

1927-28

107 Mrs Gunter – Aldwark Manor York

108 Lady Durand – Langley Farm, Winchcombe Glos.

109 Mrs Baron – Holmbury House, Holmbury St Mary, Dorking

110 Hon Mrs Marcus Pelham – Hinton House, Byfield Northamptonshire

[Page 6]

1927-28

111 Mrs D. Hambro – Kidbrooke Park, East Grinsted [sic]

112 Mrs Gladstone – 26 Holland Villas Road

113 Mrs Balfour – Holton Park, Wheatley Oxon

114 Mrs Giles – Churchill, High Pine Close, Weybridge

115 Mrs Goldsmid – Hyde House, Goring Heath, Oxon

116 Mrs Hilton – Stanton-Woodhouse, Rowsley, Derby

117 Mrs Brooke – Ashton Grange, near Chester

118 Barnet By Pass

119 Stewart – Farmside, Park Road, Banstead

120 Saling [?] – Holmwood, Wimbledon Common

121 J. Fox – Pennant, Wellington Som.

122 Mr Guffy – Courtlands, Park Road, Banstead

123 Holland Hibbert – Grove House, Beckley, Oxford

1928

124 Hon Mrs Whitbread – Coopers Hill Lodge, Englefield Green

125 Mrs Hodgkinson – Tyne Hall, Bembridge, Isle of Wight

126 McCombie – Brick House, Felsted, Essex

127 Mrs Inglis – Bramble Rough, Hartfield Sussex

127a   "   "   – *cottage gdn* [?]

128 Mrs Schuyler – Coke's Farm, Chalfont St Giles, Bucks

129 John Hall Esq – Broughton Hall, Eccleshall, Staffs
   { Estate Agent – W.L. Pakenham, Broughton Hall
   { Estate Office, Wetwood, Eccleshall

130 Hambro – Merly House, Wimborne, Dorset

131 Oakley Hall Planting plan – *for Forestry Assn*

[Page 7]

132 Taylor – 33 Elsworthy Rd

133 Mrs S S. Burge – Drokes, Beaulieu Hants (648[?]) & 6 Cottesmore Gardens, West 1739

134 Mrs Peat – Ashe House, Axminster

136 Lady du Maurier – Cannon Hall, Cannon Place, Hampstead N.W.

135 *J.L. Musgrave – Rough Hay Stokepoges Bucks*

1928-29

137 G. Wheeler – Holywell, Whitchurch, Aylesbury

138 Mrs Napier – Boldre Hill, Lymington

139 Mrs Wilson – Burley Beacon, Burley, Hants

140 Lady Berwick – Attingham, Shropshire

141 R.A. Wilson Esq – 26 Wildwood Road, Hampstead

142 Mrs McCorquodale – Cound Hall, Shropshire

143   " Richardson – Rossford, Ballinamallard, Ireland

144 Miss Bates – Gray House, Chadlington Charlbury

1929

145 Lady Agnew – Stisted Hall, Braintree

146 Mrs Newton – La Brae, Buxted, Surrey

147 Miss Carver – The Quarry, Colwall, Malvern

148 Lady Phipps – Gardener Lynch – W. Stowell House near Marlborough

149 Mrs Newlands – Sandhayes, Warminster

150 Mrs Radcliffe – *Court Place W. Monkton Taunton*

151 Mrs Strauss (Mrs [?] Nichols) – *25, Cheyne Walk*

152 Stoke Poges Putting Green

153 Mrs H.C.T. Hawks [?] – *The Hyde Nr Luton*

154 Lt Col. J. Benett-Stamford – Pyt House, Tisbury

[Page 8]

155 Hon Mrs R. Barrington – Isle of Thorns, Chelwood Gate, Haywards Heath, Sussex

156 Lt. Col. Bower – Manston Dorset

1930-31

157 Mrs Gillilan – Upper House, Gt Bowden, Market Harboro

158   The Camp (Mrs Wagg) – Isle of Thorns Chelwood Gate

159   Lady Brage – Stanford Park Nr Rugby

160   Mrs Davison – Heale House Cury Rivel Taunton

161   Mrs Sclanders – Long Field, Bayleys Hill Sevenoaks

162   Miss Broughton – 76 Ellerton Road, Wandsworth Common

163   Lady Roberts – The Camp, Ascot, Berks.

164   Lady Portman – Staple Fitzpaine, Somerset

165   Brig. General H. Bateman Champain, C.M.G.

166   Ward, Maj. General H.D.O.[1] C.B – Linley Hall, Broseley, Shropshire

167   Cooke, Mrs – Stanley Old Hall, Bridgnorth, Shropshire

168   Middleton, William – Townfield, Lymington, Hants [and] Lock's Orchard, Lock's Heath Nr Southampton

169   J.H. McNeile Esq – Nonsuch, Bromham, Wilts

170   Lady Bunbury – Naunton Hall

171   E. Wrench – Dukes House, 23 Lawrence St

172   Chelsea Housing scheme – Worlds End Passage, Chelsea

173   Wycombe Abbey School – Wycombe Abbey

[Page 9]

1931–32

174   Miss Lear – Barry's Close, Long Hendon, Thame, Oxon

175   Mrs Reid – 7 Upper Phillimore Gdns, W.8

176   Mrs Holt – Lingmoor House, Kirbymoorside, York.

177   Miss Kennedy – Sarn Hill Grange, Tewkesbury *through Whitmore*

178   Mrs Griffiths – 25, Harrington Gdns, S.W.7

179   Queen Margarets School – Scarborough *through Swanley*

180   Mrs Blackett-Swiney – 12, Chester Street, S.W.1

181   Lady Rowley – Holbecks, Hadleigh Suffolk *through Mrs Richardson*

182   Sir Elliot Colvin – Gangbridge, St Mary Bourne Hants

1932–33

183   Mrs Pinching *Sept* – Ardly House, Bicester *through Mrs Knightley* [?]

184   Miss Pigot-Moodie *Sept* – 1 Essex Villas W.8 *through Whitmore*

185   Mrs Cunningham-Jardine *Sept* – Jardine, Lockerbie Dumfries *through Brooke*

186   Mrs Buxton *Sept* – Bengeo Old House Hertford

187   Lady Margaret Shaw *Sept* – Melville, Woldingham Sussex *through W.H. Baker* [?]

188   Mrs W.B. Gladstone *Jan* – 5, Stanford Road W.8

189   Lady Rolleston *March* – Martins, Haslemere Surrey

1933

190   Mrs Cookson *March* – Witheby Sidmouth Devon

191   Sir James de Hoghton *May* – The Elms, Bembridge, I.of.W (*Mrs Thorby*)

192   Mrs Abel Smith *June* – Woodhill, Hatfield

193   Admiral Nelson Ward *June* – The Dower House, Crocker Hill, Chichester (*through Pelham*)

194   Mrs Masters (*Universal Aunts*) *July* – Barrow Green Court Oxted

195   Farquharson – St Leonards Terrace S.W.3

196   Cotton – Cherry Orchard Penn Bucks

197   Watanabe – Suma, Hatchford Cobham *through Alan Thompson & Mrs*

[Page 10]

198   Ronald Smith – Old Turks, Iden Kent (through Mrs Pirie & Lady Bunbury) Nell Strong

199   Mrs Maxwell – Conderton Manor Tewkesbury (through Miss Kennedy – through Wolryche Whitmore, Warwick, McNamara)

200   Barrow Green Estate – Oxted (through Mrs Masters)

201   Mrs Holland Martin – Overbury Court, Tewkesbury *Dec 33* (through Sir H. Baker, Raynor Woods, & Mrs Maxwell)

1934

202   Craig Myle Glebe – Woldingham *Jan 1934* (the Hon A. Shaw)

203   Sir Bertram Standen – Ibthorpe Farm, Andover Hants (Direct through family)

204 Sebright School, Wolverley – through Mr Corbett

205 Sydney Schiff Esq – Abinger Manor Nr Dorking (through Ed. Maufe, and Cmdr Lambert)

206 Alexis ffrench – Fairseat Manor, Wrotham Kent (through Commander Lambert)

207 Mrs Bell [?] – Ciders Court, Alderton, Suffolk (through Nell Strong and Bunbury)

208 Colonel Woodall – Netherbury Court Beaminster Dor. *Gardener Fred* (through Mrs Swann)

209 St Felix School – Southwold Suffolk *Gardener Young* (through Mr Shaw)

210 Mrs Brocklebank – Charlton House Shaftesbury Dorset (through Mrs Gunter)

[Page 11]

211 Mrs Goschen – Woolly Grange, Bradford on Avon Wilts (through Brooke)

212 Miss Heaviside – Viewpoint, 20 N. Common Rd, Ealing (through Miss More – Miss Pigot-Moodie)

213 Mrs Dowson – Frith Manor, East Grinstead (through Commander Lambert)

Jan 1935

214 Lady Watson – Mount Hall Gt Horkesley Colchester – through family

215 Col. Mallinson – Memorial Garden Southwold *The White House Woodford Green* – through Mr Tweddle, bursar of St Felix

216 Leonard Ingram – 18 Cheyne Row – through Chelsea Show

217 Miss Freeman-Harris – Chapel Oak nr Evesham – through Chelsea Show

218 City of London Maternity Hospital – 102 City Road, E.C.1 – through Lady Bradford

219 I.N. Hooper – Monkswood Gt Hallingbury Essex – through H.E. Mozer [?]

220 Mrs George Dickson – *Struan* Wimbledon Park – through Chelsea Show

221 Mrs Hickson – Savages House, Bishops Tatchbrook nr Leamington – through Mrs Murray (through Studio Annual)

222 Mrs Burgoyne – Old House Haywards Heath Sussex – through Swanley

[Page 12]

1935

223 Mrs Hartnoll – Conigre House Bradford-on-Avon (through Mrs Goschen)

224 Mrs Stephenson – The Heronry Hurstbourne Priors Whitchurch Hants (through Abel Smith, and EGC)

225 Mrs Alexander – Hothorpe Hall, Theddingworth Rugby (through Mrs Gillilan)

226 Mrs Burton – Manor of Groves Sawbridgeworth Herts (through former work at Bengeo and Rowley [?] & Abel Smith)

227 H.E. Colvin – Oakley Hall, Ugley Essex – direct

228 Dowager Lady Buchanan-Jardine – Binfield Park, Bracknell – through photos published in Studio Annual

229 P. Horton Esq. – Leighthorn Rough, Morton Morrell Warwicks – through Commander Lambert

230 Colonel Hodgkinson – Drybrook Cholderton Wilts (previously at Tyne Hall Bembridge, see 125) – through Dewhurst?

231 Colonel Stephens – Manor House Cholderton Wilts (through Hodgkinson)

232 Maj-General Ward H.D.O. C.B. – Wenlock Abbey, Shropshire (through work at Linley Hall[2]) (in 1930 – through D. Hudson? or Whitmore)

233 Mrs Fair – Northway House Tewkesbury (through Mrs Maxwell)

[Page 13]

234 Lady Stokes – 4 Holly Terrace, West Hill, Highgate (through Miss Stokes, Swanley)

235 Mrs Dewhurst – Overdale Sandiway Cheshire (through previous work, No 75) (through Mrs Fowler)

236 Sir Bruce Richmond – Netherhampton Ho, Nr Salisbury

237 Mrs Pirie – Warren Ho, 9 Highbury Rd Wimbledon

1936

238 Wing Commander A.W.H. James – Brackley Grange, Brackley Northants (through Pelham)

239 Mrs Penrose-Thackwell – Clovelly, Merrow Guildford

240 Mrs Powles – Little Cliff, Point Hill, Rye

~~241~~[3] John Newton Esq – Corfe Cottage Taunton Som

241 Mrs Fane – Ferring Place, Kelvedon Essex (through Lady Rowley)

242 C. Russell Esq – Stubbens, North Ockendon Upminster. Essex

243 Lady Knudsen – Old Warren Farm Wimbledon (through M. Mellor)

244 Countess of Hardwick [e deleted] – 3 Cranley Pl. S.W.7 (through Mrs Gladstone)

[Page 14]

1936

245 Lady Kinnard – Langham House Rode, Bath (through Lady Phipps)

246 Miss Moat [?] – 10 Craven Hill (through Miss Pigot-Moodie)

247 Mrs Wilson – Aston Somerville Broadway (No 139 Burley Beacon Mrs Napier) [*sic*, Mrs Napier was No 138]

248 Lady de Vesci – Monk Hopton, Bridgnorth (through Mrs Ward)

[line deleted]

249 Archduke Charles Albert Habsburg – Chateau Zywiezc Poland (through 'Good Gardening')

250 Miss Briggs – 15 Belsize Squ. (through Chelsea Show)

251 Mrs Newton – Blunham House, Beds (through former work at Buxted 146)

252 Mrs Pilkington – Appledown, Frilsham, nr Newbury. Berks (through M. Mellor)

253 P.H.B. Burgoyne – Five Beeches, Dyke Rd Av, Hove – through Mrs Burgoyne

254 D.A. Stirling Esq – 1 The Grove Highgate. N.6

255 West Hill Court – Highgate (Curtis & Henson) *through Curtis & Henson*

[Page 15]

1936-1937

256 Mrs Prior – Fishleigh House, Hatherleigh, N Devon

257 A.R.W. Landon Esq – Mornington, Mayfield, Sussex – through Swanley

1937

258 Mrs Beamish – Jewell's House, Stanford Dingley, Berks – through family

259 Mrs Henry Tiarks – 67 Avenue Road, London NW

260 Lambeth Housing Movement – 320 Clapham Rd. S.W. – through Lady Allen? Coronation Planting Comm

261 Neville Gladstone Esq. – 32 Kensington Square W8

262 Miss Cross – The Manor House, Hazelbury Bryan Sturminster-Newton Dorset

263 Captain Hume – Gorsefield, Stansted, Essex – through H.E.C.[4]

264 Mrs Norris – Cross Hill Adderbury Banbury Oxon (through Mrs Brocklebank)

265 Dr Noel Sergeant – Newlands House Tooting Bec Common S.W.19. – through Robertson

266 Capt Pedder – Berden Lodge, Bishops Stortford – through H.E.C.

267 Hon. Mrs Butler Henderson – Faccombe Manor, Andover – through family through Radcliffe

268 Lady Deedes – The Old Rectory, Rendlesham Suffolk – through Whitmore and Bunbury

[Page 16]

1937

269 Mrs Roselli [or Rozelli] – [blank] – through Mrs Tennant

270 Mrs Birney – Pucks Croft, Rusper, Sussex

271 Capt Lockhart Leith – Speen Holt Newbury – through Mrs Godwin

272 Sir Edward Benthall – Lindridge, Bishops Teignton – through H.E. Colvin

273 Miss K. Newton – Holthangar, Wentworth, Virginia Water (through Col. Woodall)

274 Mrs Illingworth – The Hill House, Mulberry Green, Harlow, Essex – through Mrs [blank]

275 Mrs Douglas Pennant – Sholebroke Lodge, Towcester, Northants – through Pam Pelham

1938

276   Lord Dunsford – Eastwell Park Ashford Kent – through Universal Aunts

277   Mrs Disraeli – Testcombe, Stockbridge, Hants – through Mrs Rickards

278   Roedean School – Brighton – through Swanley

279   Hon Mrs Pretyman – Orwell Park House, Ipswich – through Bunbury

[Page 17]

1938

280   Mrs Lambert – Home Farm, Sherston, Swindon, Wilts (Reginald Hams [?] gardener) through Mary Mellor

281   Mrs White – Alassio, Italy – through Swanley

282   Mrs Chaplin – The Old Rectory, Clipsham, Oakham *nee* (*Abbotswood Stow on Wold*) through Mrs Holland Hibbert

283   Hon D. Erskine – Chilterns End, Henley – through Mrs Godwin

284   Mrs M. Buxton – Mardocks Mill Ware – through Mrs J. Buxton

285   J.T. Morgan Esq – St Nicholas, Glamorganshire – through Chelsea Show

286   Hon Mrs Whitbread – Burford House, Tenbury Wells – through former gdn at Coopers Hill

287   Lady Wakehurst – Rockley Manor, nr Marlborough – through Lady Falmouth

288   Mrs Michael Bullen [?] – Westergate Ho. Arundel (gardener Hunter) through Lady Benthall

289   Mrs Elliot – Longthorpe Ho. Peterborough – through Mrs Holland Hibbert

290   Mr Trelawney Irving – Wellwick Ho. Wendover – through Mrs Sclanders

291   Mrs Tennant – Eagles Nest

1939

292   Eaton Square trenches – for Met. Public Gdn Assn – through Miss Agar

[Page 18]

1939

293   Trench Section Sh Bush – Met. Pub. Gdns Assn

294   Mrs Leigh Barnet [?] – Wickham House Newbury – through Mrs [blank]

295   Commander Powys Maurice [?] – High House, Curdridge Hants – through Mrs Pilkington

296   St Felix School – (Craigmyle House)

297   Mr Kereth – June 1943

War years[5]

~~298~~   Mrs Brocklebank – Downhead Hall Shaftesbury

1944-5

299   H. Herd – 1 Prince Arthur Rd, Hampstead (through Miss Lancaster) *Southall*[6]

300   Greenhill Farm – Morton Bagot Studley – through Studley

1946

300   Miss D. James – Boreham House, Boreham St Sussex

301   Captain L. Impey – Chilland Cottage Nr Winchester – through Christopher Hussey

302   Capt Inglis – The Manor Wield, Nr Alresford – rough sketch plan only (through Mrs Inglis, No 127)

303   Allan Thompson [blank] (through Sch of Planning lectures)

[Page 19]

305[7]   Mrs Wilson – The Old Rectory, Aston Somerville, Broadway (former gdns Nos 247 & 139)

304   Miss Higgins – Moorend Court, Mathon, Malvern – rough sketch plan only (through Margaret Lancaster)

305   Mr Seligman – 33 Camp Road, Wimbledon – through Mr Jellicoe

306   Mr Liquorish – 81 Higher Drive, Banstead – Ewell 4105 – through Selfridges inf. [?]

1947

307   Charles Cavendish Esq – Leadervale, Earlston, Berwickshire (E. Crookshank, now Mrs Cavendish)

308   Port of London Authority – Trinity Square – through I.L.A., Bolton, and P. Mawson

~~308~~   L.H. Bolton – reconsideration of plan No. 110 Hinton Ho.

309 Haverhill & District Housing Society Ltd
Haverhill, Suffolk – Parkway Estate – through
I.L.A.

310 Samuel – 75 Avenue Road N.W. – through
Country Life and Mr Blairman

311 Sir Thomas Beecham Bart – 39 Circus Road N.W.
– through Esther Turner and Avril Haslett

312 P.A. Green Esq. – Grimscott, Coleshill
Warwickshire – through C.P.R.E. and Jellicoe

[Page 20]

1948

313 Plunkett – Kilmore, Chobham Surrey – through
Thompson & – [dash]

314 Ashton Roskill Esq – Cox's Newtown, Newbury –
direct – Planting plan only

315 Mrs Verey – 13 Palace Gardens Terrace – through
Mrs Wilson

316 Mrs Mommersteeg [?] – Mills Croft, Higham
Ferrers Northants – through I.L.A

317 Lady Forteviot – House of Ross, Perth – (through
Cavendish) (307)

318 David Astor – The Manor, Sutton Courtenay
Oxon – (through John Hill)

319 Miss Brodrick – Plas Llewelyn, Abergele, N Wales
(through Lady Moyra Loyd [sic])

320 J. More Esq – Lindley Hall, Shrewsbury Salop

1949

321 Stanstead Abbots Church Yard Memorial – for
Burton Esq. [?]

322 Derbyshire C.Co [blank]

324 Herts County Council – Schools planting
programme – (through School of Planning)

325 Swan Cottage, Swan Walk, Chelsea – Mrs
Chaplain [?] through Rosamund Sands

[Page 21]

326 Rowntree Village Trust – New Earswick, Yorks
(through Louis de Soissons)

327 E. Robinson – 241 Petersham Rd, Richmond
(through lectures and book)

328 Mrs Clifford Curzon – The White House,

Highgate – through lectures and book and Kate
Hawkins

329 C.H. Aslin – Herts County Arch?

330 Herts Co. Co. – Grounds of County Hall

331 Warton Crag Quarry – I.L.A.

332 Leavesden Hospital – I.L.A.

333 Crofthead Quarry – Hill & Cawdor (Lanark C.C.)

334 ~~Sparrow Pit~~ Eldon Hill Quarry Derbyshire

335 Mrs Impey – The Old House, Guilsborough,
Northants

1952

336 Keadby Housing – Farmer & Darke (through W.
Henderson)

337 Keadby Power Station – Farmer & Darke
(through W. Henderson)

338 Stourport Power Station – Farmer & Darke
(through W. Henderson)

[Page 22]

1952

339 Lambhill Cemetery – through Mr Coin [?]

340 Lady Evershed – through G. Jellicoe – King's
Lynn, Norfolk

341 Simon Nowell-Smith – 9 Pembroke Gdns W.8

342 Lady Watson – 29 Montpelier Pl S.W.7

343 St Albans Primary School – Holborn (Miss
Harris, Norman & Denham [?])

344a ~~Mrs Strettell Howe Park Tattenhoe, nr Bletchley Bucks – through Mrs B [?] and L. Colvin~~

345 Bairnswear – Worksop, Mr Gerrard (through tree
book)

344 Titsey Hill

348 North London Collegiate School – Canons Park
Edgeware – through Wye & RHS

346 Bradmede ? School – L.C.C.

347 Eliot Place School – L.C.C.

[Page 23]

1953

349 Roehampton School – L.C.C.

350 Thorn – Yew Hedge, Chandlers Cross,
Rickmansworth (I.L.A.)

351 Strettel – Howe Park, Tattenhoe, Nr Bletchley, Berks – through Mrs Beauville & L. Colvin

354 Reginald Abel Smith – Datchworth Close, Nr Knebworth Herts (see No 192)

353 Sir Bruce Richmond – The Old Rectory, Islip

352 Dark – 30, Hyde Park Gate

355 David Astor – 12 & 14, Elm Park Road, N.W.1

356 Loewy Engineering Co Ltd – Poole (Farmer & Dark) (through W. Henderson)

357 Oliver Poole – Redheath House, Croxley Green (through Col [blank])

358 David Astor – Compton Beauchamp House

359 Whiteknights Park – Reading University

360 Lady Gater – The Barn House, Church Stanton, Oxon

[Page 24]

1954

361 Cheshire Foundation – Liss, Hants – Le Court (*through Lady Mund*)

362 R. Gimson – 37 Chapel Lane, Knighton, Leicester (*through Land and Landscape*)

363 Lady Helen Smith – Aston Tirrold Manor, nr Didcot (*through Clough Williams Ellis*)

1955

364 Little Peacocks, Filkins – own garden

365 Michael Behrens Esq – Culham Court, Henley – in collaboration with F. Dark

366 John Buxton Esq – Morley House, Wareside, Herts

376 Provident Mutual Life Assurance Assoc – Hitchen – *planting for F. Dark*

368 Ian Hooper – Doubleton, Penshurst, Kent

369 H. E. Colvin – Nunton Ho, Nr Salisbury

370 Vincent House – Pembridge Square (R.H.S.)

371 Sandye Pl – Bedfordshire – *book?*

372 Poole Potteries – Poole, Dorset (Mr Carter) (through & for F. Dark)

373 Old Westfield Farm – Lighthorn Rough, Moreton Murrell, Warwicks – Mrs Vaughan – See No 229 (Horton) [spellings differ from those in No 229]

[Page 25]

1955

374 Ecton Copper Mines – Peak Planning Board

375 Mrs Bryson

376 Boyd Alexander – Prospect House, Upton, Didcot, Berks

1956

377 Bowater – New Thames Mill, Northfleet (Farmer & Dark)

378 Count Seilern [?] – Hog Lane Farm, Ashley Green, Chesham – through Wanda

379 Lady Rupert Nevill – Uckfield House, Uckfield Sussex (G. Jellicoe)

380 Sir Ian Walker – Salisbury Crematorium Okeover Hall, Derbyshire – (G. Jellicoe)

381 Grounds Peace[8] – Filkins

382 The Hon Mrs Trower [?]

383 Miss Graham – Ripsley Cottage, Liphook (through Boyd Alexander)

384 Lady Nicolson – Norton Lavant Manor, Wilts – through H.E.C. and [?]

385 R. Abel Smith – Datchworth Church Herts – Churchyard

386 Mrs Gunn – Saxons, Top Park, Gerrard's Cross (Youngman)

[Page 26]

387 Salisbury Crem – Salisbury Crem

388 Sir Anthony Lindsay Hogg – Acryse Manor, Kent (through Mr Dark)

399 Lady Patricia Ward – Box House, Bampton

400 H.H. Maharanee of Baroda – Box Hill (through Langley Taylor)

401 Sir Ian Walker-Okeover – Okeover Hall (G.A. Jellicoe)

402 Bowater Paper Corp – Merseyside (Farmer & Dark)

403 Hotel at Ch[?]- Beyrut, Ch[?] (Farmer & Dark)

1957

404 Mrs Colvile – Weald Manor, Bampton Oxford (through Goodenoughs?)

405 Maurice Farquharson

406 T. Abel Smith – Woodhall Pk. Hertford (through R. Abel Smith)

407 The Countess Alexander of Tunis – through Anstey Gibbs

408 Major Ramsden M.P. – Old Sleningford Hall, Ripon (through Mrs Wilson)

409 Messrs Curry Ltd – Chilcomb Lane, Winchester (through Co. Pl. Officer)

[Page 27]

1957 cont

410 Salisbury Precision Eng Co (through Rackham Pl. Officer)

411 Lady Cripps – ~~New House~~, Minchinhampton – Derham's House

412 John Cripps – St Peter's House, Filkins

413 Oxford High School for Girls – Belbroughton Rd – through Boyd Alexander

414 Dr P.H. Walker – Thatcham, Berks (through Arch. press books)

415 Mrs Frank Sargent – Old Rectory, Bighton, Alresford, Hants

416 Col R.L. Broad – Bradon Farmhouse, Devon (through G.A. Jellicoe)

1958

417 Michael Hope Esq – Colebrook House, Blockley (through Sir Gordon Russell)

418 Mrs Blake Tyrer – Fisherton Delamere House, Wylye Wilts

419 Dr T.H. Hughes – 571 High Road, Wembley, Middx (Engl Forestry Assn)

[Page 28]

1958

420 John Summers & Sons – Steelworks – through S. Crowe – Shotton, Chester

421 Dr K.E.M. Allen – Bushcombe Lane, Woodmancote

422 Dr G. Paterson – Mulberry Cottage, Wonersh – through Miss Ledeboer

423 Sir Francis Hopwood, Bingham's Melcombe – through G. Jellicoe

424 Commander J Oram – Whitwick Manor, Herefordshire – through Gladstone Lulworth job

1959

425 E. Raymond Cochrane – Guiting Power Manor – through H. Farquharson

426 Mrs Clive Morton – 2 Westbourne Park Rd London W2

427 Nurses Home Hostel of God – North Side Clapham Common – through Miss C. Fenwick

428 Frankland Dark – Snape Barn, Wadhurst, Sx – Former client

[Page 29]

1959

429 J. Burder, Falcon Close, Woolton Hill, Newbury – personal friend

430 D. Gomme Esq – Busto House, West Marden, Nr Chichester – through Messrs [blank] & S. Crowe

431 Lady Phipps – Yew Tree Cottage, Wilcot – former client

432 Drakelow C Power Station – Burton on Trent, C.E.G.B.

433 Peter Stuceley Esq – The Old Parsonage, Buscot, Faringdon – through Mrs Wansborough

434 Elizabeth Gardens, Salisbury – Salisbury Corporation. Former client

435 Lea Castle Hospital – Kidderminster Rd A449 – Regional Hosp. Bd. Bm [?]- through S. Crowe

436 Colonel Head – Bourton on the Hill House, Glos. – through G. Jellicoe

437 Brockenhurst Park – Hon Mrs Hoare (Aynho)

1960

438 Trinity College Oxford – through the President, Mr Norrington – through Oxford High School for Girls

[Page 30]

1960

439 Mrs Woodruffe, The Glebe House, Sacombe – through Mrs Timothy Abel Smith

440 Spicer, Idbury House – through [blank]

441 Inner Temple Garden – through Ashton Roskill

442 Finchley CEGB – Farmer & Dark

443 Morgan Crucible Co Ltd – Farmer & Dark

444 Shardeloes, Hoare – Hon. Mrs Hoare – through former work, Aynho & Brockenhurst

445 Eweline Sports Fields – (Nowell-Smith)

446 Gomme – Hyde Park Gardens

447 Gomme – Lower Farm, Up Marden

448 Down House Red Marley – through Oliver Roskill – N. Rog Robinson

449 Hursley House, Winchester – Farmer & Dark – I.B.M.

450 Adders Moss – Over Alderley Cheshire – Basil Ferranti through architects Cruikshank & Seward

451 Locksash Farm Locksash Cheshire Mr Ferranti through J Seward

[Page 31]
1961

451 Ferriby Hill – Needler – North Fernby, E. Yorks – through Mr Johnson

452 Drakelow Canteen – Farmer & Dark – Squires Lane? C.E.G.B. S. District

453 Peters Finger[9] – Salisbury Council – Salisbury Sewage Works – Former Client

454 Eggborough Pr Station – C.E.G.B.

455 The Folly, Eastleach – Sir Thomas Bazley

456 Gomme Estate – Watergate Woodlands – Locksash Farm

457 Halls of Residence Belfast University – through Mr Seward (Ferranti)

458 Ferriby Mount – H. Needler. Yorks

459 Mr Malcolm – 32, Marlborough Place – through Richmonds

460 Samuel Fox & Co (Steelworks. Wire & Cables) – Sheephouse Wood. through P.Officer West Riding

[Page 32]
1961

461 West Thurrock Generating Stn – CEGB Southern Group – Squires Lane, Finchley

462 Scorton – Hoveringham Gravels – H. Needler

463 Kencot Hill Farm – Lord Ebrington

464 Eyemore Fm later known as Trimpley Reservoir – Birmingham Water Board – through Shepherd Fidler

465 Gale Common – connected with Eggborough – Ash Disposal Scheme Pr Station

466 Michael Hope – Blockley, Churchill Close – through Sir Gordon Russell

467 Hoveringham Gravels – Head Office (Needler)

468 Cheescombe Farm – Mrs Erskine

469 Malone Playing Fields Belfast – Munce & Kennedy architects, Belfast

470 Watergate Farm – Mr Gomme

471 Broughton Poggs – Mrs Wansbrough

[Page 33]
1962-3

472 Oxford Bishopric – Church Commissioners (Mrs Chick) – New See House Cuddesden

473 St Georges Hall, Kings Lynn – The National Trust (Lady Evershed)

474 U.C.W. Aberystwyth – University of Wales (through Mr Marsden [?])

475 Truck Maintenance depot – Esso Petroleum (Essex Pl. Officer)

476 Messrs Elliot Bros – Sportsfield. Borehamwood. (through Mrs Fanleones)

477 Aldershot New Military Town – Aldershot Planning Group B.D.P. (C. Tandy)

478 River Severn Scheme – B'ham Water Dept Alternative Scheme for Trimpley

479 Watergate House – E.D. Gomme

480 Mere, Fairford – Maj. A.J. Crawdon [?]

481 Rockley Copse, Bessels Leigh – Christopher Harris Woodland Management

482 Yorkshire Inst of Agric

483 Aldershot Sewage Area – A.P.G.

488[10] Horowitz

484 L.C.C. Finchley Rd Widening – L.C.C.

485 A.C.C. Barracks

486 Gurston Manor – Potter and Hare

487 Trinity College New Court – Oxford – follow-on from No 438 (1960)

489   Mrs Matarasso

490   Rugeley C.E.G.B.

491   "   Ash disposal

[Page 34]

1964 + 1965

492   C.H. Priestley – Puddle End Farm

493   Ramillies Park, Aldershot

494   Willems-Warburg Aldershot

495/1   Tangley House – M. Colvin

496/1   Michael Piggott – Upper Througham

497/1   Gawcombe – advice only

498/1   Langley Mill – through Tony Pasley

499/1   Kempton Park Racecourse – Sir George Langley
        Taylor (C.P.R.E.)

500/1   Duntisbourne Abbots

501   ~~Qu. Univ. Belfast. Rangers Houses~~ – Michael
        Hornby (through G. Jellicoe) – W.H. Smith,
        Swindon

502   Rev. Nagel – Kencot

1966

503   Cross, Home Farm, Shoreham, Kent – Sir G.
        Langley-Taylor

504   Sodbury – Kingsgate Pk (ILA)

505   De Mawney – Little Farringdon

506   Meaford Pr Stn – through Region

507   Queens, Belfast Ranger's Houses

508   Lady Evershead [sic] – Castle Ave

509   Ruth Lady ~~R~~ Fermoy – through Evershed. carried
        on by [blank]

510   Styal Village – National Trust

511   University of East Anglia – through Redhead
        (Lasdun's Partners) Landscape

512   Mrs Gaskell – Gillow Manor (through Mr
        Wordsworth)

513   Lady Baird – Reeves Green, Herts

514   U.E.A. Playing Fields

[Page 35]

1967

515   Arley Old Orchards – M Turner – Through
        Trimpley

516   Swansea – Potter – through ILA list

517   Slade, Mr & Mrs M.G. – Garden at W. Kington, Wilts

518   Cubberley, Ross-on-Wye – Lord Greville – in assn
        with Claude Phillimore (through J. Trafford and
        Robinson Gdn, Down Ho.)

519   M. Koster. Ringwood – Kington Vale, through book
        on small gdns by S. Jellicoe and Lady Allen

1968

520   Dukes Park M.S.Q.   }

521   Blenheim Park   }Aldershot ASSO

522   Dev Arcor 10 and 11   }

523/1   Aston Magna – Lord Dulverton (through G.
        Jellicoe)

524   Aldershot Alison's Road

525   Inglesham Caravan Site – New College Oxford

[526–530 Filkins office]

526}[11]   Old Vicarage Ashbury – Airey-Neave through
        C. Beauchamp

527}   Compton Beauchamp – Astor (New No)

528} }   Astor [?]

529} }

530}

[531–540 Aldershot office]

531}   HQ Group Catering [?]

532}   AO car park

533}

534}   Contract 17

535}   DA 66

536}   Garrison seargeants [sic]

[Page 36]

1968

537}   A325 dualling

538}   Revised Master Plan

539}   73/4 DA – 74/5 – 75/6

540}   76/7 DA Programme}

[541–550 London office]

541}

542}

543}

544}

545}   London

546}

547}

548}

549}

550}

1969

551(1) Patrick Sterling Civic Trust – Farmington Old Rectory

552(X) John Williams The Glebe – Williams & Winkley

553(1) 1 and 2 Spenser Pk – Basil de Ferranti – see No 450

554(1) Turville Church & Glebe – R. Gaynes, The Old Vicarage – Through John Piper & Graham Thomas

555(1) Dr Gibson, Charlbury

556(X) Williams & Winkley (St Margarets, Twickenham)

557(X) D. Cripps – Goodfellow

558(1) Pyrton Manor – Maj. Farrell (through G. Jellicoe)

559(1) Mrs P. Hellyer – Silver Spring Cottage, Lower Chedworth (I.L.A.)

~~560 Major Farrell – Watlington Oxon Repton Manor – through G. Jellicoe~~

[Page 37]

1970–71

560(X) Lesser Wildwood – J Williams

561(1) Mrs Mitchell – Axel Cottage – through Jellicoe book, *Small Modern Gardens*

562(1) Tadmarton Ho. Frm. – Col. G. Lewis

563(1) Salisbury Place – L.D. Spicer – Former Client (see 554)[12]

564(X) White Horse Hill – D. Astor

565(X) Own House – H. Moggridge

566(X) Brenig Reservoir – Dee & Clwyd River Auth. through Binnie

567(2) Townleigh Reservoir – CPRE

568(X) Bristol Polytechnic – Bristol City (probably thro' Landscape Research Group)

569(1) Lady Margaret Hall – Oxford (Principal Dame Lucy Sutherland)

570(1) Shotton Steel Works – J. Summers (Extension for 420)

1971

571(2) Little Peacocks, Office Extension – Colvin & Moggridge

572(X) Sainsbury – Peterborough – Scott [two words illegible] through Aldershot

573(1) Garden at 59 Parktown, Oxford – Dame Lucy Sutherland

574(X) Wessex Water Order

575(2) Warborough Pig Unit – Mr Plint, Simmons (sec) [?]

576(X) Youlbury Garden

577(1) Downington Green – Rev & Mrs Nagel, Lechlade

578(X) Aberystwyth – Ove Arup & Ptnrs

1972

579(X) St Elf…[unclear] Church, Wal…[unclear] Williams & Winkley – S. Race

580(1) Combe – Lower Farm – Mr & Mrs Fawcett through Poll

581(X) Aberaevon – Aberystwyth U.D.C.

582(X) Coca Cola – Williams & Winkley

583(X) Aberystwyth St Michael's Churchyard – Aberystwyth U.D.C.

[Page 38]

1972

~~584 Coca Cola, Durham – Williams & Winkley~~

584(X) Neuadd Wen

585(X) Old School, Shilton

586(1) Michael Hope – Blockley – Former Client through Sir Gordon R.[13]

587(X) Marriage Farm – M. Waterfield

588(X) Aldergate Wood – C. Green

589(1) Sherborne Ho, Lechlade. H.S. Mullaly (through Nagel 577)

590(2) Somerton – through L&L

591(X) Grove End House – Williams & Winkley

592(1) J.L. Haag, Stratton Pl. Cirencester (Harpers article)

593(X) Tan-y-Bwlch Beach, Aberystwyth (see 578)

594(1) Martin Koster, 20 Palace Rd. E. Molesey –
Former Client (519)

1973

595(X) Crownhill Police Station Plymouth – Eliz.
Chesterton

596(1) 133 St Georges Rd – London?

597(1) Datchet Reservoir – C.P.R.E.

598(1) Netherton Farm, Mr & Mrs Wigan – (Baird,
Fawcett) see also plan 267

599(1) Hyde Grange. Mr & Mrs Gilbert – through
Arnold Browning ARIBA

600(X) Jews Wood Comprehensive School – Plymouth
C.A.

601(2) Teds Stable Kencot – gdn for converted barn

602(X) Brenig – Control House – Part of Reservoir
Wales

603(1) Church Crookham 64 MOQ – (Aldershot
Extension)

604(X) Snowdon Summit – Elizabeth Chesterton

605(X) Bodmin Bypass   – ?

606(2) Hillslope Oxford (saw the New House)

607(1) Mrs Bemrose, Coln St Aldwyns – through M.
Thirkettle & others

[Page 39]

1973

608(X) Brenig – Bryn-hir – Farmhouse restoration

609(2) Naunton, Mill buildings – conversion

610(1) CME, Millbank – thro' Page, DOE,
Chessington

611(1) Aldershot – AYSC St. Omer Barracks

612(X) 3M (UK) New Office – Alex Sondern &
Partners

613(1) Aldershot 1974/5 Dev. Area Planting – part of
tenn [?] commission

614(1) Packford Boars Hill – ? ILA

615(X) Torr Works – E. Chesterton

1974

616(1) Basingstoke Canal Report – Aldershot
extension

617(X) Uplands Landscape – Countryside Commission

618(1) Houses @ Burford Road, Carterton – Oxford Co.

619(X) Broadoak Reservoir – Wrights

620(1) Aldershot D.A. Recosting – part of general

621(2) Gorse Hill, Swindon – Martin Cobden
501(1) (74) W.H. Smith & Son Swindon –
(adaptation of 1965 plan – adapted to
proposed extension) Rush & Tomkins

622(X) Crumbles, Eastbourne – L.M. & P.

623(X) Benghazi, Libya (Ahmed Rafiq Corniche) –
Rendel, Palmer & Tritton

624(X) Coach House, Hemingford Abbots

1975

625(2) Leafield, the Laurels – Mrs S. Osmond

626(X) Darnbrook Farm, Arncliffe, Yorks – Farm
buildings: Mr J. Moores

627(2) St John's Primary School, Bristol – Thro'
County of Avon, Bristol Polytechnic

628(1) 10 Turn Again Lane, Oxford – Mr Beard –
Thro' Oxford Architects Ptnership on behalf of
Oxford Preservation Trust

629(X) Byford House, Shilton – Dr Richards saw New
House

630(2) Stanton Barns – Wallace & Hoblyn, architects

[Page 40]

1976

631(X) Roadford Reservoir – South West Water
Authority

632(X) Milton Brook Reservoir – South West Water
Authority

633(X) Woodland Reservoir – South West Water
Authority

634(X) Abbey Meads, Chertsey   - R.M.C.

635(X) Wimpey – Toothill Swindon – thro' Bristol
Poly

636(X) Ffynon Llugwy Road N. Wales – Brenig

637(X) Roof Garden, 51 Eaton Mews S – W & W

638(X) Demonstration Farms Project – Countryside
Commission

639(1) Mrs Dunipace Sketch and advice memo
Through Gilbert (599) (Foxhills, Cirencester)

640(1) Aldershot, Hospital Site

641(X-2) Upton Wold Farm (ILA)

642(2) Leeds & Bradford Boiler Co – through A. Leitch

643(X) Hamilton Lodge[14] (gift)

644(X) St Benedict's School – W & W

1977

645(2) Hilton House Garden Mrs Young – Lord Southborough Bingham's Melcombe

646(X) Kencot Lodge (conversion) – Yapps

647(1) R.G. Taylor, Hollen Ho, Buckland – through Miss Pugh (sec White Ho Hill)

648(1) Cuxham Mill – William Clarke

649(1) Solvay la Hulpe – ?

1978

650(X) Northleach Bypass – CPRE

651(2) Canvey Island – ORL

652(1) 6 Chapman's Piece [?] – Mrs Osmund

[Page 41]

653(1) Langford Ho, Little Faringdon – Lord and Lady de Mauley – through Simon Wilding

654(X) Lakes Park, Benghazi – Rendel, Palmer and Tritton

655(1) Mrs Barrington, Oddington Lodge – through: Geo. Foster Ltd. (Mr Peel)

656(2) Mr A.R.E. Pretor-Pinney, Somerton Erleig (through job No 590)

657(X) Theale Shed for Foster Yeoman – through Elizabeth Chesterton

658(2) The Old Vicarage Garden, Gt. Durnford Russells, through Lord Southborough

1979

660(2) The Old Farm Ampney Crucis – Butler, through Fletcher Watson and Wishart [unclear]

659(2) Aldershot: A325 dualling

661(X) Farnham depot for Foster Yeoman – through Elizabeth Chesterton

662(X) Stevens Close, Jesus College – through L.I.

663(X) Carnon Valley, Cornwall (Billiton UK Ltd) through L.I.

664(2) Thamesmead House (Mrs McLeod)

665(X) Leeds Castle, Kent – through Ralph Cobham

666(X) Ham Estate, Wantage (Mr Tony Rosser) – through Ralph Cobham

667(X) Haringey, London (Williams & Winkley)

668(X) Ten Flats, Wroxton – Col. Lewis

669(X) W. Oxon D.C. (Sundry schemes)

670(X) W.O.D.C. (Sundry housing)

671(X) Aldershot N. Camp Amenity Gdn

1980

672(X) Liverpool Bay Golf Complex Formby

673(X) Mr Coombes Squall's Farm -through P. Goodhart

674(X) Evenlode Cottage (Dr & Mrs Nixon)

675(X) Thenford House (Heseltine) – thro' Basil Street

NOTES

1. 'H.D.O.' are Major-General Ward's initials. See also No 232.

2. No. 166.

3. Presumably further work for Mr Newton at Corfe Cottage, No 33.

4. 'H.E.C.' is her brother, Hugh Colvin.

5. Colvin's own note.

6. It is not clear whether 'Southall' refers to 299 or 300.

7. Arrows indicate that this entry and the next should be transposed, but the following entry was mis-numbered as a second 305.

8. Dr John Groundes-Peace was Colvin's GP in Filkins. They had an arrangement whereby he would visit her at home rather than expect her to attend surgery and in exchange she designed areas of his garden.

9. The location for the sewage works in Salisbury.

10. An arrow indicates that 488 should be moved to its correct position under Trinity College New Court.

11. Jobs 526 to 530 are bracketed together with 'Filkins' written beside them, and Jobs 531 to 536 are bracketed with 'Aldershot' beside them – indicating which office was handling the work. Some work was also handled in London.

12. Possibly 440.

13. 417 and 466.

14. Hamilton Lodge School for deaf children in Brighton.

Index

The abbreviation BC refers to Brenda Colvin. Subentries under the entry for Brenda Colvin are in chronological order followed by some more general entries. Page numbers in *italic* refer to illustrations. Page numbers in **bold** refer to the biographies on pages 228–31.

Picture credits

The publishers would like to thank those listed below for permission to reproduce the images on the following pages:

© Aerofilms and Aero Pictorial Ltd, 171

© Airviews (M/cr) Ltd, 156

© Sylvia Grace Borda, 100

© The British Library Board, 16 below

© Central Electricity Generating Board, 163 above

© Chris Carter, 9, 86 centre, 92, 103, 211–13

© Colvin & Moggridge, 11, 22, 23, 106, 114, 128, 133 above, 134–7, 143, 146, 148, 152, 154, 150–5, 157–61, 165–6, 167 above, 169-70, 172, 173 top and bottom, 174–9, 186, 188, 195–6, 197 above, 198, 209–10

Harriet and Julian Cotterell, 45–7, 48 below, 87 below

© CPRE archive, Museum of English Rural Life, University of Reading, 39

Dennis Emery, 203

© Trish Gibson, 26 (by kind permission of Lady Redman), 58–9, 60 above (by kind permission of Jane Carr), 74–5 (by kind permission of Molly and Robert Wheatley), 89, 127, 153 above, 163 below, 187 below, 201 (by kind permission of Julia Joynt), 204–5 (by kind permission of Sir Peter Walker-Okeover)

Alan and Debbie Griffiths, 68

Pat Grover, 8

Julia Joynt, 14–15, 16 top, 20, 21

© Knight Frank, 192

Landscape Institute Library and Archive, 33, 35, 37, 44, 62, 85, 101, 104, 110 top, 112, 138, 140, 144, 168, 206 below

Sacha Maxwell, 56

© Oxford Mail, 184

© Percy Lund, Humphries & Co. Ltd, 98–9

Lady Redman, 24–25

© Henk Snoek and Associates, 133 below

Swanley Town Council, 12, 17

© Taylor Woodrow, 173 centre

UEA Society, 149

University of Wales, Aberystwyth, 145

The Wimbledon Club, 18

All the remaining illustrations are Brenda Colvin's own photographs, © Colvin & Moggridge.

Author's acknowledgements

Like so many books before it, this study of the life and work of Brenda Colvin would not have seen the light of day but for the freely given help and enthusiastic support of many. My journey of discovery has been a long but fascinating one, hindered at least in part by Colvin's self-effacing nature – as I hope I have demonstrated, she was no self-publicist – and the consequent lack of any organised archive of her work. I have however been generously helped along the way by those who knew her and worked alongside her over the years as well as by the owners of gardens that she designed. I am very grateful to them all.

From the time of my first tentative visit to Colvin's former home and the offices of Colvin & Moggridge at Little Peacocks, Hal Moggridge has been a constant supporter and I owe him a tremendous amount. From the start, he willingly shared his memories and opinions of Colvin and her work, and allowed me to make use of the collection of her papers, notes and photographs held at his office; more recently I have much appreciated his considered advice and comments on Colvin's larger landscape work and his provision of a large part of the relevant illustration. Similarly Chris Carter, consultant to Colvin & Moggridge, has generously shared his memories and views on Colvin and her work, and provided photographs of the garden at Little Peacocks. I must also note that Hal and his wife Cass and Chris and his wife Stephanie, those who probably knew Colvin best towards the end of her life, all made a most useful contribution to what I hope is a rounded portrait of her in later life as well as offering valuable insight into her beliefs and character.

Following my first meeting with Hal Moggridge, John Brookes and the late Anthony du Gard Pasley both agreed to share with me their views on Colvin's character and on her contribution to the worlds of landscape architecture and garden design. Their strongly held belief in what they both saw as her undervalued importance and their favourable view of her personality encouraged me to delve further. Their generosity with their time and memories has since been echoed by others who worked with her: the late Ivor Cunningham, Diana Ford, Pat Grover, Carol Møller, Barbara Moth, Barry Newland, Barbara Oakeley, James Riley and the late Peter Youngman. Laurie Fricker, although he never actually worked with her, kindly shared his memories of his meetings with her, and her niece Julia Joynt added much valuable information about her family background. I thank them all.

Garden owners too have been generous with their time, responding to my enquiries, allowing me to visit their gardens and see what plans or other information they might have about Colvin's creative input. I am grateful to Bridget Astor, Sir Michael Bunbury, Jane Carr, Harriet and Julian Cotterell, Dennis Emery, Alan and Debbie Griffiths, Sacha Maxwell, Lady Redman and Felicity and Jeremy Redman, Jane and Jonathan Ruffer, Sir Peter Walker-Okeover, and Mollie and Robert Wheatley. As gardeners, Inara Gipsle at Sutton Courtenay and Jerry Shenton at Okeover have kindly shared their particular insights into Colvin's work. Lastly, Donald Lewis provided much useful information about the current state of the gardens of the New Castle at Zywiec in Poland.

At the Landscape Institute, first Sheila Harvey and then Annabel Downs and Kate Lander were all most willing to help with my enquiries. Esmé Hodge of the Hextable Heritage Centre has been unsparing in her research on my behalf into the archives of Swanley Horticultural College.

In more general terms, this book would not exist had I not encountered two enthusiastic garden historians. Toby Musgrave first whetted my appetite for the subject with his course at the University of Bristol Botanic Garden. This led to my meeting Tim Mowl, Professor of History of Architecture and Designed Landscapes at Bristol University. I owe him an enormous debt for his inspirational and enthusiastic teaching which, in turn, has encouraged me to complete this work on Colvin.

Of course, the book also needed the right expertise and support to get it published. My thanks go to my editor Jane Crawley, designer Anne Wilson and to John Nicoll and Andrew Dunn at Frances Lincoln who in publishing it have brought Brenda Colvin the wider recognition she deserves.

Most important of all, those closest to me have encouraged, enthused and, when necessary, cajoled me through what has been a long and demanding process. My son Sam and daughter Hannah have both been immensely supportive and I trust they know that their help has been much appreciated, as is Sam's patient and sensitive work on retouching and improving Colvin's photographs. But without the loving support of my husband Jeremy, this book would almost certainly not have been completed. That it exists is in very large part due to his patience, his strength and his invaluable input.